Training for

Results

*Key Tools and Techniques
to Sharpen Trainers' Skills*

BY SCOTT B. PARRY

Ordering information: Books published by the American Society for
Training & Development can be ordered by calling 800.628.2783 or
703.683.8100.

Library of Congress Catalog Card Number: 99-68258
ISBN: 1-56286-132-8

TABLE OF CONTENTS

How to Use This Book

Teaching and learning are two sides of the same coin. An instructor has not *taught* you anything until there is a behavior change (learning) on your part. The instructor has *told* you many things, but nothing has been taught until you have changed your performance. In short:

- ◆ Teaching is not synonymous with telling (imparting information).
- ◆ Learning is synonymous with behavior change (performance improvement).

Unfortunately, many trainers and educators have never been taught how to teach. When confronted with the need or opportunity to give instruction, they unconsciously follow the models provided by the hundreds of past teachers they've had. Instructors tend to teach the way they've been taught. And their models haven't always been the best ones if their purpose is to change behavior and improve performance.

I've been privileged over the past 40 years to conduct more than 400 train-the-trainer workshops for thousands of instructors and course designers. In the process I've developed a wealth of handouts: readings, self-assessments, planning sheets, training tools, and other forms of learning exercises that have proved to be effective in sharpening my participants' instructional skills.

This book is the result. It consists of 40 chapters divided into nine sections. At least one of these learning exercises appears in each chapter. They are arranged in the natural flow of activities associated with the preparation and instruction of a new course. The sections and chapters cover the following information:

- ◆ Section 1, "Training: The Key to Performance Improvement": learning and behavior change, andragogy and pedagogy, history of training and development, education or training
- ◆ Section 2, "Analyzing the Need for Training": three types of data, linking training to the business plan, 12 reasons for conducting a needs analysis, tools and techniques for doing the job
- ◆ Section 3, "Designing a Training Program": architect and contractor analogy, 26-step planning sheet, human behavior as knowledge, attitude, skill, preparing objectives, blueprints, make or buy
- ◆ Section 4, "Developing a Training Program": systems model (five stage), input (acquisition) and output (application), lesson plan formats, a sample lesson on fire fighting

- Section 5, "Sharpening Your Instructional Skills": who needs an instructor, small stimulus-response-feedback links in the instructional chain, using questions effectively, using subgroups to improve learning

- Section 6, "Teaching Inductively and Deductively": lecture method versus Socratic instruction, programmed instruction as a deductive model, three exercises in converting inductive lectures into deductive discussions

- Section 7, "Using Training Tools Effectively": flipchart uses and abuses, preparing and using overhead transparencies, games, simulations, in-basket exercises, dos and don'ts of role play in class

- Section 8, "Transferring Behavior From the Workshop to the Workplace": 20 techniques and 50 factors that affect transfer, using action plans and managers' briefing and contracts, examples such as meeting announcements and recaps

- Section 9, "Measuring the Effectiveness of Training": evaluating at each of Kirkpatrick's four levels, 10 questions to ask when evaluating, 12 lessons on evaluation, four ways to calculate training's return-on-investment.

While there is a logic and flow to this book, its main value to you does not depend on your reading it from cover to cover. A detailed table of contents precedes each of the nine sections, listing the concepts and skills of each chapter and outlining the objectives that you should be able to meet when you've completed each section.

I see two major uses of this book. Workshops and courses on human resource development can benefit from the activities and exercises contained in its chapters. And individuals who want to sharpen their instructional competencies can use this book as a self-study program.

A word about the Internet: According to *Computer Industry Almanac,* the number of people who connected to the Internet between 1996 and the end of 1998 jumped from 61 million to 150 million. This enormous increase in traffic led 34 universities to band together to build special lanes for videoconferencing and distance learning. To date, several hundred universities are delivering courses via the Internet.

According to a prediction in *Training* magazine's October 1999 issue, corporate training departments will soon benefit from the technology and will catch up with the universities. However, the Internet is simply another means of delivering training. The principles of instructional design and the psychology of learning as discussed in this book apply to courses on the Internet as well as in any other delivery system.

I've enjoyed assembling and describing the tools and techniques in this collection. If you find the book helpful, then we'll both have benefited from the experience.

Scott B. Parry
Princeton, NJ
March 2000

SECTION 1

TRAINING: THE KEY TO PERFORMANCE IMPROVEMENT

Workers, methods, machines, materials, money. These are the resources that organizations need to achieve their goals. The primary resource, of course, is the workers because all the others exist to extend the effectiveness of the human resource.

The purpose of training is to enable people to use these resources to the best advantage. Organizations that are seen as world class have done a better job than their competitors in training and developing their employees.

The chapters in this section describe the process of training and how that process has changed over the years. Following is a description of each chapter:

Chapter 1, "Learning and Behavior Change," describes the process of learning, 10 factors affecting learning, six kinds of learning (sensory, motor, verbal, ideational, procedural, and discovery), and four types of behavior change used to monitor learning (accuracy of response, speed of response, rate of learning, and degree of forgetting).

Chapter 2, "A Comparison of Andragogy and Pedagogy," outlines the ways in which adults learn differently from children, with nine principles drawn from the work of Malcolm Knowles.

Chapter 3, "A Thumbnail History of Training and Development," traces the evolution of the field from 1900 to the present, with significant activities noted for each decade.

Chapter 4, "Education or Training?" distinguishes each process from the other with regard to objectives, methods, content, roles of instructors and learners, and the dependency of each on the other.

Upon completing this section, you should be able to:

- ◆ give two definitions of learning
- ◆ list at least three examples of knowledge, attitudes, and skills
- ◆ describe the S-R-F learning model (criteria for each part)

- compare Knowles's andragogy and pedagogy to McGregor's theory X and theory Y
- state at least five principles that describe how adults learn
- describe the shift from K to A to S from the 1960s to the present
- explain why many instructors tend to perpetuate the past
- define *education* and *training,* noting at least four differences.

CHAPTER 1

LEARNING AND BEHAVIOR CHANGE

The ability to learn, to communicate that learning to successive generations, and to build empirically upon prior learning is what sets us apart from all other forms of animate creation. Without learning, humans would be capable only of reflex action and instinct. With learning, we can rise above our environmental constraints and master the situations that come our way.

Our behavior during the first year of life was reflexive. We cried when hungry or tired, we rolled over in our cribs when the light was in our eyes, we rapidly withdrew our fingers after touching a hot object. But during the first few years of life, we learned how to use words to give and get information, convey our feelings, and respond to other people's feelings. From then on, most of our learning has been verbal—reading, writing, listening, and speaking.

Learning has been defined as new behavior not due to maturation or instinct or drugs. A six-day-old child cannot pick up a pencil. A six-month-old child can pick it up but cannot draw or write, actions that a six-year-old child can perform. These stages illustrate maturation. The new behavior depends on the growth and development of hand muscles, eye-brain coordination, and nerves.

What about instinct? Many animals have a sixth sense that we call instinct. You can take your dog or cat for a ride and deposit the animal in an unfamiliar place several miles from home. Your pet will find the way home: The new behavior can only be explained by instinct.

What about drugs? Whether prescribed or not, they are able to alter moods and perceptions dramatically, inducing new behavior that is unnatural and unlearned.

Let's modify our earlier definition of learning to exclude the effects of maturation, instinct, or drugs. Learning is the process of acquiring knowledge, attitudes, and skills to produce new behavior. Table 1-1 gives examples of each of these three components, referred to in some psychology texts as the cognitive, affective, and psychomotor domains.

Table 1-1. Examples of the cognitive, affective, and psychomotor domains.

Knowledge (Cognitive) What We Know	Attitudes (Affective) How We Feel	Skills (Psychomotor) What We Can Do
Facts	Feelings	Psychomotor (e.g., manual dexterity and assembling)
Concepts	Beliefs	Reasoning (e.g., problem solving, decision making, organizing, and prioritizing)
Rules	Values	
Theory	Perceptions	Perceptual (e.g., visual, auditory, and tactile)
Principles	Style	
Policy	Opinions	
Procedures	Drives	
Generalizations	Biases	

Nature versus Nurture

Is all behavior learned? Or did we inherit certain patterns of behavior? What roles do heredity and environment play in influencing our behavior? Three centuries ago, John Locke explained that the mind of a baby is a *tabula rasa,* or blank tablet, and that each generation can start anew without the jealousy, biases, and emotional conflict of prior generations. Clearly a vote for environment over heredity.

The nature versus nurture argument is largely moot today. Were the many children of J.S. Bach gifted musicians because of inherited traits or because they grew up surrounded by music? Are the graduates of Princeton, Harvard, or Yale successful in life because of their superior education (nurture), or did their superior genetic endowment (nature) help them to get into these schools?

Perhaps the best resolution of these questions is to realize that the issue is not nature versus nurture but nature and nurture. We are all products of the interaction of heredity and environment. **Learning is the grindstone that sharpens the tools of inherited ability.**

Factors Affecting Learning

Following is a list of 10 factors that educators and psychologists have identified as variables that can help or hinder learning.

♦ **The desire to satisfy a need:** Jim is studying Spanish because he wants to travel and do business in South America. Marianne is buying recordings of musical classics because her boyfriend is a musician. Tom is reading books on automotive repair so he can take care of his antique car. Of course, if the need is satisfied or withdrawn, the learning may stop. If Marianne breaks up with her boyfriend, she may stop buying classical CDs.

◆ **The desire to avoid punishment:** Jim, Marianne, and Tom were looking for rewards as the motivation for their learning. Equally powerful is the desire to avoid painful or unpleasant situations. This is how you learned how to avoid touching a hot stove, or stepping into a shower without testing the temperature first, or unplugging an electrical appliance before attempting to repair it, or apologizing to someone whom you have wronged.

◆ **The relevance of the material:** The more interesting or useful the material to be learned, the easier it is to learn it. Although our formal education included many courses that seemed dull and irrelevant, it may well be that the fault lay with the instructor or the text rather than with the subject. The challenge to trainers and educators is this: Don't attempt to give instruction until you can bring the relevance of your subject to life for your students. There are no dull subjects: only dull instructors or writers.

◆ **The immediacy of the application:** If reinforcement is to be immediate, we must give the learners immediate opportunity to practice and apply what they just learned. Psychologists view learning as a chain of stimulus-response-feedback (or reinforcement) links, as figure 1-1 shows. The shorter the links, the stronger the chain. This is the problem with the lecture method: Too much stimulus (information) is given to learners before they have an opportunity for response and the chance to practice and apply it. People learn best not by being told (S) but by experiencing (R) the consequences (F) of their thoughts and actions.

Figure 1-1. Learning as a chain of stimulus-response-feedback.

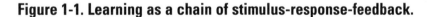

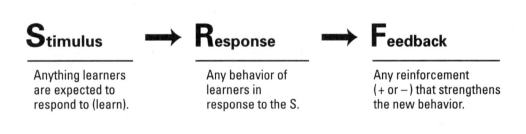

Stimulus	➡	**R**esponse	➡	**F**eedback
Anything learners are expected to respond to (learn).		Any behavior of learners in response to the S.		Any reinforcement (+ or −) that strengthens the new behavior.

◆ **The immediacy of the reinforcement:** As soon as learners have shown a new behavior (that is, new learning), they should be given reinforcement. They should receive positive reinforcement if the behavior is acceptable and negative reinforcement (correction, not punishment) if it is unacceptable. It is much more reinforcing to return a graded test with feedback to your learners if done immediately rather than a week later. Reinforcement, whether positive or negative, is defined as any action that increases the chances of getting the desired behavior in the future. The more immediate the reinforcement, the stronger the new behavior.

◆ **The relevancy of the response:** Since people learn best from their Rs and not from their Ss, we must elicit Rs that are relevant to the behavior we're teaching. Asking learners if they understand or if they have any questions will elicit Rs, but not relevant ones. Similarly, giving a true-false or multiple-choice test will elicit Rs. But these responses are a far cry from the behavior we expect of our learners in the situations for which we are preparing them. A response is relevant when it duplicates or simulates the learner's desired behavior in the real world.

◆ **The intrinsic nature of the reinforcement:** Much of the learning that takes place in school is induced by extrinsic rewards, such as grades, honor rolls, report cards signed by parents, punishments for failure. Such learning is often shallow and short-lived when compared with the learning that results when students seek answers to issues in which they are deeply interested and the motivation is intrinsic (that is, a personal and compelling need is being met and the learner's new behavior is inherently satisfying).

◆ **The internal logic of the subject matter:** Many things can be learned more effectively if the logic and internal relationships are explained. Examples include learning a foreign language vocabulary by recognizing related words in English or remembering a formula (for example, converting Fahrenheit to Celsius) by deriving it or learning how the formula was put together. Even when no logic is evident, we can make use of mnemonic rhymes like the following to help us to learn:

   — Thirty days hath September, April, June, and November.
   — In fourteen hundred ninety-two, Columbus sailed the ocean blue.
   — Red skies at night, sailors delight, Red skies at morning, sailors take warning.

◆ **The opportunity to apply new learning:** Athletes must exercise regularly to stay in shape. So must our learners if their new behavior is to be retained. The more often a person must apply new learning, the stronger that learning will become. Trainers use the term *just-in-time training* to explain why we shouldn't teach new skills until they are needed. For example, they wouldn't teach team building to employees until they are assigned to a team and can go through the course with their fellow team members.

◆ **The reinforcement of new behavior following learning:** In class an instructor can reinforce the learner's behavior. But when class is over, the learner returns to an environment that is not always supportive of the new behavior, and may even be hostile to it. Parents of public school children must be taught how to recognize and reinforce new behavior whenever possible. Similarly, in the workplace, managers and team leaders must learn how to get the maximum transfer of learning when members of their group return from a training program. Without this, the return-on-investment for new learning will be far below its potential.

The Instructor's Role

We've just looked at 10 factors that affect learning. They are stated as psychological principles. Now let's reword them as instructor guidelines to be applied whenever you teach.

1. Know your learners' needs and relate each topic to these needs.
2. Show learners how new behavior will benefit them and help them to avoid punishing situations.
3. Make learning relevant. (There are no dull subjects, only dull teachers.)
4. Elicit responses every five to six minutes. (Break information into S-R-F chains.)
5. Give immediate feedback (reinforcement) on the appropriateness of responses.
6. Elicit relevant responses that describe or simulate real world behavior.
7. Avoid extrinsic rewards in favor of intrinsic reinforcement.
8. Teach the *why* (internal logic) as well as the *what* and the *how to*.
9. Arrange opportunities to apply new learning following the instruction.
10. Prepare others to recognize and reinforce new behavior (transfer).

To assess progress and the impact of their teaching, instructors must measure their learners' performance, both during the course and after the program is over. The methods they use must depend on the kind of learning that took place: sensory (that is, making visual discriminations), motor (for example, keyboarding, assembling), verbal (such as languages, sales presentation), ideational (for example, time management, decision making), procedural (planning and scheduling, project management), and discovery (creativity, problem solving).

Instructors may measure learning performance in terms of one or more of the following behavioral changes:

◆ **Accuracy of response:** Reduction in the number of errors over time (for example, data entry, and verbal skills).

◆ **Speed of response:** Where timeliness is important (for example, emergency procedures, and number of transactions processed per hour).

◆ **Rate of learning:** Is it accelerating or slowing down (usually shown by plotting a learning curve of performance over time)?

♦ **Degree of forgetting following instruction:** Measured by recall, recognition, and relearning (plotted on a retention curve).

The educator makes heavy use of paper-and-pencil tests to measure learning in courses that teach history, English, civics, math, and sciences. The trainer often has the advantage of being able to simulate workplace situations and measure learning by observing the learners' behavior in role plays, case method, in-basket exercises, and other simulations of conditions at work. The closer an instructor can get to creating the conditions a learner is expected to deal with throughout life, the better will be the measurement of actual behavior change.

CHAPTER 2

A COMPARISON OF ANDRAGOGY AND PEDAGOGY

In 1973, Malcolm Knowles introduced trainers and educators to the concepts of andragogy and pedagogy in his book *The Adult Learner: A Neglected Species.*

Knowles's thesis, simply stated, is that the instructional methodology used in schools (from the primary grades through college and university) is not appropriate for teaching adults. The teaching of children, or **pedagogy,** is based on different values, needs, and assumptions than is the teaching of adults, or **andragogy.**

Pedagogy places emphasis on the imparting of information by an instructor and the absorption of it by learners (whether through memorization, memory aids, concept formation, or insight and understanding). Andragogy places emphasis on experiential learning and the role of an instructor as a catalyst, facilitator, and arranger of experiences. Learners are seen as self-directed and responsible for their own learning.

Knowles's contribution to the field of education and training bears a striking parallel to the work of Douglas McGregor in the area of management style (theory X and theory Y). McGregor taught us that the way a manager supervises depends upon the following:

◆ the assumptions the manager makes about the nature of the work and of the employees who perform it

◆ the goals (purpose and mission) of the organization and how they have been translated into a manager's expectations of employees

◆ the personality and characteristics of the manager as shaped by heredity and environment.

In the statements above, if you substitute the terms *instructor* for manager, *learner* for employee, and *course* for work, you will have a fairly direct translation for converting McGregor's theory X and Y into Knowles's pedagogy and andragogy.

Pedagogy is based on the existence of a static culture, such as an organization or society, and the importance of perpetuating it by teaching its members the lore of knowledge and values associated with it.

Andragogy is based on the existence of a dynamic culture and the importance of preparing its members to deal with change and uncertainty as they face the world.

Back in school, our teachers filled their roles mainly as pedagogues; they imparted information that we absorbed and were then tested on to measure our retention and understanding. We have had relatively few teachers who saw us as independent adults and saw themselves as catalysts helping us to grow. Thus, when we are called upon to give instruction to others, we unconsciously follow the models we have had for so many years. We may want to embrace the values and beliefs of andragogy, but our behavior with students is largely pedagogical. Table 2-1 summarizes some of the differences in how adults and children learn.

Charles Dickens ([1854] 1981) illustrates an example of pedagogy at its most extreme in his book *Hard Times*. The scene is a schoolroom where the teacher, Dr. Thomas Gradgrind, is holding forth. He calls on Sissy Jupe, who has spent her life traveling with her father, a horse trainer. Many days and nights have found Sissy grooming, training, and caring for horses—they are her family. Not wishing to neglect her education, her father has just enrolled her in Gradgrind's school. Our visit takes place on her first day of school.

Thomas Gradgrind, sir. A man of realities. With a rule and a pair of scales, and the multiplication table always in his pockets, sir, ready to weigh and measure any parcel of human nature, and tell you exactly what it comes to.

Thomas Gradgrind now presented himself to the little pitchers before him, who were to be filled so full of facts. He seemed a kind of cannon loaded to the muzzle with facts, and prepared to blow them clean out of the regions of childhood at one discharge. He seemed a galvanizing apparatus, too, charged with a grim mechanical substitute for the tender young imaginations that were to be stormed away.

"Girl number twenty," said Mr. Gradgrind, squarely pointing with his square forefinger. "I don't know that girl. Who is that girl?"

"Sissy Jupe, sir," explained number twenty, blushing, standing up, and curtseying.

"Sissy is not a name," said Mr. Gradgrind. "Don't call yourself Sissy. Call yourself Cecilia."

"It's father as calls me Sissy, sir," returned the young girl in a trembling voice, and with another curtsey.

"Then he has no business to do it," said Mr. Gradgrind. "Tell him he mustn't. Cecilia Jupe. Let me see. What is your father?"

"He belongs to the horse-riding, if you please, sir."

"We don't want to know anything about that here. He doctors sick horses, I dare say?"

"Oh yes, sir."

"Very well, then. He is a veterinary surgeon, a farrier, and a horse-breaker. Give me a definition of a horse."

(Sissy Jupe thrown into the greatest alarm by this demand.)

"Girl number twenty unable to define a horse!" said Mr. Gradgrind for the general behoof of all the little pitchers. "Girl number twenty possessed

Table 2-1. Comparison of learning in adults (andragogy) and children (pedagogy).

Factor	Andragogy	Pedagogy
Definition	Giving instruction on the basis of how adults learn.	Giving instruction on the basis of how children learn.
Purpose	To teach people how to learn and function for themselves; to release from dependency on the instructor.	To perpetuate a static culture and an in-group based on knowledge the group's members have acquired; to control.
Time Orientation	Forward looking: prepare people for tomorrow—teach them how to deal with the unknown.	Backward looking—pass on the knowledge and lore of yesterday, the knowns.
Self-concept of Learner	Independent, autonomous individual—adult.	Dependent on teacher and authority figures—child.
Student's Role	Students are resources, learning from one another's experience.	Students are sponges absorbing information.
Teacher's Role	Catalyst—arranger of experience.	Expert—imparter of information.
Methods of Teaching and Learning	Deductive—group discussions, experiential learning, hands-on exercises, consultations, self-assessment.	Inductive—lecture, presentations, text, tests, mainly one-way communication with little interaction.
Rewards	Intrinsic—ability to solve problems, make decisions, and think for oneself.	Extrinsic—grades, admission to further studies, career options, and the like.
Assumptions	◆ Students will exercise self-direction and self-control in pursuing learning objectives to which they are committed. ◆ Self-evaluation is more effective than instructor evaluation, and feedback from other learners can speed the process. ◆ Success depends heavily on how you use what you know.	◆ Students cannot be trusted to know what they need to learn to pursue their own learning program without extrinsic rewards. ◆ The instructor is the primary or sole source of evaluation and feedback to learners because they lack the ability to assess their own performance. ◆ Success depends heavily on what you know.

of no facts in reference to one of the commonest of animals! Some boy's definition of a horse. Bitzer, yours."

The square finger, moving here and there, lighted suddenly on Bitzer...whose skin was so unwholesomely deficient in the natural tinge that he looked as though, if he were cut, he would bleed white.

"Quadruped. Graminivorous. Forty teeth, namely twenty-four grinders, four eye-teeth, and twelve incisive. Sheds coat in the spring; in marshy countries, sheds hoofs, too. Hoofs hard, but requiring to be shod with iron. Age known by marks in mouth." This and much more from Bitzer.

"Now, girl number twenty," said Mr. Gradgrind. "Now you know what a horse is."

One of the characteristics of pedagogy is that the instructor assumes the "parent" role (authority figure) and places the learner in the "child" role (ignorant, highly dependent, not capable of self-help). Sissy's knowledge of horses was real, adult (mature), and far more extensive than Thomas Gradgrind's. Had he practiced andragogy, Gradgrind might have used Sissy as a resource and gotten the class to ask her questions and take advantage of her experience. However, Gradgrind is the quintessential pedagogue: an expert rather than a catalyst, an imparter of information rather than an arranger of learning experiences, an authority figure rather than a catalyst.

Following are a number of principles that describe how adults learn. An understanding of these principles will help you to design and deliver more effective instruction:

- ◆ Adults are problem centered or opportunity centered—they look at how to—rather than subject-matter centered. Focus is on need to know rather than on nice to know.

- ◆ Adults want immediate, hands-on examples where they can practice and apply their new knowledge in typical, real-world situations.

- ◆ Adults bring a wealth of experience to the learning environment. This should be built upon and channeled. Each learner is a resource to other learners.

- ◆ Adults need a high degree of control over the learning process—pacing, sequencing, degree of participation, feedback, and recognition.

- ◆ Adults learn at different rates and styles. The instruction should be varied and designed so as to accommodate a wide range of learner differences.

- ◆ Adults need to know the big picture—the why behind the how to, the part-to-whole relationships, the sequence and flow of the course.

- ◆ Adults can help one another. Learning exercises should make use of subgroups, pairs, teams, task forces, the buddy system, and so on.

- ◆ Adults have a short attention span, about eight minutes for the average manager, according to the American Management Association. The pace must be brisk.

- ◆ Adults have an awareness of the value of their time. Learning should be efficient and cost-effective with a short-term return on the investment.

References

Dickens, Charles. (1854; reprint 1981). *Hard Times.* New York: Bantam Books.

Knowles, Malcolm. (1973). *The Adult Learner: A Neglected Species.* Houston: Gulf.

CHAPTER 3

A THUMBNAIL HISTORY OF TRAINING AND DEVELOPMENT

Probably the earliest known forms of group training occurred when the armies of countries surrounding the Mediterranean needed to learn how to coordinate an attack, move a battering ram into place against a walled city's gates, and march in phalanxes. This was three millennia ago.

During medieval times, the guilds took up the responsibility for training their members. Masons, carpenters, shipbuilders, tanners, and scores of other trades moved craftsmen through the three stages of apprentice, journeymen, and master. Some of these guilds still exist in England today (for example, the Worshipful Order of Skinners).

But our concern with the history of human resource development (HRD) might well begin with the 20th century, when the Industrial Revolution was transforming America from an agricultural society to an industrial age. Let's examine the evolution of HRD by decade:

- ◆ **1900-1910:** Most of the training that took place was in the form of on-the-job apprenticeship in which a supervisor or seasoned employee taught the new hire. This worked well in service industries—banking, insurance, hotels, retail, hospitals, and other relatively small organizations. However, Henry Ford, Thomas Edison, and others were introducing mass production that gave impetus to formalizing the training function.

- ◆ **1910-1920:** The outbreak of World War I brought unprecedented demands on manufacturers to convert men and women from farmers to factory and foundry workers. Charles Allen introduced a four-step process and taught instructors how to show-tell-do-check, a procedure that has been followed ever since. Companies began to set up training departments and conduct courses.

- ◆ **1920-1930:** Colleges began to set up business education programs. Schools of business formed alliances with larger employers to provide them with secretaries, accountants and bookkeepers, and clerical personnel. High schools began to teach vocational courses, such as automotive, electrical, metalworking, woodworking, and printing for young men and domestic skills for young women.

— Sidney Pressey, a professor at Ohio State University, developed a testing and teaching machine and used it with his students in the years 1924 to 1927. This innovation led to B.F. Skinner's work at Harvard a quarter century later, thus paving the way for programmed learning and self-instructional courses.

— The National Home Study Council was established in 1926, providing accrediting standards for home study programs. International Correspondence Schools became the best known, offering several hundred courses containing more than 2,000 instruction units, each requiring an average completion time of 12 to 17 hours.

◆ **1930-1940:** The Depression killed many fledgling training programs because there was a surplus of skilled, unemployed workers. However, the Roosevelt Administration launched many programs that required training of unemployed workers for government projects (for example, the CCC, or Civilian Conservation Corps, and the WPA, or Work Projects Administration).

◆ **1940-1950:** The first national society of trainers was established (National Society of Sales Training Executives, NSSTE) in 1940, followed by the American Society of Training & Development's (ASTD) organizational meeting in 1943 and the first national convention in 1946. National Training Labs (NTL) began human relations training in 1947. The National Association of Foremen ran a conference for training directors and the War Manpower Commission conducted training institutes to prepare civilians for jobs in the burgeoning defense industries, where vestibule training and on-the-job training (OJT) became the primary methods of imparting instruction.

— World War II brought a tremendous surge in research into how people learn, with study programs funded by the U.S. Office of Education, the Office of Naval Research, the Air Force Personnel and Training Research Center, and the Department of the Army's HumRRO, which published guidelines for developing instructional programs based on measurable performance objectives.

— In 1942, the Army Institute was established and expanded the next year to become USAFI, the U.S. Armed Forces Institute. Located in the Education Center of military installations, USAFI made courses available at the high school, college, and technical-vocational levels. USAFI also administered the General Educational Development (GED) test that enabled U.S. military personnel throughout the world to complete their high school equivalency studies and receive diplomas.

◆ **1950-1960:** Courses moved from pure lecture method to include role playing, case method, in-basket exercises, and other forms of simulation. The American Management Association published a Top Management Business Decision Simulation. The new technology of reel-to-reel tape recorders and closed-circuit TV entered the classroom to capture and replay interactions for analysis. Educational TV came of age; by 1958 there were 32 stations in operation, many offering training programs for adults. The widespread use of computers in the office, robots in the factory, and video in the classroom led many people to fear that automation would replace humans in the workforce.

◆ **1960-1970:** ASTD and McGraw-Hill published the first edition of the *Handbook of Training and Development* (Craig and Bittel, 1967). Programmed instruction came of age. Robert Mager (1961) wrote a paperback titled *Preparing Objectives for Programmed Instruction* that has been through 18 printings. The National Society of Programmed Instruction was formed in 1962 (now the International Society for Performance Improvement). Sensitivity training and T-groups, or therapy groups, blossomed. Under President Lyndon Johnson, the Job Corps and the National Alliance for Business were formed, and government grants were given to employers who would hire and train the so-called hard-core unemployed in basic reading and writing as well as job skills. Many well-known behavioral scientists published their theories and research during the 1960s, including the following:

— Chris Argyris. (1960). *Understanding Organizational Behavior.* Homewood, IL: Dorsey.

— Robert Blake and Jane Mouton. (1964). *The Managerial Grid.* Houston: Gulf Publishing.

— Peter Drucker. (1966). *The Effective Executive.* New York: Harper & Row.

— P. Hersey and K. Blanchard. (1969). *Management of Organizational Behavior.* Englewood Cliffs, NJ: Prentice-Hall.

— Frederick Herzberg. (1966). *Work and the Nature of Man.* New York: World Publishing.

— Abraham Maslow. (1968). *Toward a Psychology of Being.* New York: Harper & Row.

— David McClelland. (1961). *The Achieving Society.* New York: Van Nostrand.

— Douglas McGregor. (1960). *The Human Side of Enterprise.* New York: McGraw-Hill.

— Carl Rogers. (1961). *On Becoming a Person.* Boston: Houghton-Mifflin.

With the heavy infusion of theory and concepts into the literature of training, the major emphasis of management development and supervisory training was on acquiring knowledge and better understanding of human behavior.

◆ **1970-1980:** The term *HRD* began to replace *training and development.* Organization development (OD) became a recognized area of activity to which many senior trainers migrated. Universities now offered degree programs in HRD and OD and instructional technology. Assessment centers appeared as a way of evaluating job applicants and employees to determine their strengths and developmental needs. More than 1,000 training consultants offered their services to clients. Dozens of innovative organizations were founded, providing customized and off-the-shell training programs. In 1978, they created the Instructional Systems Association (ISA), whose member companies currently number close to 200.

— Given the interest in affirmative action and equal employment opportunity generally, assertiveness, transactional analysis (TA), open communications (the free, or public, area of the Johari window—named for its creators, Joseph Luft and Harrington Ingram [1961]), and getting in touch with one's inner self, the focus of training moved toward courses dealing with attitudes and values. Outdoor training at remote sites took trainees through exercises designed to develop cooperation, trust, self-confidence, stamina, and other personal traits. Hundreds of self-assessment exercises appeared on the market for use in training programs.

— ASTD membership passed the 10,000 mark, and the society moved its national headquarters from Madison, Wisconsin, to Alexandria, Virginia.

◆ **1980-1990:** Japan became a world leader in productivity and quality, prompting U.S. firms to install quality circles and employee involvement programs (self-directed work teams). The universality of personal computers led to many computer-aided instruction (CAI) and computer-based training (CBT) programs. The new technology brought teleconferencing and satellite transmission of courses by corporations and universities. Trade associations and universities put out catalogs listing a variety of courses in adult education, and continuing education enrollments at colleges outnumbered full-time degree students four to one. Over 30 corporations set up their own degree-granting colleges for employees and families. Videocassettes became the most popular medium for imparting training, with behavior modeling as the new method. The emphasis of courses was on how-to-do-it skills training, and the training of trainers shifted from imparting information to facilitating learning via more participative instructional techniques. Trainers were influenced by a number of books that came out during the 1980s, including:

— Kenneth Blanchard. (1982). *The One Minute Manager.* New York: William Morrow.

— Stephen Covey. (1989). *The 7 Habits of Highly Effective People.* New York: Simon and Schuster.

— John Naisbitt and Patricia Aburden. (1985). *Reinventing the Corporation.* New York: Warner Books.

— Tom Peters and Nancy Austin. (1985). *A Passion for Excellence.* New York: Random House.

◆ **1990-2000:** The words *performance management* and *performance improvement* have become more widespread as trainers have recognized the need to educate management to the fact that the end result of effective training has always been improved performance in the workplace and not merely in class.

As companies struggled to become more profitable through downsizing (also known as rightsizing and reengineering), training managers learned how to do more with less. Line managers became more involved in delivering training, and evaluation of training's impact moved from Kirkpatrick's (1998) levels one and two (Did they like it and learn it?) to levels three and four (Did they apply it, and did it produce return-on-investment?). Management development programs focused on leadership, and supervisory training focused on facilitation skills to support work teams. Training managers spent less time teaching and more time managing resources (suppliers, consultants, and freelance trainers).

At the risk of oversimplifying, the emphasis of training in the 1960s was on imparting knowledge, in the 1970s on influencing attitudes, and in the 1980s on teaching skills. In the 1990s, these came together in the form of competency-based training, a competency being defined as a cluster of related knowledge, attitudes, and skills that influences a person's performance in a major aspect of his or her job (such as, problem solving, planning and scheduling, communicating). Many organizations defined the behavioral standards associated with each competency of widely held jobs (managers, salespersons). Competency-based assessments and training programs became available, with tools to evaluate one's competencies before and after training.

Peter Senge's book *The Fifth Discipline* (1990) described what the learning organization should look like and pointed out that "the only sustainable advantage one organization can have over another is its ability to learn faster than its competitors." Many organizations were influenced by Senge's insights.

With the arrival of CD-ROM, the Internet, and the intranet, courses can now be delivered at a learner's PC at the learner's own time, place, and pace. It will be interesting to see how prevalent this means of learning will become in the new millennium.

As the world becomes a global village, multinational organizations have learned to face the challenges of making training available to employees in many countries (for example, cross-cultural translations, procedural differences, technology differences: video in NTSC, PAL, Beta). ASTD's training conferences have attracted as many as 25 percent of the attendees from overseas. The United States is acknowledged as the world leader in training and development, and we enter the new millennium with ASTD at representing more than 70,000 HRD professionals.

References

Craig, Robert, and Lester Bittel. (1967). *Handbook of Training and Development.* New York: McGraw-Hill.

Kirkpatrick, D.L. (1998). *Evaluating Training Programs.* San Francisco: Berrett-Koehler.

Luft, Joseph, and Harrington Ingram. (1961). *Of Human Interaction.* Palo Alto, CA: National Press Books.

Mager, Robert. (1961). *Preparing Instructional Objectives: A Critical Tool in the Development of Effective Instruction.*

Senge, Peter. (1990). *The Fifth Discipline. The Art and Practice of the Learning Organization.* New York: Doubleday.

CHAPTER 4

EDUCATION OR TRAINING?

We are all products of an education system. We've typically gone through 12 years of public school, followed by some college. Thus, we have been exposed to dozens of teachers delivering hundreds of hours of instruction. It comes as no surprise, then, that when we are called upon to design or deliver a course, we will unconsciously imitate, or model, the teachers in our past:

◆ We tend to teach the way we've been taught;

◆ We tend to teach what we've been taught.

When someone asks you to give a course on topic x, your immediate thought is, "What do I know about x that I'd feel comfortable teaching others?" This is followed by, "How have I seen x or similar topics taught before?"

In short, the design and delivery of courses is strongly influenced by what we've been taught (content) and how we've been taught (process). Nobody taught us what to teach or how to teach. Our past teachers have been our models.

Let's define the word *model*. We're not using it to suggest desirable or ideal performance. Rather, we are looking at the process of implanting. Our parents, teachers, bosses, and anyone else who has influenced our lives have been our model—for richer or poorer, better or worse.

Thus, it becomes important for anyone who teaches to look at past models critically and analytically, and ask questions like these:

◆ Where will these models help or hinder me in enabling my learners to meet the objectives of my course?

◆ Where should I perpetuate tradition (that is, It's always been taught this way)?

◆ Where should I break with tradition (that is, What the learners need is at variance with the content and process of past courses)?

◆ In short, what and how should I teach?

Let's look at three examples of our tendency to perpetuate past learning.

◆ During the 1940s and 1950s, supervisory training programs were heavy on writing skills (memos, business correspondence, and the like), taught by people with a background in English grammar and composition. Then, in the early 1960s, a firm called Basic Systems (later Xerox Learning) published a course called *Effective Listening*, which is no longer available. This topic soon became standard diet for supervisory training as trainers realized that the typical manager spends about 40 percent of the day listening and only 5 percent to 10 percent of the day writing. But before the listening course appeared, few trainers had ever seen a model showing the content or process side of how to teach listening. The need was there, but it had not been recognized until the need satisfier—that is, the published course—appeared.

◆ Similarly, for years managers have looked for ways to improve job satisfaction and productivity. That's the need. The need satisfier was typically a heavy dose of motivation theory— Maslow's needs hierarchy, Herzberg's hygiene factors, and the like. These topics probably did little to improve job satisfaction or productivity. But they were what we knew how to teach, having learned them in our freshman psychology courses. Today these topics have been largely replaced by a focus on team building, participative management, quality assurance, employee involvement, joint goal setting, and other how-to-do-it topics that are much more effective in improving job satisfaction and productivity.

◆ Communication skills have been a mainstay of courses for salespeople, supervisors, customer service representatives, and anyone else whose jobs depend heavily on interacting with others. An entire generation of trainers taught these courses with an emphasis on the communication model (sender-message-media-receiver), the barriers (semantic, psychological, physical), and demonstrations of how perception differs from reality, as found in textbooks on communications. But the 1970s brought us transactional analysis (parent-adult-child), behavior modeling, and a translation into English of Jung's work from the 1920s on communication styles—sensor, intuitor, thinker, feeler. Today the emphasis is on how to communicate rather than the theory behind the process.

The preceding three illustrations were drawn from the realm of training. To complete the picture, consider the following three examples from the realm of education.

- For years—in fact, centuries—students learned their math by focusing on drills and practice: addition, subtraction, multiplication, division, fractions, decimals, percentages, squares and square roots, and so on. The need was for clerks, accountants, and grocers who could crunch long columns of numbers rapidly and with deadly accuracy. Today, number crunching is the work of computers, hand-held calculators, and optical scanners that read labels on merchandise. The need today is to understand how computers work and how to use them. Hence the new math that came out in the 1960s, with its focus on sets, relations, and functions. This approach is much more appropriate in preparing people to think in sets and subsets for the binary world of the computer.

- In Grandma's day, students learned their English grammar by diagramming sentences. They learned to underline the subject with one line and the predicate with two and to draw arrows from the adjectives and adverbs to the words they modify or describe. The exercise was largely academic because students had already developed well-entrenched patterns of speaking and writing, and the exercise did little to improve one's ability to communicate. We now realize that the purpose of English grammar is not to make us slaves to rules but to make us masters of words and the process of converting thought into language. Today, students write and edit TV scripts, news commentaries, advertising copy, and editorials. The emphasis is on ends (effect) rather than on means (formal grammar).

- One of the attractions of the physical sciences is their empirical, logical, black-and-white structure. There are irrefutable laws, facts, relationships, and highly predictable outcomes. This has led teachers of general science, physics, and chemistry to teach the subject as a litany of formulas and constants to be memorized and recited back to the instructor on exams. All this began to change in the 1960s with curriculum reforms that now treat science as a method of inquiry, a way of solving problems, establishing relationships, and thinking analytically. New textbooks and summer institutes emerged to prepare teachers for the new content and process. The old curriculum bred scientists as technicians and people with the right answers. The new curriculum breeds scientists as researchers, inquirers, and people with the right questions and the ability to design appropriate ways to answer them.

All six examples—and others you could cite—lead us to these conclusions about the relationship of education and training:

- In both fields, course design and development tend to begin by looking backward rather than forward. Instructors faced with a new course typically ask, "How has it been taught in the past?" rather than "What do my learners need or want in order to perform effectively?" Thus, instructors tend to perpetuate the past.

◆ The models we have had are deeply ingrained. Most of us were exposed to them for 12 to 16 years. Between a half and a quarter of your life was spent in school. It's very difficult to break with the traditional role of the teacher as an expert and authority figure, an educator, and fill the role of a facilitator and catalyst of learning, a trainer.

◆ Education and training each have their place. Their objectives are different. But most courses are a combination of education and training, whether they are taught in the public schools, on the campus, or in the corporate classroom. And the instructor's role is different when educating than when training, as table 4-1 shows.

Defining the Two Processes

We've spent a lot of time discussing education and training without stopping to define the two processes. This was intentional because most people equate education with the public schools and training with the corporate classroom or on-the-job training. Both are too restrictive. Virtually all instructors, regardless of where they hang their hats, are responsible for delivering courses that are part education and part training.

The next two paragraphs contain our definition of education and training. Before reading them, you may want to take a sheet of notepaper and try your hand at defining the two processes.

Education is the process of imparting the knowledge, skills, and attitudes (such as values, beliefs, or styles) needed to prepare a person for life. The skills are broad and intended to apply in a great variety of situations (when a person would use, for example, math, grammar, or general science). The knowledge and values (history, geography, civics) are intended to homogenize the members of a given culture or society. This process, known as *socialization* or *acculturization,* is cited by John Dewey as the primary reason why education is mandatory and free (that is, tax-supported) in virtually every society. Without education and a fairly universal distribution of common coping skills and shared values, it would become difficult if not impossible for a society (or organization) to function.

Training is the process of shaping the behavior of learners so they can meet specified performance criteria (expectations) in response to specific situations. The knowledge, skills, and attitudes that go into a course are typically criterion referenced: Limits and standards of acceptability have been set that are task or job specific. There is a relatively immediate return on the training investment, and the trainee's manager has a responsibility for recognizing and reinforcing (maintaining) the new behaviors following the training sessions, so as to ensure a maximum return-on-investment.

The training process cannot proceed effectively unless learners have the prerequisite education. For example, if we're training salespeople,

Table 4-1. A comparison of education and training.

Factor	Education	Training
Emphasis of objectives	Understanding, appreciation, acquisition of information.	Doing, hands on, application of information.
Subject matter, or content	Knowledge, principles, concepts, theory background.	Skills, procedures, rules, technique, how to do it.
Instructor's role	Expert, authority figure, presenter of information.	Coach, facilitator, catalyst, arranger of learning experiences.
Relationship of learners to instructors	High dependency of learner on instructor—to know what I need to know, to help me understand, and to give me a good grade. This can lead to adversarial relationships.	Interdependency—each depends on the other for feedback on pacing, level of understanding, relevance, and the like. Tends to foster a partnership relationship.
Focus of course	Broad and generic, one size fits all, everybody can benefit from it.	Narrow and specific; only for the right people at the right time.
When it is applied	Long range, used years hence, lengthy shelf life.	Short term, immediate, quickly dated, short shelf life.
Time orientation	Perpetuating the past, passing on the body of knowledge, sharing the contributions of past leaders, to see things as they've always been.	Preparing people for tomorrow, for situations that haven't happened yet, and for things as we want them to be.
Effect	Provides a stabilizing, unifying force to the organization and to society; gives everyone common values and ways of looking at things.	An agent of change, can be disruptive or a threat (old guard, new guard; or my instructor says . . . versus my supervisor says . . .).
Effectiveness measured by	Learners' grades on progress tests, final exams, term papers, etc.	Learners' performance in classroom simulations and back on the job.
Expectations of learner performance	Normal distribution, with few high and low grades and a large number of average performances (that is, the bell-shaped curve).	Skewed distribution, with almost everyone reaching high performance criteria (the 90/90 criteria, that is, 90% of trainees score 90 or better).
How instructor is evaluated	By learners' grades or popularity of course, or both.	By performance of learners in the workplace.

they first need to be educated in product knowledge, pricing policy, and market conditions. Or, more broadly, to be trained in their jobs, newly hired employees must be educated in the business their employer is in— the history, organization, products and services, policy and procedures, and the like. (That's right. Employee orientation is education, not training.) Put the magnifying glass on a typical training course, and you'd find that the first part of the course was probably educational in nature, covering background, prerequisite knowledge, orientation to course objectives and expectations, and so on.

Similarly, education for its own sake is largely dead. Educators are being called upon increasingly to justify their courses, indeed, their existence. Greek and Latin have all but disappeared from the campus. Few students read Chaucer. Today, professors are being asked to rewrite their course descriptions so that the catalog will state what the students will be able to do after taking a course. It's ironic that Robert Mager (1961) wrote his classic paperback, *Preparing Instructional Objectives,* primarily for educators. But they weren't ready for it as much as trainers were, and the book is responsible for a whole generation of trainers whose courses are behavioral, criterion referenced, and driven by objectives rather than by subject matter. Today, 40 years after its initial publication, the book has gone full circle and is now finding acceptance among educators.

Reference

Mager, Robert. (1961). *Preparing Instructional Objectives: A Critical Tool in the Development of Effective Instruction.* San Francisco: Fearon.

SECTION 2

ANALYZING THE NEED FOR TRAINING

The objectives, content, and methods of a training program are based on needs: the needs of the organization (business needs, mission, goals) and the needs of the trainees (knowledge, attitudes, skills, or K-A-S). Thus, an organization should not launch a training program until its managers and instructors have spelled out the organization's human performance needs, the levels of understanding and performance of the people to be trained, and the gap between these two sets of behavior. This process is known as a *needs analysis.*

Many terms have been used to describe these two sets of behavior: *actual* versus *desired, present* versus *proposed, existing* versus *required.* Trainers use the terms *entering behavior* to describe the K-A-S that learners bring with them and *terminal behavior* to refer to the new K-A-S needed to perform back on the job.

The chapters in this section contain a description of the benefits of doing a needs analysis, along with guidelines and a list of tools and techniques for carrying out a needs analysis.

Chapter 5, "Needs Analysis: The Starting Point," illustrates the role of learning on the birth-death continuum, noting the effect of a dozen reinforcers and constraints that operate in the workplace, and listing the three primary reasons for doing a needs analysis.

Chapter 6, "Linking Training to the Business Plan," presents a four-stage model for needs analysis, a 12-step outline for course development, and a description of the subanalyses that go into a needs analysis.

Chapter 7, "Twelve Reasons for Conducting a Needs Analysis," should help in preparing trainers to convince management to budget the time and money needed to conduct a thorough needs analysis.

Chapter 8, "Conducting a Needs Analysis," examines the trainer's credo (six beliefs), five questions to be answered during a needs analysis, and 25 tools and techniques for collecting data for analysis.

Upon completing this section, you should be able to:

◆ distinguish between entering behavior and terminal behavior
◆ list at least six workplace factors that help or hinder transfer
◆ illustrate by examples the difference between skills and competencies
◆ describe four levels a needs analysis should go through
◆ define two criteria of course design: effectiveness and efficiency
◆ select and describe three of the five types of subanalysis
◆ state at least six of the 12 reasons for doing a needs analysis
◆ show by example how needs analysis can be built into course design
◆ give examples of internal and external factors affecting performance
◆ list the five questions to be answered during needs analysis
◆ state three needs analysis tools and techniques for supervisory training.

CHAPTER 5

NEEDS ANALYSIS: THE STARTING POINT

Instructors, whether educators or trainers, should not design or deliver courses until they have established measurable objectives. This is true whether you are an educator or a trainer. Educators can establish course objectives without doing a needs analysis. In public schools and colleges, educators can list the things they want their students to know without assessing how their students will apply this knowledge later in life. The measure of an educator's success is largely the popularity of his or her course and the students' performance on the exams.

In contrast, trainers have a responsibility for delivering performance in the workplace. Their learners must meet the expectations of management, customers, other employees, and supervisors. Trainers are not ready to prepare course objectives until they first determine what behavior (performance) is expected of their graduates. For educators, the starting point is their course objectives, which they often derive from their knowledge of the subject matter that they will teach. But for trainers, the starting point is a needs analysis and the assessment of performance, both present and desired, with an identification of all the factors that stand between present and desired.

Another difference between educators and trainers relates to their understanding of their students. Every human is on a learning continuum that began at birth and that will end with death. Each new day brings new learning—changes in knowledge, attitude, and skill (K-A-S). Learning is the process of moving from one set of behavior (K-A-S) to another. Let's agree to call these two sets entering behavior, or E.B. (what the learner enters an instructional program with—the K-A-S), and terminal behavior, or T.B. (what the learner leaves with—the new K-A-S). Figure 5-1 depicts this learning continuum.

Both educators and trainers are concerned with facilitating the learning process by moving their learners from E.B. to T.B. But they prepare for this mission in very different ways. Consider the teachers you've had, whether in sixth-grade math, eighth-grade science, college history, or

Figure 5-1. The learning continuum.

```
Birth              E.B.            T.B.                Death
 |                  |               |                   |
 |                  |——————————————>|                   |
 |        K-A-S     |               |     K-A-S         |
 |                  |               |                   |————>
 |                  |               |                   |
 |            L   e   a   r   i   n   g                 |
 |                  |               |                   |
 |                  |               |                   |
```

some other course. They knew what you had already studied in prior years. They knew your E.B. pretty well, based on your age, and students in a given course in the public schools or college tend to be at approximately the same age. In contrast, as trainers we often face a class in which our trainees are of much different ages, educational levels, and work experience. Yet we have the same need that our teachers had back in school—to know our learners' E.B. and to build on their existing K-A-S. One of the reasons for doing a needs analysis is to assess the E.B. of our learners before we design or deliver a course.

Another difference between educators and trainers relates to the setting in which new learning will be applied. The math, science, history, or other course that we learned back in school can be applied throughout life with relatively little interference from other forces. Our main concern is with memory and what we've remembered or forgotten.

Training is different. In many courses, trainees go back to the workplace and face constraints that keep them from applying what they learned. Following are some of the factors that can either help or hinder employees in applying at work what they learned during training:

- supportiveness of supervisor
- the time to do it the right way
- physical workplace conditions
- reward structure (reinforcement)
- permanency of what was taught
- enough opportunity to use skills
- the right equipment, forms, and the like
- degree of feedback trainee gets
- sufficient money and resources
- norms, culture, and climate
- peer pressure to conform
- performance of past trainees
- efficiency of systems and methods.

The issue is one of transfer. With education, transfer from classroom to life largely depends on the learner's memory and the relevance of the course. But with training, transfer from workshop to workplace depends on a variety of organizational factors in addition to memory and relevance.

In some organizations, trainers are expected to deliver courses without concerning themselves with how the learners apply their new knowledge back at work. However, during the past decade, the trend has accelerated toward defining the trainer's role as one who is responsible for performance improvement in the workplace and not just instruction in class. When this is the case, the trainer wants to identify as many of these workplace reinforcers and constraints as possible before designing or delivering a course. This enables the trainer to make the workplace more supportive of the desired behaviors and prepare trainees to deal with constraints by addressing them during the learning process.

Let's summarize. We've examined three major reasons for conducting a needs analysis. All three are based on the assumption that the instructor is primarily interested in performance improvement in the workplace (training) and only secondarily interested in improving the learner's knowledge and understanding (education). Where this assumption is not valid (for example, in the orientation of new employees), a needs analysis is not necessary.

Here then, are the three reasons we've just discussed for conducting a needs analysis:

◆ to establish the entering behavior and the present performance levels of trainees, so that we know where to start

◆ to agree on the desired outcomes, or terminal behavior, expected of trainees, so that we can deliver performance at the levels specified

◆ to identify the reinforcers and constraints that are operating in the workplace, so that we can maximize the reinforcers, minimize the constraints, and prepare trainees to deal with them.

Getting the Right K-A-S Blend

Every job or task that we prepare a trainee to fill has the three dimensions we've been discussing, which are illustrated in table 5-1. Although laying bricks is typically regarded as a skill, a master bricklayer must have the right blend of K-A-S, as shown in table 5-1.

Knowledge, attitude, and skills refer to a broad spectrum of items, as the descriptions in the table and the following definitions show.

Knowledge refers to facts, concepts, principles, rules, policies, procedures, and information: the subject matter that the trainee needs to know. *Attitude* refers to feelings, values, beliefs, expectations, style, desires, and temperament—factors that determine how the trainee will apply K and S. *Skill* refers to aptitudes and ability to do things with one's head (cognitive) or hands (manual) or eyes (perceptual) or some combination (psychomotor).

Table 5-1. Desired terminal behavior for a bricklayer.

Knowledge	Attitude	Skill
Correct proportions of sand, mortar, lime to meet different conditions of the brick, the weather (temperature and humidity), etc.	Pride in work, high degree of craftsmanship and professionalism	Cutting brick with one blow of mason's hammer or cold chisel
Procedure for testing the sand for its organic content (and, thus, its acceptability)	Appreciation of the appearance of well-laid brick—textures, shadow play	Mixing mortar to workable consistency—not too stiff, not too runny
Patterns of brick: English, Flemish, common bond, use of header courses, etc.	Neatness in maintaining work area, cleaning tools, putting materials away at end of day, etc.	Taking mortar from mortarboard to trowel to brick without spilling or discoloring the surface of the wall
Use of weep holes, expansion joints, tie-rods, reinforcing bars, etc.	Recognition of the importance of following safety rules and practices, even when they take longer	Techniques for finishing joints—flush, raked, raised, etc.
Procedures for executing jambs, lintels, corbels, vaults and arches, gables, parapets, buttresses, free-form curves, etc.	Desire to work in cost-effective manner, working as fast as possible without sacrificing quality	Use of the level and plumb line so wall is level and plumb
		Use of trowel in buttering the ends of bricks with just enough mortar

Many training courses have placed a heavy emphasis on skills development and a how-to-do-it approach to training. The instructor or videotaped actors outline and demonstrate, or model, the key learning points and steps in a procedure. Trainees then imitate these steps during a practice session. An example of this is the training of supervisors in such skills as how to correct an employee, conduct a selection interview, set goals jointly, and give praise and commendation.

However, the skills and steps taught in how-to courses are often specific to the situation. Yet if we add up all the time a supervisor spends annually in all the situations addressed in such courses, it probably does not exceed more than a dozen or so hours a year. What have we done to prepare supervisors for the rest of the year?

If we look again at the specific situations listed above, we can see that they are all applied areas of interpersonal communications, of giving and getting information in face-to-face settings. Giving clear information is a competency. Getting unbiased information is also a competency (the ability to use directive and nondirective questions, probes, and summary statements to elicit facts and feelings without exerting your own facts and feelings first).

Competencies underlie skills. They are the foundations on which certain specific procedures, steps, and strategies are built. If we can teach supervisors how to give and get information, how to plan an interaction (that is, mentally script it out) before opening one's mouth, and how to test for understanding and agreement, then we have given our participants much more than a list of specific steps and skills. We have prepared them for all the interpersonal communications they will encounter during the rest of their life. Close to 70 percent of their time is spent drawing on these two competencies; less than 2 percent of their time is spent in the specific situations that skills-based courses typically address.

Competency-Based Needs Assessment

The implication of our supervisory training example is clear. If we look only for skills and the specific needs of trainees, we may end up with courses that shortchange them by failing to deliver the broader, generic competencies that underlie their specific needs. Competencies consist of clusters of related skills, knowledge, and attitudes that interact (that is, are interdependent) and that work together to produce desired behavior in a major area of responsibility.

More recently, many corporations have done needs assessments to determine the competencies that are important to the success of their managers. Three criteria were applied. The competencies should be as follows:

◆ almost universal, applying to all managers

◆ discriminating in that they make a significant difference between excellence and merely acceptable performance

◆ improved through training and development.

The bar graph in figure 5-2 shows the performance of a typical manager against the 12 competencies that emerged from these needs assessments. Scores at the bottom of the profile show the styles and values that strongly influence how a manager is likely to apply the competencies.

The relation of skills, knowledge, and attitudes that make up a given competency is shown in the iceberg model in figure 5-3. Skills form the tip of the iceberg, readily apparent from above the surface. That is, we can watch managers perform and quickly get a feel for how skilled they are. But we cannot easily look beneath the surface to see why, to identify the knowledge and the attitudes that are supporting and, indeed, driving their overt performance.

To summarize, the advantages of competency-based needs assessment are as follows:

◆ Competencies, not skills, make the difference in the studies of superior managers done by many corporations.

◆ Skills are situation specific and deal with a limited spectrum of managerial performance.

◆ Competencies are generic, universal, and apply to virtually all managers and to a broad spectrum of performance.

Figure 5-2. Performance proficiency against 12 competencies.

SAMPLE PROFICIENCY PROFILE

Managerial Assessment of Proficiency MAP

Date 08/14/98

MARC   CASE

	0%	25%	50%	75%	100%

MANAGING YOUR JOB		
Time Management & Prioritizing · · · · ·		46%
Setting Goals & Standards · · · · · · · · · ·		76%
Planning & Scheduling Work · · · · · · · ·		31%
ADMINISTRATIVE COMPOSITE · · · · · · · · · · · · · · · · ·		**51%**

RELATING TO OTHERS		
Listening & Organizing · · · · · · · · · · · · ·		68%
Giving Clear Information · · · · · · · · · · ·		69%
Getting Unbiased Information · · · · · · · ·		23%
COMMUNICATION COMPOSITE · · · · · · · · · · · · · · · · · ·		**53%**

BUILDING THE TEAM		
Training, Coaching, & Delegating · · · · ·		60%
Appraising People & Performance · · ·		54%
Disciplining & Counseling · · · · · · · · · · ·		79%
SUPERVISORY COMPOSITE · · · · · · · · · · · · · · · · · · ·		**64%**

THINKING CLEARLY		
Identifying & Solving Problems · · · · · ·		86%
Making Decisions, Weighing Risk · · · ·		52%
Thinking Clearly & Analytically · · · · · · ·		47%
COGNITIVE COMPOSITE ·		**62%**

PROFICIENCY COMPOSITE ·		**58%**

THEORY X (Parent-Child) · · · · · · · · · · ·		35%
THEORY Y (Adult-Adult) · · · · · · · · · · ·		45%

EMPATHIC	41		98%
CRITICAL	0		11%
SEARCHING	4		6%
ADVISING	15		33%
THINKER	18		8%
INTUITOR	25		76%
SENSOR	30		73%
FEELER	27		79%

n = 1

Figure 5-3. An iceberg model of skills, knowledge, and attitudes.

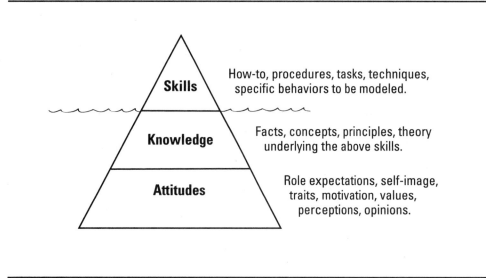

CHAPTER 6

LINKING TRAINING TO THE BUSINESS PLAN

Good training doesn't cost. It pays, but only if it is linked to the organization's business plan, goals, and objectives. The vast majority of training programs are conducted without linkage or reference to organizational objectives. Companies offer a rich smorgasbord of courses in an attempt to provide the greatest good for the greatest number and something for everyone, sort of an internal community college.

During the 1990s, corporations throughout the United States realized that education and training were growing at an enormous rate, often without direction or quality control. In the words of Jack Bowsher, former director of education at IBM, "Education...had no central direction. People were trying out every kind of delivery system.... We were reinventing too many things. We had lots of duplication and yet there were voids. Costs were going up without control and quality was going unmeasured. We figured out that IBM was spending $900 million a year on education...four percent of its total operating budget" (Galagan, 1989).

Like many companies, IBM had hit a plateau in its growth in the 1980s. This prompted a heavy expense control program throughout the company, including a request from the management committee to cut the cost of corporate education and training by $200 million. This led IBM to adopt the systems approach to education and training, shown in figure 6-1. Course design and delivery begin and end with the business requirements of the organization. The value-added impact of a course must be demonstrated before it is added to the catalog.

Two Criteria: Effectiveness and Efficiency

Courses are effective to the degree that they produce improved performance in the workplace and thereby contribute to the achievement of the organization's mission and objectives. Effectiveness should always be

Figure 6-1. A systems approach to education and training.

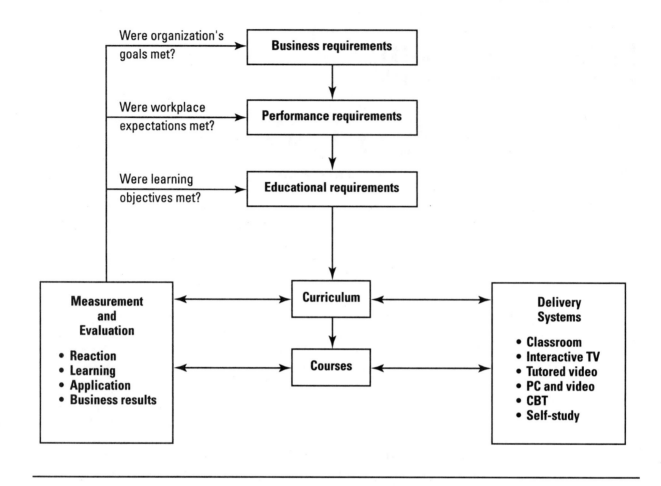

measured in quantitative terms—reduced waste, increased sales, shorter production time, and fewer accidents.

Courses are efficient to the degree that they make people effective in less time or with less money than is required with alternative modes of getting people to perform. Efficiency is thus dependent on effectiveness. It is a waste of time and money to make an ineffective course more efficient. Courses can be made more efficient in three ways: by reducing learning time, by increasing transfer of training from workshop to workplace, and by reducing the costs of delivery. Let's look at each.

◆ **Reduced learning time:** Can a five-day course be taught in three days without significantly reducing its effectiveness (for example, by making prework assignments or eliminating tangential issues)? Can a workshop or classroom experience be converted to self-study (workbooks, videotape, audiotape, computer-based training, satellite transmission, and the like)? Courses prepared in the self-instructional formats are usually

25 percent to 40 percent more efficient (by requiring less time) in getting the participants up to the desired levels of performance. Even when hands-on workshop activities are required, a five-day workshop can be reduced to, say, one or two days devoted to practice and application if the participants have learned the concepts and procedures previously via one or two days of self-study.

◆ **Increased transfer of training:** We can get participants to retain and apply a higher proportion of what they learn by improving the instructional design and by strengthening the maintenance system that recognizes and reinforces the desired behavior in the workplace. Instructional design can be improved in many ways: more hands-on learning and less lecture, better visualization of content, more deductive and less inductive instruction (that is, more Socratic, discovery method and less information dump). The maintenance system can be improved by preparing the supervisors and managers of participants to recognize, coach, and reinforce their new performance immediately after training.

◆ **Reduced costs of delivery:** A lot of time, money, and effectiveness is lost, through travel, hotel, facilities rental, and the like, by bringing trainees to a course when it happens to be offered instead of bringing courses to trainees at the time they need the training. Just-in-time training is far more effective than are courses taken well before or after the participant needs the training. Delivery costs can be reduced by using self-instructional modules, by decentralizing training and offering courses where the participants are concentrated, and by doing training in facilities designed for the purpose.

A 12-Step Process for Ensuring Return on the Training Investment

We have just examined three ways to improve the efficiency of training and education. Now let's look at a 12-step procedure for ensuring the effectiveness of instruction by linking it to an organization's mission, objectives, and needs, both immediate and long range. The model is shown in figure 6-2.

Implementing the 12 Steps

Steps one through six are usually referred to as *needs assessment* or *needs analysis.* They are concerned with organizational and individual needs, and the methods and tools used to collect data should give the organization and its employees insights into areas for improvement.

Figure 6-2. A 12-step procedure for ensuring instructional effectiveness.

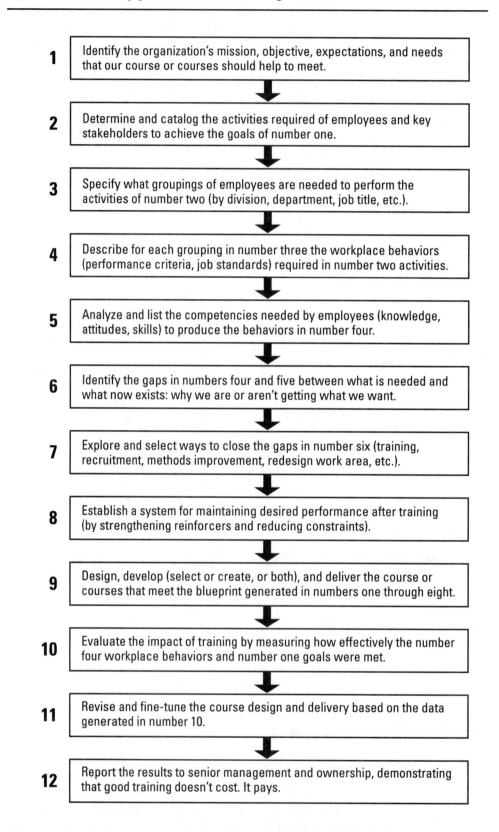

1. Identify the organization's mission, objective, expectations, and needs that our course or courses should help to meet.

2. Determine and catalog the activities required of employees and key stakeholders to achieve the goals of number one.

3. Specify what groupings of employees are needed to perform the activities of number two (by division, department, job title, etc.).

4. Describe for each grouping in number three the workplace behaviors (performance criteria, job standards) required in number two activities.

5. Analyze and list the competencies needed by employees (knowledge, attitudes, skills) to produce the behaviors in number four.

6. Identify the gaps in numbers four and five between what is needed and what now exists: why we are or aren't getting what we want.

7. Explore and select ways to close the gaps in number six (training, recruitment, methods improvement, redesign work area, etc.).

8. Establish a system for maintaining desired performance after training (by strengthening reinforcers and reducing constraints).

9. Design, develop (select or create, or both), and deliver the course or courses that meet the blueprint generated in numbers one through eight.

10. Evaluate the impact of training by measuring how effectively the number four workplace behaviors and number one goals were met.

11. Revise and fine-tune the course design and delivery based on the data generated in number 10.

12. Report the results to senior management and ownership, demonstrating that good training doesn't cost. It pays.

A needs analysis includes such subactivities as:

◆ **Systems analysis:** studying the systems, methods, and procedures with a view toward finding the best ways of doing the work

◆ **Task analysis:** breaking a task or operation down into its simplest steps and determining the best sequence for performing them

◆ **Job analysis:** breaking a job or position down into its subordinate duties and responsibilities, weighing each, and exploring work redistribution

◆ **Behavioral analysis:** breaking human activities down into the knowledge, attitudes, and skills needed to support the desired behavior

◆ **Workplace environment analysis:** studying the reinforcers and constraints that are operating in the workplace to support or squelch good performance.

Steps seven through nine are concerned with what is sometimes referred to as the *performance system* or *maintenance system.* Employees perform as they do for a variety of reasons, of which training is but one. Other factors influencing performance include the degree and quality of supervision, well-designed work environment, appropriate rewards and punishments, peer support, and a positive organizational climate. All of these factors should be examined and, where appropriate, improved so as to create the most supportive environment possible.

Steps 10 through 12 recognize that training is an iterative process and that the 12-step approach enables us to improve a course each time it is presented. Although the instruction is often evaluated at Kirkpatrick's (1998) levels one (Did they like it?) and two (Did they learn it?), our real interest when we link training to the business plan is in evaluating effectiveness at levels three (Did they apply new learning back on the job?) and four (Did it produce a return on the investment?).

On many courses, it is difficult if not impossible to collect data at levels three and four. But when trainers and line managers work together in obtaining answers to steps one through eight of our 12-step process, they have already agreed on what data will be collected and how it will be used to measure and maintain success.

References

Galagan, Patricia A. (1989, January). "IBM Gets Its Arms Around Education." *Training & Development, 43*(1), 34.

Kirkpatrick, D.L. (1998). *Evaluating Training Programs.* San Francisco: Berrett-Koehler.

CHAPTER 7

TWELVE REASONS FOR CONDUCTING A NEEDS ANALYSIS

Managers are often not aware of the time required for a needs analysis or the benefits that come from conducting one. Sometimes they assume that once a need or a desire is made known, the trainer can create or select the appropriate instruction without getting additional information. This chapter provides 12 reasons why it is important to perform a needs analysis. These explanations should help trainers who must convince management to budget the time and money needed for a needs analysis.

1 **To find out the present level of performance:** By establishing a bench level of present performance, we can measure change over time and document improvement. That is, a needs analysis will give us pretraining measures that we can compare with our posttraining measures and thereby evaluate the impact of a course, that is, the performance improvement that is attributable to training.

Example: Many needs analysis tools can be used before and after training to measure needs initially and to document the impact of a training program. Examples include assessments of proficiency, from administrative assistants' command of grammar to supervisors and their performance on managerial competencies.

2 **To determine why present performance is what it is:** Why are people performing the way they are? What reinforcers are maintaining the desired behavior in the workplace? What constraints are preventing better performance (such as outdated equipment, lack of management support, inadequate time to do a task as taught)? What is the relative strength of each of the factors affecting performance, both positively and negatively? What can be done to increase the positive and reduce the negative?

Example: A major commercial bank ran a selling skills program for calling officers and experienced no increase in business as a result. The bank then conducted the needs analysis that should have been done before launching the course and discovered the many factors contributing to the nonperformance of officers in the area of soliciting new business. (Examples included high level of acceptance when in the office but a high level of polite rejection when making calls; promotions based on what college people attended and not the sales they made; officers majored in economics and finance, not marketing; and officers who perceived selling as demeaning.)

3 **To prepare performance standards to be met back on the job:** In most organizations, job descriptions exist, but specific performance standards do not. Before running a training program, it's important to establish job standards, that is, the expectations an employer (supervisor) has of employees. This is much easier to do with entry-level jobs than with jobs that are farther up the organization chart. However, they are part of any well-designed course and must be communicated and, when possible, met during training (and not left as a hope or desire that they will be met back in the workplace).

Example: In a train-the-trainer workshop, the instructor surveys training managers to determine what qualities they look for in their instructors. The instructor converts this information to a 48-item checklist that he or she uses during the workshop. Participants take the checklist with them to be assessed against these standards in the courses they deliver.

4 **To assess the entering behavior of our trainees:** What do we know about our learners? What knowledge, attitudes, and skills do they bring to the course? What strengths can we build on? What deficiencies do they possess? How universal are these? Will one course fit all? Or do I need different courses or tracks to meet the needs of all my trainees? Who are my strong and weak trainees? Should I make subgroup assignments and use the buddy system of pairing stronger and weaker participants to work together?

Example: Prior to attending a management development program, participants go through a one-day video-based, computer-scored assessment of their proficiency on 12 managerial competencies. Participants receive a bar graph showing percentiles that compare their own performance with nationwide norms. Participants know, therefore, where to focus their attention in the workshops that follow. The organization also knows which topics to offer based on where managers' needs are greatest.

5 **To determine criteria and prerequisites for enrollment:** What minimum levels of knowledge, skill, and experience do participants need? Who is and isn't eligible to attend a course? By answering these questions in concert with the managers who will be releasing their people to attend class, we can minimize misfits (that is, participants who don't belong in class because of wrong timing, wrong person, under- or overqualifications, and so on).

Example: Preworkshop assignments can be used to determine who is and who isn't qualified to take a course. These assignments can take many forms, such as a case study, a script for critique, an assessment exercise, or a questionnaire. Materials must be returned in advance of the workshop so that the instructor can contact misfits and counsel them on alternatives.

6 **To assess the work environment within which the trainee operates:** How supportive is the organizational climate, culture, and norms? Will it nourish the behavior we plan to shape through training? Or will it discourage it and cause it to die? What can we do to improve the climate? How can we prepare our trainees to deal with the climate and perhaps improve it?

Although this factor looks similar to number two, in the earlier example of selling bank services, the problem lay with human expectations and the need to change them, whereas the concern here is in changing the environment to make it more supportive of the desired performance.

Example: Many organizations have conducted employee attitude surveys to evaluate the health of their work environment. The survey can evaluate the work group level (whether a unit, a section, or something else). This means that supervisors and managers attending a training course can obtain data on the strengths and weaknesses of the climate within their own work group. They can repeat the same survey several months after the course to measure improvement. Figure 7-1 illustrates a number of these factors.

7 **To examine the systems and procedures used:** Are there ways of working smarter? Is it possible to eliminate or simplify procedures, forms, or tasks? Are we training people for yesterday's methods rather than tomorrow's? Let's not teach old ways of doing things if improvements are

Figure 7-1. Factors in the work environment that affect the organizational climate.

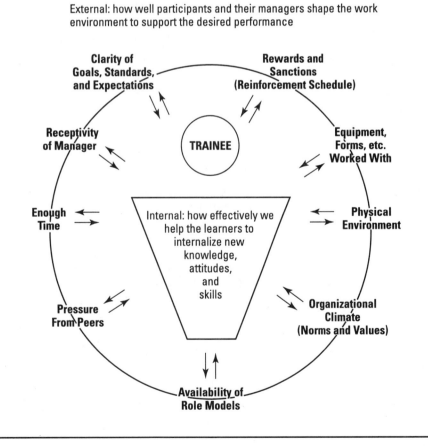

External: how well participants and their managers shape the work environment to support the desired performance

Clarity of Goals, Standards, and Expectations

Rewards and Sanctions (Reinforcement Schedule)

Receptivity of Manager

TRAINEE

Equipment, Forms, etc. Worked With

Enough Time

Internal: how effectively we help the learners to internalize new knowledge, attitudes, and skills

Physical Environment

Pressure From Peers

Organizational Climate (Norms and Values)

Availability of Role Models

needed and can be made before developing or delivering our course. This aspect of needs assessment is known as task analysis or systems analysis.

Example: A major corporation was having difficulty getting the managers in its four divisions to set goals, negotiate priorities, budget, and take the company's management by objectives (MBO) program seriously. The forms and procedures were studied, simplified, and redesigned on one form that went to all managers and that contained instruction for its use. The course then focused on having managers complete the form during the workshop.

8 **To establish the terminal behaviors and course objectives:** What are the measurable goals of the training? What are the terminal behaviors to be measured in the workplace and, when possible, in class? What competencies are needed to do the job? Will all trainees be required to meet all objectives (that is, to be proficient in all competencies)? Or should we distinguish between core competencies (required of all) and optional competencies (elected by the trainee in concert with the supervisor)?

Example: Prior to setting up a management development or supervisory training program, many organizations send out surveys and assessments that ask future participants and their managers to evaluate their needs on each of a number of competencies, rating the relevance of each and their proficiency on each. This evaluation enables the training department to offer those topics where the need is greatest.

9 **To establish policy and make decisions:** Many questions must be answered before an organization decides to make or buy a course. What materials already exist? In what format? At what cost? How well will the course meet our objectives? Does it need to be tailored or supplemented? How much time is needed for the course? How much time are participants' managers willing to release them for? What equipment (hardware, facilities) is needed?

There are many trade-offs that can affect the design or selection of a course. Some of them are listed below. Although they look like either-or decisions, the same course may embody both factors:

- ◆ initial versus continuation training (how much to teach now versus later)
- ◆ formal versus on the job (what we teach in class versus the supervisor teaching at work)
- ◆ make versus buy (what must be developed in-house versus purchased as a package)
- ◆ head versus book (what trainees must know cold versus what they can look up as needed)
- ◆ centralized versus decentralized (training in one location versus taken on the road)
- ◆ individualized versus group learning (self-study versus workshop).

Example: The publisher of an assessment exercise (Managerial Assessment of Proficiency, or MAP) and a training program (EXCEL) wanted prospective users to identify all the pros and cons of purchasing the program—the potential advantages and drawbacks. The publisher prepared a list of 20 advantages and 20 disadvantages, with space to rank each on a four-point rating scale. The resulting decision is a much better informed one.

10   **To involve line managers:** To be fully successful, training programs require the active support (and not just lip service) of managers, as supervisors of your trainees, as subject matter experts, as budget approvers, as consumers of the skills your graduates will possess. It's much easier to solicit management support of training before it is launched than afterward, which may be too late. By involving managers in the needs analysis, you will begin to form a partnership as they see their inputs to the course design or selection. Training should be seen as belonging to everyone and not as your course for their people.

Example: Prior to designing or selecting a supervisory training program, the training department surveys all second-level supervisors (that is, the managers of first-line supervisors), asking them to rank the importance of each entry on a list of 10 reasons for running training and on a list of 17 skills and abilities that they feel their people need.

11   **To generate course material:** The surveys, interviews, assessments, and observations you collect during the needs analysis will provide a wealth of data and illustrations (examples, case studies, role plays, and the like) to bring your training program to life and make it highly relevant to participants' needs. Some of your instructional time can be devoted to an analysis and interpretation of the exercises (for example, management-style inventory, climate survey, communication skills assessment).

Some courses can have a preworkshop assignment serve as a need assessment, thereby providing each participant with a detailed understanding of personal needs. Such an assessment should be interpreted as a group exercise at the start of class, so that the instructor and participants begin with a clear picture of the group's needs. Following are some examples of this type of needs assessment:

Title of Training Program	Needs Assessment Exercise as Prework
Time Management	Weekly time log
Writing Skills	Letter or memo to be edited and rewritten
Leadership Style	Style inventory to be completed by trainee and boss
Problem Solving	Case study to be analyzed
Selling Skills	Script of sales call to be evaluated
Instructional Skills	Lesson plan to be prepared for short presentation
Career Planning	List of values and work qualities to be rank ordered

Example: In courses that make use of case studies or brief, work-related illustrations of the learning points, instructors can ask each participant to submit before class a written illustration of something that happened at work that shows the appropriate or inappropriate behavior specific to the topic. By reviewing these illustrations, instructors can assess the needs and then select appropriate examples to use in the course.

12 **To establish a maintenance system:** As discussed in numbers two and six, the workplace environment is not always fully supportive of the behavior participants learn in class. For transfer of training to be effective, we want to set up a maintenance system that will recognize and reinforce the desired behavior back on the job. The best time to begin this work is during the needs analysis, for it is here that we are dealing with the factors that help or hinder our trainees, whether these factors are employees or the supervisor, or the right equipment or forms or procedures, the presence of standards and a system for tracking and rewarding individual performance, and so on.

Example: Instructional designers who attend a workshop on design and development skills must specify what measures will be taken in the workplace to maintain the new behavior of trainees as they return from a course. A list of 20 tools and techniques is provided during the workshop.

CHAPTER 8
CONDUCTING A NEEDS ANALYSIS

Why Do It?

Many factors influence people's behavior, or performance, at work. Some of these factors are internal to an individual and can be taught. We refer to knowledge, attitudes, and skill, or K-A-S. Others are external to the individual and include such things as:

♦ the organization's culture, norms, and climate

♦ the expectations of one's manager, peers, subordinates, and customers

♦ the equipment, procedures, forms, and systems used at work.

Internal factors are what the individual brings to the job, whereas external factors are what the job brings to the individual. It is the interaction of these two factors that produces behavior change, as figure 8-1 shows.

Figure 8-1. Interaction of internal and external factors.

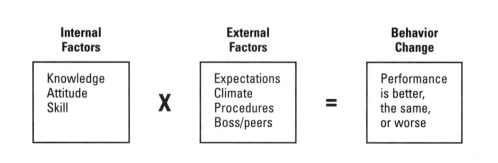

Internal factors (K-A-S) can be shaped through training and development. External factors are more resistant to change, and often require management action to initiate the process of behavior change.

To produce the desired behavior change (that is, to develop employees with the competencies that were determined earlier), trainers must design, select, and instruct their courses in such a way as to address both the internal and the external factors. Both types of factors influence the results of training (in much the same way that the area of a rectangle is the product of its length and its width, and it is academic to ask which is more important).

Another way of depicting the relationship of internal (K-A-S) and external (work environment) factors is shown in figure 8-2. Each of the factors shown in the work environment can act as a reinforcer or a constraint, helping or hindering employees as they leave training and attempt to apply new concepts and skills on the job.

Herein lies a major difference between education and training. Educators need not concern themselves with the external factors that affect their students after the course is over. The effectiveness of their curriculum, their instruction, and their students is usually measured solely in terms of K-A-S that was transferred from teacher to learner. Thus, educators have no need to conduct a needs analysis. Rather, they set forth a curriculum or a catalog of course offerings, and it is the student's job to select what is needed. (To be sure, educators may conduct surveys to see

Figure 8-2. Relationship of internal and external factors.

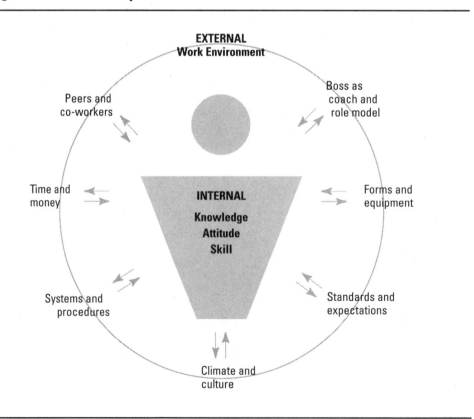

what courses students might want, but let's not confuse a wants analysis with a needs analysis.)

In contrast with educators, trainers have a responsibility to deliver performance in the workplace and not merely in class. This is a far more demanding charge than educators face. Professional trainers have accepted a belief in training as a process, and their credo goes something like this:

◆ Training cannot be deemed effective until trainees perform in desired ways on the job, ways that were spelled out in the course objectives.

◆ There are many external factors besides the internal K-A-S that influence a person's behavior on the job.

◆ Some of these organizational factors (such as, the climate and culture and the expectations of boss and peers) can be influenced and improved over time as successive cycles of employees are trained.

◆ But other environmental factors will always pose a barrier to trainees as they try to practice at work what they learn in class (for example, having the time to do it right, having a distraction-free and conflict-free work environment like the one in class).

◆ The purpose of training is to improve performance both in the trainee and in the work environment.

◆ Trainees should thus be viewed as catalysts and agents of change whose impact on the work environment will produce organizational growth and development in desired directions.

The Trainer-as-Salesperson Analogy

Salespeople can make cold calls and deliver a canned presentation, which yields a relatively low closing ratio. Or they can research the needs of the organization and individuals on whom they call, thereby enabling them to tailor their presentation, know what to sell and what not to sell, and avoid wasting time with people whose needs are not aligned with their products or services.

Trainers make similar choices. They can run courses without researching the needs of the organization and its trainees, an approach that yields a relatively low return-on-investment. Or they can invest time in a performance audit, thereby enabling them to tailor the course, know what K-A-S to include and exclude, and avoid wasting time with people whose needs are not aligned with their offerings.

Let's continue the sales analogy one step further. A salesperson calls on present customers and on new prospects. The approach to each is quite different. So it is with trainers. At times, we trainers set up courses for new hires. These are like the salesperson's new prospects: their entering behavior (K-A-S) is hard for us to tap, yet we must if we are to succeed. At other times, we are called on to train seasoned employees whose present behavior on the job is easier to access and, hence, to assess. As with the salesperson, our approach to these two audiences must be different.

Questions to Be Answered

The professional trainer seeks to answer five basic questions before launching a training program. The purpose of a needs analysis is to provide answers to these questions as well as to other questions that may be specific to certain types of training. Here are the basic questions:

◆ What is the present behavior of job holders? This is asked when we are called on to train experienced employees. When training new hires, the question is often worded as follows: What is the entering behavior (E.B.) of the trainees? What common K-A-S do they possess that we can build on?

◆ What is the desired terminal behavior (T.B.) of our trainees? What do we expect of them back on the job? What are the organization's performance standards and expectations for these job holders?

◆ What reinforcers and constraints exist in the workplace that will help or hinder people from performing at the desired levels? What can be done to establish a maintenance system for reinforcing the desired behavior?

◆ What opportunities exist for doing things better or smarter? Let's not assume that the purpose of training is to impart an acceptance of the way we've always done it. How do we want it done tomorrow that is different from the way we did it yesterday?

◆ On the basis of the foregoing questions, how can we best close the gap between E.B. and T.B.? What changes are needed besides training? And, as for training, what will be its content, format, length, frequency, location, cost, and so on?

The NIH (Not Invented Here) Syndrome

There is always the danger that participants will view training as a Little Red Schoolhouse experience. It's nice to know about, but not as relevant as it might be to the real world of work they face daily. As trainees sit in class, they are thinking about all the reinforcers and constraints they will face as they try to transplant what they have learned into practice back on the job. The course materials and exercises, whether developed internally or purchased, are seen as not invented here because they fail to address the problems and situations trainees need help with.

Moreover, the support that each trainee needs from the immediate supervisor would probably not be forthcoming if these supervisors had not been consulted when the course was developed or selected. If they and their subordinate trainees see training as something that the human resource development (HRD) people do for them, then there is little reason for them to buy in and see training as their responsibility as well.

By involving trainees and their immediate supervisors in the needs analysis, we can virtually eliminate the NIH syndrome. When training programs are seen as a response to needs that were articulated by managers, commitment to the programs is that much stronger.

Methods and Tools

There are five major methods for collecting data in a needs analysis. Following is a list of those methods, along with examples of the tools for generating new information (as in examples one and two) or for capturing existing information (as in example three). A typical needs analysis uses no more than two or three tools. Organizational audits (example three) are best because they do not take employees away from their work and because they are more likely to yield data with high reliability and validity. However, these methods are often not acceptable to management, and trainers must use survey research (example one) and simulation assessments (example two) to generate information:

- ◆ **Example 1: Survey Research**
    - — interviewing: present job holders, new trainees, supervisors, customers
    - — questionnaire: mailed or filled out at work, alone or in researcher's presence
    - — climate survey: to measure morale, commitment, work environment, attitude
    - — tests of proficiency: writing skill, knowledge of supervisory practices, circuitry
    - — attitude survey: management style, communication style, and the like
    - — critical incident research ("Recall a recent situation in which...")
- ◆ **Example 2: Simulation Assessments**
    - — assessment lab in managerial skills, via videotape or live experience
    - — in-basket and managerial appraisals
    - — role playing (for example, selling skills, interviewing, supervisory skills)
    - — case analysis (for example, in problem-solving and decision-making skills)
- ◆ **Example 3: Organizational Audits**
    - — **Type A: Task Analysis and System Analysis**
        - • flow charting of procedures and work flow
        - • work distribution study and analysis of time sheets

- methods improvement and work simplification
- present versus proposed analysis of work elements
- operation analysis, human-machine analysis

— **Type B: Observation on the Job**

- participant observer (as co-worker)
- nonparticipant observer: obtrusive and unobtrusive research
- shopping survey: retail sales, banks, airlines, and the like
- telephone shopping of employees at work

— **Type C: Records Check**

- reports on file: call reports, incident reports, grievances, and the like
- systems and procedures documentation (such as flow charts)
- methods and procedures manuals, training guides, and so forth
- complaints, error rates, rejects, squeaky wheel data
- job descriptions and performance appraisals, for example
- library research: trade association data, competitors' data, studies by industry, use of experts, commercially available courses, and so forth.

SECTION 3

DESIGNING A TRAINING PROGRAM

This section deals with course design, and the next section addresses course development. What's the difference? And is it important?

The roles of course designers and course developers are comparable to those of architects and contractors. Although architects and contractors must understand one another, each brings unique skills to the task of creating a new building.

Course designers are architects, drawing on their understanding of human behavior and educational psychology and on their ability to convert performance expectations into required knowledge, attitudes, and skills.

Course developers are contractors, drawing on their creative abilities as writers, illustrators, media specialists, programmers, and production specialists converting the designer's blueprints into finished course materials.

In today's era of high-tech training, courses are often designed internally by training specialists and developed externally by media experts. Of course, the trainer, as architect, is responsible for the outcome of both processes, design and development.

The chapters in this section explain the reasons for doing a needs analysis, how to prepare course objectives that are based on developmental needs, and how to specify the content, methods, and media that will meet the objectives and serve as a basis for the make-or-buy decision. Following is a description of the topics in each chapter:

Chapter 9, "Behavioral Analysis," illustrates the process of listing the entering behavior (E.B.) and desired terminal behavior (T.B.) for a sample course (business writing) in three categories: knowledge, attitudes, and skills.

Chapter 10, "Preparing Course Objectives," outlines the criteria for generating behavioral (observable, measurable) course objectives of two types: mediating (classroom) and terminal (workplace).

Chapter 11, "Programmed Instruction: An Example," provides a pretest, self-study spelling lesson, and posttest, followed by the behavioral analysis that illustrates how the lesson was designed.

Chapter 12, "Course Design Blueprints," presents two formats for outlining the four components of a course and showing their relationship to each other: objectives, content, methods, and criterion test.

Chapter 13, "Make or Buy," lists 10 benefits of making and of buying a training program, followed by a 26-step planning sheet for use in making (designing) a course.

Upon completing this section, the learner will be able to:

- ◆ illustrate from a course on safety one E.B. and its desired T.B.
- ◆ evaluate this learning objective: "Trainers will be able to understand the . . ."
- ◆ define and illustrate mediating behavior and terminal behavior
- ◆ state at least four criteria for effective course objectives
- ◆ apply the S-R-F model from chapter 1 to explain how programmed instruction works
- ◆ describe the four components of a good course outline
- ◆ indicate which of two outline formats is preferred and why
- ◆ list at least four benefits of making and of buying courses
- ◆ identify the five phases of course design, from analysis to delivery.

CHAPTER 9

BEHAVIORAL ANALYSIS

Determining Present and Desired Behavior

A need for training exists when—and only when—there is a gap between the present behavior and the desired behavior of a population. That population may be employees, students, customers, volunteers, or any other group. Behavioral analysis refers to the process of identifying and describing these two sets of behavior.

Let's agree first on a definition of *behavior.* Perhaps the closest synonym is performance, which can be observed (if the behavior is overt) or non-observable (if the behavior is covert, as when you are thinking or feeling something). Trainers and educators are concerned with both the overt and covert aspects of their learners' behavior.

Human behavior takes place in three arenas: knowledge, attitudes, and skills. Psychology textbooks refer to these three arenas as the cognitive, affective, and psychomotor domains. Putting it in simplest terms, our behavior in any situation can be attributed to what we know, how we feel, and what we can do. Moreover, most human behavior depends on all three factors working together. Table 9-1 shows examples of the components of these arenas.

Behavioral analysis is concerned with identifying and describing the desired knowledge, attitudes, and skills of a group or an individual, and then taking an inventory of that person's present, or existing, knowledge, attitudes, and skills (K-A-S). The gap between these two sets of behavior will determine the nature, scope, and content of a training program (or any other intervention that might close the K-A-S gap, such as mentoring or counseling).

Putting it another way, behavioral analysis is the process of identifying the gaps between what we want our people to know, feel, and do (in order to perform at desired levels) and what they presently know, feel, and do.

Table 9-1. Three arenas of human behavior.

Knowledge (Cognitive) What We Know	Attitudes (Affective) How We Feel	Skills (Psychomotor) What We Can Do
Facts	Feelings	Psychomotor (e.g., manual dexterity and assembling)
Concepts	Beliefs	Reasoning (problem solving, decision making, organizing, prioritizing, etc.)
Rules	Values	
Theory	Perceptions	
Principles	Style	Perception (visual, auditory, tactile, etc.)
Policy	Opinions	
Procedures	Drives	etc.
Generalizations	Biases	
etc.	etc.	

If there is no gap, there is no *need* for training. There might be an *opportunity* for training if we want to upgrade our expectations of those people's performance. However, if existing and desired K-A-S are one, there is no need for training.

Preparing a Behavioral Analysis

In courses where the standards or desired outcomes are well known, it is usually easier to start a behavioral analysis by first listing the terminal behaviors—that is, the things we want our learners to know, feel, and do in the workplace. A course on business writing skills is an example because the standards of good writing are well established. Table 9-2 shows a list of entering behavior and terminal behavior.

Moreover, we are much better prepared to know what K-A-S to look for when we go to our population of trainees if we have already listed the behaviors we want to see in the workplace. As we examine their present writing and their thoughts about the writing process, we will know much better what questions to ask and what behaviors to observe.

In contrast, when we are faced with preparing a behavioral analysis for a job, task, or situation that has never existed before, we might find it easier to study present behavior first and then decide how much improvement is realistic or possible. An example might be a course in time management. Even where courses have been given before (such as supervisory training), it may be desirable to observe and list the present levels of K-A-S on such predetermined topics as team building, company policy and procedures, performance appraisals, interpersonal communications, and the like before setting terminal behaviors that might be unrealistic.

Table 9-2. Behavioral analysis for a business writing skills course.

	Entering Behavior (Present)	Terminal Behavior (Desired)
Knowledge (facts, rules, theory, concepts, and procedures)	Sentences long and sometimes rambling. Writers unaware of this. Common use of passive voice ("it was decided that…it has been brought to our attention that…"); no knowledge of why passive voice is poor writing. Low readability due to many long, imprecise words (e.g., facilitate, coordinate, retain, obtain, endeavor—"Every endeavor will be undertaken to facilitate the successful implementation of your program").	Sentences should not exceed an average of 17 words. Shorter is better. Conversion to active voice ("The team decided that…we've noticed that…"); passive used only when subject (person acting) is unknown. At least 75% one-syllable words to give high readability (e.g., help, work with, keep, get, try—"I think we can help to make your rollout a real success").
Attitudes (feelings, values, perceptions, beliefs, and the like)	Long sentences and a polysyllabic vocabulary with many unfamiliar words are the mark of an educated writer. Management will think I have not thought things through or done my homework if I don't deliver a multipage document. There's a certain formal style to business writing that I should model: "This department intends to facilitate an increased exchange of information…"	Key executives and busy, successful people get a lot of message into a crisp, lean writing style. Less is more (readability, attention, etc.). Management has had poor models. Give them a brief document with attachments that provide depth for those who want it. The formal style of the past is as useless today as powdered wigs. Write the way you speak: "I'd like to see more swapping of ideas…"
Skills (manual, cognitive, perceptual, that is, things we do)	Little or no outlining or planning prior to writing, free flow of thought, not always logical or consecutive. Heavy use of business jargon; dull, ponderous, imprecise, or pompous writing; not conversational. First dozen or so words often wasted: "I have just received your letter dated March 12, in which you inquire about the availability of our…"	Writer knows before starting that a letter (memo, report, etc.) will have five paragraphs (four sections, etc.); good organization and flow. Use of colorful, interesting, memorable expressive words, analogies, and figures of speech: conversational. Key message is up front, usually in first paragraph: "Yes, our 1997 model is still available. I'm delighted that you're interested in…"

Three assignments follow. On a sheet of paper, create a behavioral analysis for the one most relevant to you. Follow the format used in table 9-2, labeling the vertical columns *Entering Behavior* and *Terminal Behavior,* and the horizontal columns *Knowledge, Attitudes,* and *Skills.* Try to find at least three entries for each category: knowledge, attitudes, and skills. Under the heading *Entering Behavior,* list the assumptions you feel safe in making about the population of trainees for whom you're designing the course. (You would, of course, want to test these assumptions with research if you were really designing the course.) Under *Terminal Behavior,* list the behavior you want of your trainees after the course, specifically what they must know, feel, and do. The choices are as follows:

◆ **Selection interviewing:** The Human Resources Department conducts employment interviews to screen job applicants, but the supervisor conducts the final selection interview. Supervisors have never been trained to do so, and you have been asked to perform a behavioral analysis prior to designing or selecting a training program.

◆ **Running a meeting:** Although a survey indicates that employees spend an average of 20 percent of their time in meetings, no one has ever trained the people who run these meetings. Time is wasted. Follow-up is weak. Prepare a behavioral analysis for the meeting leadership course you've been asked to create.

◆ **Changing a tire:** The local women's club has asked you to give a one-hour talk on how to change a flat tire. To make your course as effective as possible, you've decided to prepare a behavioral analysis.

How Did You Do?

In doing a behavioral analysis, trainers often find it helpful to state the desired terminal behaviors that are difficult to obtain, followed by the entering behavior, either assumed or observed, that is blocking attainment of the terminal behaviors. Let's look at one or two examples in each of the three courses you had as choices.

Selection Interviewing

One terminal behavior is to ask the job applicant questions that are unstructured, or nondirective, so as to get the applicant doing most of the talking. Often the entering behavior of a supervisor is to ask directive questions that elicit short answers and give little information. Another example is the terminal behavior of avoiding questions that violate the guidelines of equal employment opportunity. Unfortunately, a common entering behavior is for supervisors to ask a female applicant if she is married or if she plans to have children.

Running a Meeting

Some terminal behaviors for the person running a meeting are to control digressions and to limit questions and contributions not on the agenda. Not wanting to offend anyone, the meeting leader often lets the group wander into areas of discussion that are irrelevant. The leader should say, "I'm having trouble relating your comments to our agenda. Can we get back to our agenda and our objectives for this meeting, please."

As for the weak follow-up to meetings, another terminal behavior is to have the meeting leader or a recorder make entries on a flip chart each time a decision is reached, an action taken, and an assignment made. This can then be reproduced and distributed immediately after the meeting.

Changing a Tire

One terminal behavior is to loosen the lug nuts before jacking the car up. Unfortunately, the common entering behavior is to put the jack in place and raise the tire off the ground. Thereafter, any attempt to loosen the lug nuts will only spin the wheel. Another terminal behavior is to test a spare tire before installing it to make sure it is fully inflated. The entering behavior is that a spare tire may have developed a slow leak and may be unfit to use. It would be foolish to discover this after installing it when the simple test of bouncing the tire on the roadway will confirm whether the tire is fully inflated.

CHAPTER 10

PREPARING COURSE OBJECTIVES

Robert Mager's book *Preparing Instructional Objectives* set the guidelines for specifying the desired outcomes of a course. The key word in a learning objective is the verb. It must describe a behavior that the learner performs after instruction, and it must be both observable and measurable. Consider two examples. The verbs in the first one are not observable or measurable. The verbs in the second can be observed and measured.

- ◆ Upon completing the course, the learner will be able to appreciate the value of new customers, understand the importance of spelling their names correctly on the account information card, and treat them with respect.

- ◆ Upon completing this course, the learner will be able to state the average annual dollar value of a new customer, spell the customer's name correctly on the account information card, and use that person's name twice when greeting and saying good-bye to the customer.

The following learning objectives are taken from a course that teaches the principles of flight to persons qualifying for their private pilot's license. Although it is unlikely that you know how to fly a plane, you should nevertheless be able to tell which of them satisfy our criteria for a behavioral objective and which do not. After each one, write "yes" if it qualifies, and "no" if it doesn't.

Upon completion of this lesson, the student pilot will be able to:

1. completely understand the aerodynamic properties of airfoils _____

2. write, in his or her own words, the definition of an *airfoil* _____

3. state the physical law by which an airfoil produces lift _____

4. be motivated to a degree that is enough for the student pilot to be able to know the meaning of *chord line* _____

5. list the four forces that act on a plane in straight-and-level flight _____

6. *really* understand Bernoulli's principle and apply it to an aircraft's wing _____

7. discriminate between statements that are true or false concerning angle of attack and angle of incidence _____

8. select, from a given list of aircraft parts, those that are considered airfoils _____

9. fully appreciate and grasp the significance of the ability of a plane to fly _____

10. understand and enjoy the experience of small-aircraft flying _____

11. spell correctly the words *aerodynamics, Bernoulli, incidence, stratosphere,* and *vacuum* _____

Let's see how you did. The first objective rates a no because we can't observe or measure the verb *understand*. Numbers two and three are both acceptable and get a yes. The fourth objective is no because we don't know how to observe or measure *motivation*. Besides, motivation isn't the behavior we want. The simpler wording of "define chord line" would have earned a yes. Number five rates a yes; six, no; and seven yes, although the writer didn't have to tell us that true and false items would be used. Simpler wording would have been "discriminate between angle of attack and angle of incidence." Objective eight gets a yes, and both nine and 10 are no. Objective 11 gets a yes because it is probably the easiest objective to observe and measure. But does it have anything to do with flying a plane? Probably not. So let's add another criterion to our guidelines: Course objectives should contain words that are observable, measurable, and relevant.

Parts of a Behavioral Objective

In addition to creating training objectives that are observable and measurable, we should also include quantitative criteria whenever possible so that we can evaluate the degree of acceptability of our learner's behavior. For example, suppose we are teaching someone to keyboard and set one of our objectives as follows: "The trainee must be able to keyboard rapidly and with accuracy." This is a poor objective as it stands. What does rapidly mean? What is accuracy?

A better training objective is this: "The trainee must be able to keyboard at least 40 words per minute (average of 10 minutes), and must have no more than three corrections per 200 words." This objective is observable and measurable.

When we are preparing objectives for courses that are primarily concerned with the teaching of procedures or techniques, our behavioral objectives should contain the following three elements:

♦ the condition (event, situation) that the trainee must respond to

♦ the behavior (response) we want the learner to make

♦ the criteria of acceptability for evaluating the learner's behavior.

Let's look at an example of an objective taken from a course designed to train retail sales clerks. This particular lesson deals with handling money and making change. The three parts of an objective are labeled beside it:

Condition (S) { Given a customer paying for merchandise with paper money whose face value exceeds the price,

Behavior (R) { the sales clerk will follow the correct procedure (five steps) for making change,

Criteria (F) { with no more than two omissions over six transactions (that is, two out of 30 steps is our tolerance).

In learning theory, the smallest unit of behavior is the stimulus-response-feedback unit (S-R-F). A learning sequence consists of a chain of S-R-F links. If we now look again at the sample objective above, we see that the condition is the stimulus (that is, the event or situation that stimulates the learner to respond). The behavior is the response we want the trainee to make. And the criterion enables the trainee and the instructor to have feedback on how well the learning is progressing. (Notice the letters *S, R,* and *F,* indicating the three parts of the objective, printed in front of the appropriate part.)

The objective we just examined is mainly concerned with the sales clerk's skill in following procedures correctly. Trainers sometimes prefer objectives that focus on knowledge rather than skill. Here's an example of the preceding objective, rewritten to stress knowledge:

Condition (S) { Upon completing the lesson dealing with handling money and making change,

Behavior (R) { the sales clerk will be able to list the five steps to be followed when a customer needs change,

Criteria (F) { giving them in correct sequence and stating why each is important to the accuracy of the transaction.

Incidentally, the five steps referred to in both of our sample objectives are as follows:

1. Acknowledge the size of one or more bills: "That's $3.95 out of $20."
2. Place the bill on the ledge of the register until the transaction is complete (don't put it in the drawer).
3. Select change from the drawer, working from smallest size up; give it in the same sequence.
4. Count the change on the counter or as you put it into the customer's hand; state when to do each.
5. Thank the customer for shopping here; place the bill in the register.

Mediating Versus Terminal Behavior

In preparing objectives, we must distinguish between mediating behavior (which occurs in class) and terminal behavior (which can occur in class as well as on the job). The verb is the key to whether an objective is mediating or terminal. Table 10-1 lists behaviors that illustrate the difference:

Table 10-1. A comparison of mediating and terminal behavior.

Course	Mediating Behavior	Terminal Behavior
How to Change a Tire	Trainee must be able to name the three parts of a standard automobile jack and describe where the jack should be placed to raise a flat tire off the ground.	Trainee must be able to assemble the jack, place it correctly on the automobile, and operate it so as to raise a flat tire off the ground.
How to Cash a Check	Bank teller must be able to state the five things to look for in cashing a check (negotiability factors) and to describe the procedure for dealing with problems with each.	Bank teller must be able to process a mixed batch of checks that contain errors, determining whether or not to cash each check.
How to Punctuate	Writer will be able to identify dependent and independent clauses, words used in apposition, words in series, and conjunctions used to separate two clauses or sentences.	Writer will be able to punctuate correctly, inserting commas where needed (to separate clauses, appositives, words, in series, two clauses or sentences, etc.).

Mediating behaviors usually contain verbs and phrases like *state, name, describe, identify, explain, show, define,* and *give an example.* These behaviors occur in a class but not in the real world. For example, we don't expect writers to identify the dependent clauses and the appositives in the copy they generate, but we do expect them to punctuate their copy correctly.

Terminal behaviors usually contain verbs and phrases that are observable, such as *assemble, conduct, perform, produce, process, fill out, complete,* and *arrange.* These are the behaviors we want of the learner in the real world.

The question arises: Why have mediating behavior at all? Don't we always want to state our objectives in a way that reflects what the learner does in the real world? Perhaps we do. However, it is not always possible to measure or observe our trainees under the actual conditions for which we are training them. Suppose, for example, we are developing a course to train nurses how to evacuate the hospital and move patients in the event of fire. We could develop a simulation, of course. But it would cost time and money, and would not be likely to induce the element of panic and fear. So we might settle for mediating behavior instead: "Describe the process of evacuating a ward, noting the five steps to be taken and three precautions to be observed."

The training of firefighters, police cadets, airline pilots, military personnel, nuclear power plant supervisors, and the like involves the development of many behaviors that can be simulated but never duplicated. In such cases, trainers may have to accept the trainees' verbal descriptions (mediating behaviors) of their real-world performance in situations that all of them hope will never occur.

How Do These Objectives Rate?

Table 10-2 lists sample learning objectives from different courses. Your job is to evaluate each against six criteria, entering your evaluations in the last column in the table. Then use a separate piece of paper to rewrite objectives or portions of them, as required. The criteria are as follows:

1. Is it mediating or terminal?
2. Are the initiating conditions (stimulus) specified?
3. Are the criteria (response acceptability) spelled out?
4. Is it a relevant (useful) objective?
5. Is it behavioral (measurable)?
6. Is it sufficiently discrete (small, workable)?

Table 10-2. Sample learning objectives.

Course	Objective	Evaluation
Letter-Writing Course	Given a letter of complaint from a customer, the branch manager will be able to (a) identify the purpose of the reply, (b) select the most appropriate style and format for the reply, and (c) describe some of the things to be included in the letter (apology, restatement of problem, statement of empathy, corrective action taken).	
Structural Steel Framing (a design course)	Given a blueprint showing the elevations (cutaway) of six different nuclear boiler installations, the designer will be able to specify the appropriate cross-bracing (system design and size and type of structural members) in at least five of the six installations.	
Management Development Program	Upon completing the session on motivation, the participants will be able to distinguish between Herzberg's "motivators" and "hygiene factors," indicating which is intrinsic and which extrinsic, and giving at least four examples of each that are operating in the participant's work group (section, department, etc.).	

How Did You Do?

Our sample objective from the Letter Writing course is good as far as it goes. But the verbs express mediating behaviors: identify, select, and describe. Let's add a final verb that describes the terminal behavior: "and write an appropriate letter in response to the complaint."

The structural steel framing example seems to be okay as it stands. The only question we might have relates to the criterion "at least five of the six installations." If the design of nuclear boilers is critical to safety and the life or death of thousands of people, then we might want the learner to know all six. But this is an issue that the subject matter experts would have to decide.

The objective dealing with motivation is acceptable for the part of the course that deals with the theory of motivation. The question arises: Will managers be any more adept at fostering a highly motivated work group after meeting the criteria of this learning objective? We'd like to see a terminal objective in which managers take stock of the relative strength or weakness of Herzberg's motivators and hygiene factors in their own work group, perhaps even with each of their staff members.

Reference

Mager, Robert. (1961). *Preparing Instructional Objectives: A Critical Tool in the Development of Effective Instruction.* San Francisco: Fearon.

CHAPTER 11

PROGRAMMED INSTRUCTION: AN EXAMPLE

Linear Frames Form a Lesson on Spelling

The instructional sequence that follows illustrates the kind of detailed behavioral analysis that must be done before preparing self-instructional material that must stand on its own without a live instructor. Your role is to go through the lesson and then study the behavioral analysis.

Directions: You are about to take a pretest, a self-instructional spelling lesson, and a posttest. Here's how the exercise works.

Step A. On a blank sheet of paper, write the numbers 1 through 18. Then select the correct spelling from the two options in each sentence below, and write this word on your numbered sheet.

Step B. Score yourself by referring to the correct spelling in the answer key that follows the self-study program.

Step C. Go through the nine "frames" of programmed instruction in table 11-1. Cover the answer column with a blank sheet of paper, and slide it down the page to reveal the correct answers or preferred spellings following your response to each frame.

Step D. Repeat the pretest printed below, using the same procedure outlined in steps A and B.

Step E. Enter your pretest and posttest scores:

Pretest score: _____

Posttest score: _____

Change: (+ or −) _____

1. We shall remain steadfast in (<u>abhoring</u>/<u>abhorring</u>) smut.
2. They went (<u>caroling</u>/<u>carolling</u>) on Christmas eve.
3. We are not (<u>committing</u>/<u>commiting</u>) ourselves at this time.
4. Dr. Smythe is (<u>counseling</u>/<u>counselling</u>) one of his students.
5. James (<u>piloted</u>/<u>pilotted</u>) the ship into the harbor.
6. We were (<u>traveling</u>/<u>travelling</u>) over the holidays.
7. He (<u>prefered</u>/<u>preferred</u>) not to be contacted about the matter.
8. The annual report (<u>focused</u>/<u>focussed</u>) on environmental issues.
9. The policy had been (<u>canceled</u>/<u>cancelled</u>) two months before.
10. He (<u>admited</u>/<u>admitted</u>) that he had never been to see her.
11. Jackie had always (<u>exceled</u>/<u>excelled</u>) at math.
12. I'm (<u>infering</u>/<u>inferring</u>) from his comments that he's not convinced.
13. Using a flashlight, he (<u>signaled</u>/<u>signalled</u>) for help.
14. Washington's ragged army (<u>repeled</u>/<u>repelled</u>) the attack.
15. A racist's actions are invariably (<u>bigoted</u>/<u>bigotted</u>).
16. Funds for the project were (<u>alloted</u>/<u>allotted</u>) in fiscal 1999.
17. Wines that are (<u>labeled</u>/<u>labelled</u>) "Estate Bottled" are select.
18. I can't think of any (<u>minuses</u>/<u>minusses</u>).

Table 11-1. A sample program on spelling.

Answer Column	Questions
answered don't	1. answer control follow propel slobber prefer ransom admit When these words take endings like **–ed,** and **–ing,** we must decide whether or not to double the final consonant before adding the ending. For example, you know that when we add **–ed** to the word *answer,* the correct spelling is (answerred/answered). In other words, we (do/don't) double the final consonant on *answer* before adding an ending.
admitted consonant or letter	2. When we add **–ed** to the word *admit,* the correct spelling is (admitted/admited). In this case, we have doubled the final _____ before adding the ending.
vowels consonants	3. Often we must decide whether or not to double the final consonant before adding an ending. It happens with all words that end with the consonant-vowel-consonant combination. We call them C-V-C words. As you recall from past courses in English grammar, the letters *a, e, i, o,* and *u* are called_____and the other letters are called_____.

Table 11-1. A sample program on spelling. *(continued)*

Answer Column	Questions
shrug pedal infer	**4.** shrug pedal bake paint push infer Three of the preceding six words end with a consonant-vowel-consonant. Circle these three.
do	**5.** Now look back at the eight words listed in question one. As you can see, all of these words (do/don't) end with the consonant-vowel-consonant combination.
last double	**6.** Here's the rule governing such words: If the last syllable is accented, you must double the final consonant before adding the ending. Say the word *admit* to yourself and you'll see that the (first/last) syllable gets the accent. This is why we must _____ the final consonant before adding the ending.
did not does not	**7.** Now say the word *answer* to yourself, and you'll see that the reason we (did/did not) double the final consonant before adding **–ed** is that the accent (does/does not) fall on the last syllable.
must	**8.** Of course, some words that end with a consonant-vowel-consonant have only one syllable: win tip split sit spit tan slug rob throb The rule still holds: Because the last syllable—the only syllable—is accented, we (must/must not) double the final consonant before adding the ending.
answer ed propel led ransom ed control led slobber ed admit ted follow ed prefer red	**9.** Now we're ready to add endings to the words we looked at in question one. Write the correct spelling of each of these words when you add the ending **–ed** to each: answer _____ control _____ follow _____ propel _____ slobber _____ prefer _____ ransom _____ admit _____
	Answers to test: 1. abhorring 6. traveling 11. excelled 16. allotted 2. caroling 7. preferred 12. inferring 17. labeled 3. committing 8. focused 13. signaled 18. minuses 4. counseling 9. canceled 14. repelled 5. piloted 10. admitted 15. bigoted

Behavioral Analysis of the C-V-C Rule of Spelling

The content and sequencing of the nine frames you just went through were determined by the behavioral analysis shown in table 11-2. Notice that each frame is constructed in a manner calculated to close the gap between the learner's entering behavior and the desired behavior.

Table 11-2. Behavioral analysis of the C-V-C rule of spelling.

Desired Behavior: Upon completing the lesson on when to double the final letter (consonant) before adding the ending, the learner will be able:	Entering Behavior: Here is the prerequisite behavior the learner brings to the lesson (assumptions to be confirmed):
to recognize that some words do and some don't require the final letter to be doubled (questions one and two)	already knows how to spell easy words like *answered* and *admitted*
to distinguish between consonants and vowels (question three)	remembers learning about vowels and consonants but needs review
to discriminate between words that do and don't end in a consonant-vowel-consonant combination (questions four and five)	can identify final syllables that end in C-V-C
to determine by pronouncing a word whether or not the last syllable is accented (questions six and seven)	knows how to pronounce English words
to state and apply the rule that requires doubling of the last consonant if the C-V-C syllable is accented (questions six and seven)	no prior knowledge needed
to recognize that all one-syllable C-V-C words are accented and thus must have the final consonant doubled (question eight)	an exception: C-V-C words that end in *x* do not get doubled (fixing, boxing, taxing); but learners are not likely to double an *x*
to practice applying the rule on a group of C-V-C words, some of which do and some of which don't require the final consonant to be doubled (question nine).	no prior knowledge needed; only application of everything taught in the lesson.

To summarize, the objective for the lesson on spelling and the C-V-C rule is as follows: Given a root word ending in a C-V-C syllable to which an ending is to be added *(-ed, -ing, -er, -or)*, the learner will be able to double the final consonant before adding the ending whenever the C-V-C syllable is accented.

Chapter 12

Course Design Blueprints

Two Useful Outline Formats

The final stage of course design is the creation of an outline that serves as a blueprint for the construction, or development, of the course. The writer or writers who will develop the learning exercises must know four things that a good course outline will contain:

♦ **The desired behavior:** course objectives and performance expected of the learners, in class (mediating behavior) and in the workplace (terminal behavior)

♦ **The subject matter:** the knowledge, skills, and attitudes— course content—that must be taught in order to produce the desired behavior

♦ **The methods and media:** instructional tools and techniques to be used to impart the subject matter (lecture, video, lab, role plays, and the like)

♦ **The criterion tests:** learner responses to be elicited by the instructor as feedback needed to monitor and evaluate progress.

These four are interdependent, of course, and a good outline will show the relationship of each to the others. Two such outlines are shown in tables 12-1 and 12-2 and have been filled in to illustrate the nature and scope of the entries. Table 12-1 uses a tabular format to outline the course. The format of table 12-2 is an outline for one objective of the same course. Both formats show the behavioral objectives, the course content, the methods and media, and the criterion tests.

The degree of detail that a course designer provides depends on the writer's familiarity with the objectives, content, and methods and media (in much the same way that an architect may provide a more detailed blueprint to a new contractor than to an experienced contractor or to one who had worked closely with the architect on past projects).

The four-column format in table 12-1 can accommodate a number of course objectives on the same page. In contrast, table 12-2 requires a separate page for each course objective (desired behavior). To illustrate their relationship, we've selected one of the objectives from the first form and reproduced it on the second one.

Study the two forms. Then answer the following questions. (The desired behavior for this exercise is that you select the form best suited to your needs, and use it in your future course designs.)

Advantages and Disadvantages of Each

Questions on Tabular and Outline Formats

The following questions should help you understand the ways in which tables 12-1 and 12-2 differ as well as the appropriate uses of each. After you've responded to each, compare your answers with the feedback that follows it.

1. What are some of the advantages of the format in table 12-1? What are some advantages of the format in table 12-2?
2. Do you see any benefit in using both? Or would you only use one? Why?
3. Which do you prefer? Why?
4. Imagine a training department in which every course is on disk and filed in hard copy in a three-ring binder containing a detailed outline (on one of these two formats). What are some of the uses and benefits you can see for this type of course documentation?
5. What do you think of the sample entries on table 12-1 or table 12-2 (that is, the outline of a course on delegation for supervision)? Is this outline too spare? Too detailed? About right?
6. How would the blueprints for your own course design be similar or dissimilar to the ones shown on the prior pages? Explain.

Possible Responses

1. Table 12-1 shows a larger segment of the course (that is, an hour compared with 15 minutes in table 12-2). The instructor might prefer this more inclusive outline. Also, anyone wanting to see an overview of a course would probably prefer table 12-1.
2. There are benefits to using both. Use table 12-2 during design. Then, after the course is field tested and revisions have been made, the course can be presented in final form on table 12-1.
3. Your answer here depends on the roles you fill as a trainer.
4. There is real value in having each course on disk and in a binder. Disk copies are easy to print out, send by computer, and revise. It's also easy

Table 12-1. A blueprint for a course on delegation, using a tabular format.

Behavioral Objectives: What the learners will be able to do after the course (in minutes [min.]).	Subject Matter (Course Content): What you will tell or show the learner; the information learners need to meet the objectives.	Methods and Media: How you plan to get the message across.	Testing (Responses): How you will know the objectives have been met.
List three to four reasons why supervisors may not want to delegate work. (5 min.)	◆ No faith in subordinates, past disappointments. ◆ More comfortable doing than supervising. ◆ Desire for personal credit or visibility. ◆ "If you want a job well done, do it yourself." ◆ Not enough time to develop another person. ◆ Subordinate may feel imposed upon ("It's not my job."). ◆ "The buck stops here" . . . I am ultimately responsible.	Deductive discussion with instructor listing contributions on flipchart.	Ability to come up with examples and actual experiences.
Identify at least four benefits of delegating (conditions when you should delegate). (10 min.)	◆ Need more time to do supervising and managing. ◆ To develop staff (flexibility, growth, morale). ◆ When it's not seen as favoritism or as dumping. ◆ When you are willing to take the time. ◆ When the task can be done by a subordinate. ◆ When employees are looking for challenge. ◆ When the subordinate has skills you lack.	Subgroups brainstorm. Instructor reconvenes groups, then uses a round robin format to call on each group for one benefit until all have been given.	Their contributions during subgroup discussions (instructor circulates among groups).
Outline the steps and procedures to be followed in delegating a task or project. (15 min.)	◆ Determine whether the task should be delegated. ◆ Select the people carefully. ◆ Spell out objectives, resources, criteria, deadlines. ◆ Set intermediate checkpoints and targets. ◆ Prepare all individuals who are affected. ◆ Follow up. ◆ Reward the performers appropriately.	Transparency on overhead projector; each step hidden by sliding mask. Discuss how to and get examples on each step. Distribute delegation planning sheet.	Their ability to suggest the steps and elaborate on the procedure for each step.
Apply the procedure to a task to be delegated. (30 min., two enactments of 15 min. each)	Working in groups of three or four, one participant is supervisor, one is subordinate, and one or two serve as observers who evaluate and lead the postenactment discussion. Roles then rotate to allow two enactments in each group.	Role-play in subgroups. Handout spells out the assignment and the criteria on the rating sheet.	Scores obtained on the rating sheet used in each subgroup during the postenactment discussion and critique.

Table 12-2. A blueprint for one objective from a course on delegation.

Human Resource Development	TOPIC: Basics of Supervision		TIME (est.): 15 min.
	AUTHOR: J.S. Donovan	SOURCES: Black and Ford: *Front Line Management,* Chapter 26 Terry and Rue: *Supervision,* Chapter 5 AMA: *Leadership on the Job,* Chapter 6 Training House: EXCEL, Module 7	
	UNIT NO: Delegation		

OBJECTIVE: Upon completing this topic, the trainee will be able to:

Outline the steps and procedure to be followed in delegating a task or project (seven steps).

SUBJECT MATTER: (Course content to be taught in order to produce the terminal behavior outlined above):

Determine whether the task should be delegated.

Select one or more people carefully.

Spell out objectives, resources, criteria, deadlines.

Set intermediate checkpoints and targets.

Prepare all individuals who are affected.

Follow up.

Reward the performers appropriately.

Discussion of how to do each of the above, with examples provided by participants.

METHODS, MEDIA, TECHNIQUES, INSTRUCTIONAL SERIES:

Seven steps are listed on transparency on overhead projector; each step is hidden by sliding mask to reveal one at a time. The delegation planning sheet is distributed at the end of exercise.

CRITERION TEST: (How will you know that trainee has met the objective?)

Trainees' ability to suggest the steps and to provide examples of how each step should be carried out. (Also, the next exercise is a role play that serves as the ultimate criterion test of whether the delegation process has been mastered.)

to print out for use in a notebook. In a notebook format, every objective can be shown on table 12-2, followed by the supportive learning material (that is, a copy of every handout, workbook page, overhead transparency, or test that is needed to meet the objective). Such a binder has several uses, including the following:

◆ Anyone can review or preview a course without attending it.

◆ Future instructors can prepare to teach the course.

◆ Designers of future courses can see what has already been taught.

◆ Counselors can advise employees on which courses to take for certain skills.

5. The question of whether too much or too little information has been given depends on the level of experience and knowledge of the persons using these outlines.

6. Your organization must have lesson plans or instructor guidelines or teacher manuals for the courses offered. Do they have any advantages over table 12-1 and table 12-2? Or do you see some advantages to the two formats presented in this chapter?

CHAPTER 13

MAKE OR BUY

An Evolution of Choices

The electronic age has had a sweeping effect on training. Prior to the 1970s, trainers rarely raised the make-or-buy question. They had to make the courses they taught. To be sure, there were training films available on a variety of subjects, but packaged courses containing participant workbooks, instructor guidelines, audiovisual support material, handouts, tests, job aids, and the like had not yet arrived on the scene.

Today, nearly 200 firms are members of the Instructional Systems Association, a professional group committed to creating and marketing packaged courses of proven quality. Training managers can scan a half dozen directories that describe the thousands of training programs now available. The technological innovations that have produced CBT, distance learning, satellite transmission, Internet, intranet, and CD ROM are largely responsible for this wealth of choices.

Prior to 1960, course development was largely synonymous with the writing of a training manual. The result was a heavy binder crammed with policy, procedures, and reprints. The reading levels were difficult, illustrations and white space—margins around written copy—were virtually unheard of, and audiovisual support (if any existed) referred to overhead transparencies and flipchart pages.

An electronic age has enabled trainers to use methods and media that are far more effective in imparting information and in providing opportunities for learners to apply it to computer-based training, videocassettes, interactive video, PC-linked keypad response systems, touch-screen video, and so on.

Today's trainees have been raised on TV and the PC. They have come to expect technology in the classroom and in self-study programs. And the effectiveness of the new electronic methods and media, when used appropriately in an instructional design, cannot be disputed.

The challenge facing training managers is greater than ever. In the 1960s, the average cost of a course per trainee per hour was well under five dollars (excluding salary and facilities). By the end of the 1990s, this same figure hovered between $25 and $35. It is a lot more expensive to produce videotapes and computer software than it is to write a training manual. Thus, the make-or-buy decision is more critical than ever.

Although training is expensive today, it is more available in that learners do not have to be brought to the same place for training. Moreover, the training is now available when the learner needs it and not when the course happens to be given.

Help in Deciding

Two simple lists can help you decide whether to make or buy the courses you want to offer. Following are 10 statements that support making a training course and 10 that favor buying one. You can think of these statements as a decision matrix. Next time you are faced with a make-or-buy decision, assign a value to each statement to reflect its relative importance. We suggest using a four-point scale, as follows: 3, extremely important; 2, somewhat important; 1, slightly important; and 0, not relevant.

Benefits of Making Your Own Course

Following are 10 benefits of developing your own courses. Assign one of the numbers on the scale to each statement:

1. The content and objectives are unique to your organization and cannot be purchased as a package course. ____

2. You have skilled writers, media experts, and course designers on staff and want to take advantage of their talent. ____

3. Your audience of trainees will assign more credibility and relevance to training if it is developed internally. ____

4. Your management expects you to create training programs rather than purchase them in packaged form. ____

5. You don't have the budget to purchase courses, and the payroll costs of developing them is not viewed as an expense. ____

6. The large number of trainees in your target audience makes the cost per person of packaged course prohibitively high. ____

7. The course content will need frequent updating, which is easier to handle when you own the course. ____

8. Some firms that supply packaged courses require licensing of instructors which you feel is expensive and unnecessary. ____

9. You've examined the packaged course or courses and would have to make too many modifications to meet your learning objectives. ____

10. It's a policy of your organization to develop your own training rather than purchase it from outside sources. ____

The total score favoring development of courses is ____ .

Benefits of Buying Your Own Course

Following are 10 benefits of purchasing a packaged course. Assign one of the numbers on the scale to each statement:

1. The content and objectives of the available courses fit our needs; why reinvent the wheel. ____

2. The quality of graphics and audiovisual material is superior to what we can produce ourselves. ____

3. We cannot afford professional talent of the caliber used to create the packaged courses. ____

4. Success on the initial offerings is more likely with a program that has a proven track record. ____

5. The course objectives are more likely to be achieved on a packaged course that has been field tested and validated. ____

6. By using packaged courses where they fit, our development time is free to create courses that we must design (that is, that don't already exist). ____

7. Because the supplier's developmental expense is spread over a number of clients, our cost is usually less than it would be by developing a course ourselves. ____

8. A support network exists: other clients, the supplier's staff, consultants who teach the courses. ____

9. The quality of delivery is maintained through detailed instructor guidelines, train-the-trainer workshops, and users' conferences. ____

10. It's more cost-effective to buy a course if it fits our needs and criteria by 70 percent or better. (We can always develop or modify the other 30 percent ourselves.) ____

The total score favoring the purchase of a packaged course is ____ .

What Should You Do?

Compare your two scores to see which of the two options received the higher score. Of course, these options are not mutually exclusive. Most organizations run courses that contain generic components that were purchased and specific, custom-designed components that were developed by the organization's trainers or their consultants.

New Course Planning

A new course design planning sheet is a useful tool whether you make or buy a training program. Figure 13-1 shows one that contains a list of 26 activities that typically go into the design of a training program. Read the list and cross out any activities that do not apply to your own course design. Then enter each estimated completion date in the first column. As each activity is completed, enter the actual date in the second column. If time was lost or gained between estimated and actual completion dates, examine the estimates on forthcoming activities to see where you can make adjustments to keep your project on target.

Figure 13-1. Planning sheet for making or buying a training program.

New Course Design: Planning Sheet		
Course Title: _____ Designer: _____		
Client: _____ Date: _____		
(individual and organization and department)		

	Estimated Dates	Actual Dates
ANALYSIS		
1. Prepare Request for Training (feasibility analysis)	_____	_____
2. Meet to agree on resources, costs, schedule	_____	_____
3. Conduct needs analysis to identify E.B., T.B., and workplace + and –	_____	_____
4. Report results and recommend broad objectives	_____	_____
DESIGN		
5. Prepare specific course objectives (mediating and terminal behaviors)	_____	_____
6. Select and sequence content; reference the sources	_____	_____
7. Determine appropriate instructional methods, both input and output	_____	_____
8. Select appropriate media and delivery system	_____	_____
9. Specify how learners' performance will be evaluated (methods and media)	_____	_____
10. Complete course blueprint and get approval	_____	_____
DEVELOPMENT		
11. Review content and intent (objectives) for congruence	_____	_____
12. Prepare scripts, text, visuals, and hands-on exercises (role plays, case methods, simulations, lab work, etc.), module by module	_____	_____
13. Seek independent review and edit by writer, subject matter experts, instructional technologists, client	_____	_____
14. Prepare end-of-course assessment of learners' proficiency	_____	_____
15. Revise course materials based on input from step 13	_____	_____
16. Prepare instructor guidelines	_____	_____
17. Produce tryout edition and run pilot cycle of course	_____	_____
18. Revise course based on results of tryout	_____	_____
PRODUCTION		
19. Conduct briefing and obtain approval to go into production	_____	_____
20. Produce components of course (videotapes, PC disks, workbooks, etc.)	_____	_____
21. Announce course availability and dates; promote success story	_____	_____
22. Assemble and store all components of course	_____	_____
DELIVERY		
23. Conduct instructor training workshops, if appropriate	_____	_____
24. Ship course material as ordered	_____	_____
25. Monitor course delivery and evaluate impact (step 14)	_____	_____
26. Prepare success story and cost-benefit analysis, if appropriate	_____	_____

SECTION 4

DEVELOPING A TRAINING PROGRAM

Most instructors did not create the training programs they teach. Their course materials were developed by other persons, and the instructors inherited them. However, as they use these materials in class, a number of things may happen:

◆ Over time, some of the content may become dated.

◆ Instructors will see better ways of bringing the content to life.

◆ Instructors will incorporate learners' contributions into future offerings.

◆ Managers may want the instructors to cover additional topics.

◆ Instructors will discover that some learning activities are weak and beg for revision.

For these and other reasons, the instructors of courses they inherited are often in the best position to make changes and additions to the programs they teach. In this regard, every instructor should understand program development and be able to create new material that will make the course more effective.

The chapters in this section will provide instructors with an introduction to program development, the selection of appropriate instructional methods and media, and preparation of lesson plans for instructor-led courses.

Chapter 14, "A Systems View of Training," describes the five major phases of a training program (preparation, acquisition, demonstration, application, and maintenance) along with a description of the purpose, content, and methods of each.

Chapter 15, "Instructional Design Planning Sheet," provides a form that course designers and developers can use to outline the actions to be taken at each of six stages: needs analysis, setting objectives, specifying input materials, specifying output materials, planning for transfer, and evaluating impact.

Chapter 16, "The Ins and Outs of Instructional Design," examines 14 instructional methods and media (seven for learner input and seven for learner output), with an exercise in listing the advantages and disadvantages of each.

Chapter 17, "Integrating the Lesson Plan, Handouts, and Transparencies," makes use of a technical example (hydraulic pump capacity) to illustrate how a lesson plan can be keyed to the visuals, handouts, and end-of-lesson mastery test.

Chapter 18, "Sample Lesson on Fire Fighting," illustrates the ties between a lesson plan overview, scripted instructor guidelines, handout and test, and job aid.

Upon completing this section, you should be able to:

- ◆ describe the activities in the evaluation, instruction, and maintenance systems
- ◆ explain why the demonstration stage of instruction can be input or output
- ◆ use the design planning sheet to outline actions at each of six stages
- ◆ list at least four input methods, with the advantages and disadvantages of each
- ◆ indicate how case method can be used as an input or output method
- ◆ integrate lesson plans with their accompanying learner materials
- ◆ prepare scripted instructor guidelines, following the example.

CHAPTER 14

A SYSTEMS VIEW OF TRAINING

Training can be viewed as three distinct systems: evaluation, instruction, and maintenance. These systems describe the events that occur before, during, and after the learning process. The following three separate and distinct activities make up each of the three systems, and figure 14-1 illustrates them.

- ◆ **The evaluation system:** Before designing or delivering instruction, trainers should evaluate three things (a process often referred to as needs analysis or performance analysis):
  - — the entering behavior of the trainees (that is, their knowledge, attitudes, and skills)
  - — the terminal behavior after the course (that is, the desired performance of trainees at work)
  - — the work environment (that is, the factors that help or hinder performance back on the job)
- ◆ **The instruction system:** The design and delivery of a training program typically follows a three-stage learning model, as shown in figure 14-1:
  - — acquisition (that is, the trainee must acquire new knowledge, attitudes, skills)
  - — demonstration (that is, examples, illustrations, cases, and models bring the K-A-S to life)
  - — application (that is, the trainee must practice and apply new K-A-S with hands-on activities)
- ◆ **The maintenance system:** After trainees have completed a course, we must maintain three things to ensure full return on the training investment:
  - — Performance on the job must be inspected, recognized, and reinforced.

— The course itself must be refined, revised, and kept current with needs.

— Evaluation measures, or data, are needed so as to maintain performance and the course.

Figure 14-1. The three component systems of a training program.

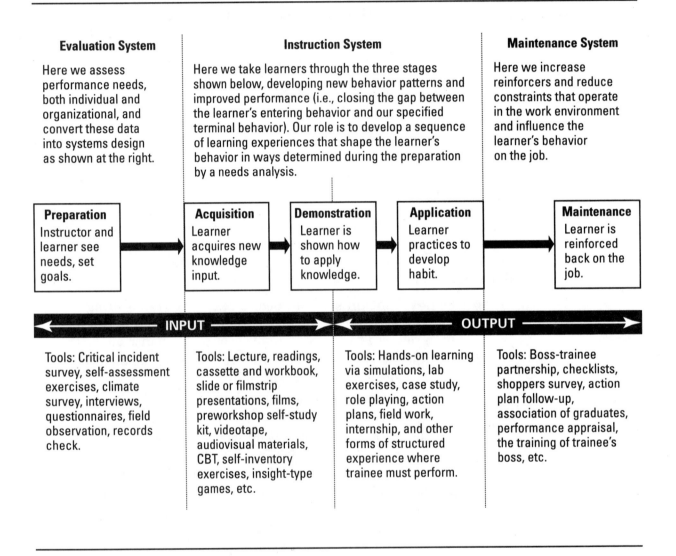

The five stages of development that appear in figure 14-1 as a horizontal flow chart appear also in table 14-1. In the table, the information appears as a vertical flow in the first column. The three other columns provide the following additional information: the typical purpose, content, and methods appropriate to each of the five stages.

Following are questions that should help you to apply the systems view of training to your own courses and to identify areas where their design or development might be improved.

1. In a survey of more than 200 instructors conducted by Training House, respondents indicated the percentage of time they divide among these three systems. Their responses typically fell into the following ranges:

   ◆ evaluation system, 15 percent to 20 percent

   ◆ instruction system, 75 percent to 80 percent

   ◆ maintenance system, 0 percent to 5 percent.

   What would you estimate your own percentages to be in these three areas of activity? Is this the most appropriate allocation of your time? What would the ideal percentage be, given the status of your course or courses and the nature of your trainees and their work environment?

2. In the course or courses you are responsible for teaching or designing, what methods and media do you make frequent use of in each of the three stages of the learning model: acquisition, demonstration, and application? (Refer to the "tools" entries at the bottom of figure 14-1 if you need help.)

3. Look at the three activities that make up the evaluation system (that is, identifying entering behavior, terminal behavior, and workplace environment). How would you score yourself on each? Use a scale of one to 10 to indicate how well your organization has done on each. What actions do you feel are called for to improve your course's effectiveness during evaluation?

4. Recall that three activities make up the maintenance system: reinforcement of desired behavior, revision of the course, and evaluation of the improved performance. Using the same scale of one to 10, how would you score yourself on each? Again, what actions do you feel are called for to improve your course's effectiveness during maintenance?

5. Consider the three stages of instruction. What percentage of time during the course is devoted to acquisition? To demonstration? To application? Do you feel this allocation is appropriate, or are you robbing Peter to pay Paul? (There is no rule of thumb or ideal set of numbers because many factors influence the appropriateness of the allocation. For example, the teaching of skills may require a higher proportion of application and practice exercises than, say, a course that consists mainly of knowledge.)

Table 14-1. Guidelines for developing five stages of the training process.

	Purpose or Goal
Stage one, **preparation,** in which we prepare both ourselves and the trainee for the task at hand.	We must first prepare ourselves: Have we established the trainee's entering behavior and the desired terminal behavior? Do we have the needed materials at hand? Is the location for training ready? Is it free of interruptions? Have we allotted enough time? Then we must prepare the trainee by explaining the terminal behavior in a way that will create a desire to learn, establish rapport, and begin the instruction on an interactive, trainee-centered basis.
Stage two, **acquisition,** in which we tell the trainee the new information that is needed to perform.	We must impart the knowledge, skill, and attitudes that the trainee needs. We must define new concepts and terms, and relate them to what the trainee already knows (as established in stage one).
Stage three, **demonstration,** in which we show the trainee how to apply what we've just taught.	We must demonstrate how the trainee is to apply what we have just taught in stage two. Our purpose is to clarify and bring to life new knowledge by providing examples: ◆ model examples that show ideal, correct behavior that trainee can imitate ◆ typical real-world examples that show correct and incorrect behavior for the trainee to discriminate between.
Stage four, **application,** in which we give the trainee hands-on practice in applying the things taught in stages two and three.	We must provide the trainee with the opportunity to practice and to experience the consequences of correct and incorrect performance. Our purposes are to get feedback that tells us what the trainee does and does not understand; to build correct patterns, or habits, and thus improve the trainee's retention (and transfer of training back on the job), and to develop the trainee's self-confidence.
Stage five, **maintenance,** in which we check out and reinforce the trainee's performance back on the job.	We must inspect what we expect, giving and getting feedback on how well our training objectives (terminal behaviors) were met. Our purpose is to measure the effectiveness of our training and improve future efforts accordingly, to get return on our investment (better transfer of training), and to show the trainee that correct performance is important and that we do care.

Table 14-1. Guidelines for developing five stages of the training process. *(continued)*

Content	Methods and Techniques
We find out what the trainee already knows so we can tell where to begin. We learn what interests, hobbies, etc. the trainee has (so that we can pick analogies and examples that will relate to the trainee's frame of reference). We tell the trainee what he or she will be able to do at the end of the training session, and why it is important.	Ask questions, use survey research (for larger groups of trainees, get a brief autobiographical sheet from each trainee listing related knowledge, skills, training, education, experience, etc.). Give trainee a brief outline of the topics to be covered (and possibly a training schedule with dates, topics, places). Often it is appropriate to have the trainee briefly observe employees at work, doing the things that the trainee is about to learn.
We introduce the trainee to the subject matter or course content; facts, concepts, principles, policy, procedures, techniques, values, and beliefs. In short, our content consists of knowledge, attitude, and skills (K-A-S).	This stage is usually handled by lecture for groups, or one-on-one instruction for individuals. Sometimes training texts (materials, handouts, workbooks) are also used. Sometimes the material can be taught through self-study (programmed instruction).
We provide concrete, specific examples (cases, incidents, situations) that illustrate the stage two content (K-A-S) being applied at work. Sometimes the examples show model or ideal behavior; sometimes they show correct and incorrect behavior.	Demonstration can be done by the instructor or by having the trainee observe an employee at work. Demonstration can be real world or staged. Demonstration can be done live or presented through audiovisuals (CBT, videotape, audiotape, slides, etc.) in which case there is greater stimulus control (i.e., we know in advance how it will go).
We give the trainee problems to be solved, tasks to be performed, procedures to be followed, forms to be completed, etc. Our role has now shifted from teacher to observer: We are diagnosing the trainee's need for future instruction or practice.	In teaching manual skills, the trainee can be given real tasks or simulations (in which we have greater stimulus control). In teaching cognitive or verbal skills, we often simulate the real world, using case study, role playing, in-basket exercises, or other techniques that give the trainee an opportunity to apply the concepts and skills that were just acquired.
We observe the trainee on the job, giving praise for correct behaviors and constructive criticism for incorrect ones. If we are not the trainee's immediate supervisor, then we should find out how well the supervisor is filling the role of coach during the trainee's important first few days or weeks on the job. If necessary, we should prepare the supervisor for his or her role in maintaining the trainee's new behaviors.	Use checklists, observer rating sheets, shopping surveys, and whatever other forms or techniques will help to standardize the quality of the observations made of the trainee's performance on the job. Find out where the trainee felt most comfortable and least comfortable during the first few days on the job and how the training of future trainees can be improved.

CHAPTER 15

INSTRUCTIONAL DESIGN PLANNING SHEET

The pages that follow include work sheets on which you can describe the methods and media (materials) you plan to use on each component of your course design. Your descriptions should be brief because they are preliminary and serve mainly to give an overview of the design to you, your manager or client, and anyone else whom the design will affect. The pages that follow contain space for your descriptions of each of the six components. They are:

1 **Needs analysis:** How will you gather and evaluate data to establish the entering behavior of trainees, the terminal behavior expected by the organization, and the reinforcers and constraints that are operating in the workplace to help or hinder the desired performance?

2 **Objectives and outlines:** What are the major outcomes or behaviors that supervisors and the organization expect of their trainees? How should these be sequenced so that the instruction will flow in the most logical sequence (psychological versus chronological versus tautological)?

3 **Input materials:** What instructional methods and media do you plan to use to impart information to trainees during the input portion of each lesson, session, or module? How will you demonstrate the learning points or use examples to bring them to life?

4 **Output materials:** What hands-on activities and experiences do you plan to develop to provide opportunity for trainees to (a) demonstrate their ability to discriminate between correct and incorrect behavior and (b) practice and refine their new concepts and skills?

5 **Transfer of training:** What actions and materials do you plan to develop for use by trainees, their supervisors, and other stakeholders so as to maximize the transplanting of new behaviors as your graduates move from workshop to workplace?

6 **Evaluation of the impact:** What tools and techniques will you develop to measure the effectiveness of your training at each of the four levels of evaluation? When do you plan to collect data to measure impact at each level?

Figure 15-1 shows a sample layout of planning sheets for an instructional design. Because these work sheets are intended to provide a broad overview, or executive summary, of your design rather than a detailed narrative, we suggest that you include reference to any enclosures or attachments of samples (first drafts or existing training materials you plan to revise) that will illustrate the direction of your design. These samples should be numbered from one to six to tie them to the preceding list of components.

Figure 15-1. Sample layout of planning sheets for an instructional design.

Your name: _____ Organization or department: _____

Title of course: _____ Estimated number of hours: _____

Brief description of audience (who, where, why): _____

_____

_____

1	Needs Analysis	How will you gather data to establish the (a) entering behavior of trainees, (b) terminal behavior after training, and (c) workplace reinforcers and constraints?
		Please include samples, labeled 1(a), 1(b), and 1(c).

2	Objectives and Outlines	What are the major outcomes you expect of trainees following this program, both mediating and terminal (workshop and workplace behaviors)?
		Please include a sample of the mediating behaviors, the terminal behaviors, and the course outline showing flow of topics. (Sample lesson plans should illustrate nicely.)

Figure 15-1. Sample layout of planning sheets for an instructional design. *(continued)*

3	**Input Materials**	What instructional methods and media do you plan to use for the input portion of your training program?
		Please include samples in the form of lesson plans or learning materials, or both.

4	**Output Materials**	What hands-on activities and exercises do you plan to develop to provide an opportunity for trainees to discriminate between appropriate and inappropriate applications of their new concepts and skills, then practice and refine them?
		Please include samples in the form of lesson plans or learning materials, or both.

Figure 15-1. Sample layout of planning sheets for an instructional design. *(continued)*

5

Transfer of Training

What actions and materials do you plan to use and develop to enable your graduates and their supervisors to maintain and reinforce at work the behaviors that were taught in your course?

Please include samples of materials and instructions on their use.

6

Evaluating the Impact

How will you measure the effectiveness of your training program? At what levels (reaction, learning, application, return-on-investment)?

Please include samples of materials or instructions on their use, or both.

CHAPTER 16

THE INS AND OUTS OF INSTRUCTIONAL DESIGN

Components of Learning

Any formal learning experience, whether instructor led or self-study, has two components. First, the course designer has selected information as input that learners should receive to help them acquire the desired behavior (that is, to perform in certain ways at work). Second, the course designer has selected or created certain hands-on activities and exercises to obtain output from learners that gives them the opportunity to apply, practice, and refine the desired behavior.

Certain instructional methods and media are appropriate for the input portion of a course design, whereas others are associated with the learners' output. The three-stage learning model in figure 16-1 shows which instructional methods and media belong with input and which with output.

Notice in figure 16-1 that half of the demonstration box is in the input side, and half is in the output side. On the input side, demonstration by the instructor or a video is used to show the correct ways to apply what was just acquired. The model or ideal behavior is presented. On the output side, demonstration is used to present correct and incorrect applications so that learners can make discriminations and indicate which is which. They must know the difference before they move into the application stage and practice the new behavior themselves.

The terms *instructional methods and media* appeared earlier in this chapter. *Instructional methods* refer to how information is presented *to* the learner as input or *by* the learner as output. Instructional *media* refer to how the method is packaged and what technology is used.

For example, lecture is a method of input. The media used to convey a lecture are many and include live lecture, audiotape, and video (live by phone or satellite or prerecorded). Let's take another example. Programmed instruction is a method. The media used to convey it include

Figure 16-1. Three-stage learning model with instructional methods and media.

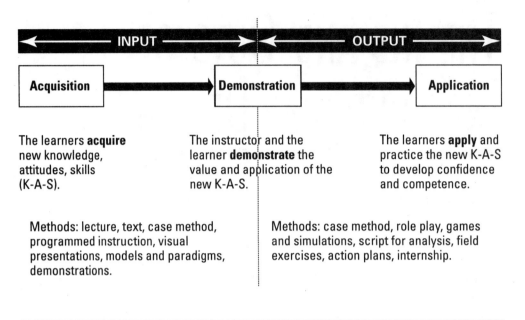

text, video, slides with soundtrack, and computer-assisted instruction (CAI), such as the Internet, intranet, CD-ROM, and PowerPoint.

Table 16-1 lists the major methods and media associated with input, and table 16-2 lists the same for output. Spaces are available in each table for you to enter the advantages and limitations of each. We have completed the first entry on each of the tables as an example.

Some Applications

Now it's your turn to design a course for four different situations—customer relations, writing skills, selection interviewing, and pipe threading. Indicate what actions you would recommend in each of the three stages of our learning model. Do not describe course content (what to teach), only the methods and media (how to teach).

1. **Customer relations:** The objective of this course is to teach all customer contact personnel how to deal with customers in a courteous manner, how to handle complaints, and how to strengthen our company's relationship with the customer. The course will last four hours.

   ◆ acquisition
   ◆ demonstration
   ◆ application

Table 16-1. Input methods and media.

Method	Media	Advantages	Limitations
Lecture (to large or small group)	Live or on audiotape or video; audiovisual aids include flipchart, board overhead transparencies.	◆ Quickly prepared ◆ Groups of any size ◆ Inexpensive ◆ Famous speakers accessible to learners ◆ Customized to needs of audience.	◆ Feedback limited ◆ Easy for learners to drift off ◆ Limits learners' ability to question or challenge ◆ Speaker controls rate of learning.
Text and Workbooks (manuals, handouts, notebooks)	Printed words and visuals, either on paper (notebook, binders) or on screen (PC or classroom projection screen).		
Case Method (to demonstrate learning points)	Video using professional talent or print in documentary or script format as a handout.		
Programmed Instruction	Print or on PC, sometimes in concert with other materials (audio, video, workbook).		
Visual Presentation	Slides or transparencies with narration, recorded or live.		
Models and Paradigms	Working scale models (larger or smaller than life) or graphic representations of a system, procedure, or concept.		
Demonstration	Live or on tape (audio or video).		

2. **Writing skills:** The objective of this course is to sharpen the skills of employees who write letters, memos, reports, proposals, and other documents. Content will focus on how to make writing clear, concise, crisp, compelling, and courteous. This will be a one-day workshop.

   ◆ acquisition
   ◆ demonstration
   ◆ application

Table 16-2. Output methods and media.

Method	Media	Advantages	Limitations
Case Method	Written word, or observed on screen (video) or live (e.g., role play)	◆ Can capture real situations ◆ Develops analytical thinking, problem solving ◆ Easy to prepare ◆ Inexpensive (written).	◆ Writer selects relevant information, but in real life, learners must do so. ◆ If based on real situations, can be embarrassing.
Role Play (two or more persons with different roles, goals, and perceptions)	Live in response to printed role assignments and rating sheets for observers.		
Games and Simulations, Laboratory Exercises, Practice Sessions	Printed instructions with hands-on materials as needed; may be computerized.		
Script for Analysis (a special form of case method)	Printed or recorded interaction in script format for critique and suggested improvement.		
Field Exercises and Assignments (outside of class)	Live. Hands-on. No media other than printed page describing the exercise or assignment and/or recording the results.		
Action Plan or Individual Development Plan	Printed form to be completed by each participant following a lesson or a workshop.		
Internship and Supervised Workplace Assignments	Live. Hands on. No media. Trainees are performing a part of their jobs, working with actual materials under workplace conditions, checked out by their supervisor.		

3. **Selection interviewing:** The objective of this course is to teach all supervisors how to interview job candidates, including how to ask questions that are appropriate and legal and worded so as to yield the information needed to evaluate the degree of fit between the candidate's qualities and the demands of the job. The course will last one day.

- ◆ acquisition
- ◆ demonstration
- ◆ application

4. **Pipe threading:** The objective of this course is to teach pipefitters how to operate the pipe threading machine and thread the standard sizes of pipe used on the job. Classes are for six to 12 trainees, and the training room contains three threading machines. The course will last one day.

- ◆ acquisition
- ◆ demonstration
- ◆ application

How did you do?

The following guidelines should help you to evaluate how well you did in selecting appropriate methods and media for each of the three stages of the learning model.

1. Customer relations: The acquisition stage could be taught by live lecture and discussion. The demonstration stage might make use of a video, either purchased or homemade. The application stage could use role play and script analysis to provide practice.

2. Writing skills: The acquisition, demonstration, and application stages could all be handled in a workbook that would outline the rules of good writing, give examples of good and poor writing, and give practice exercises in editing memos and reports and in drafting letters in response to requests, complaints, job applications, and the like.

3. Selection interviewing: The design here could be the same as the one suggested for customer relations.

4. Pipe threading: The acquisition and demonstration stages could be combined so that the class would stand in a semicircle around the threading machine. A live instructor or a videotape might be used. In the application stage, the class could be divided into three subgroups for practice exercises at the three threading machines.

CHAPTER 17

INTEGRATING THE LESSON PLAN, HANDOUTS, AND TRANSPARENCIES

One way to organize a course is to have each lesson plan on file either on computer or in a three-ring binder, followed by the transparencies (or black and white copies of them) and the handouts. Such a binder is valuable to many persons:

◆ Present and future instructors need a copy because it represents the complete documentation and set of materials needed to teach the course.

◆ Training managers and course counselors and enrollers need a copy so as to answer questions relating to objectives and content.

◆ Supervisors considering a course for members of their work group can get a quick overview and make informed decisions on enrollments.

The lesson plan should be cross-referenced to the visuals (PowerPoint, slides, flipchart exercises, transparencies, and so forth) and to the handouts (readings, assignments, tests, and the like). Copies of these visuals and handouts should be included in a computer file or in the binder, immediately behind the lesson plan that serves as its cover sheet. You'll find an example of this on the pages that follow.

The lesson plan for figure 17-1 is drawn from a technical training course and deals with how to calculate the capacity and rate of delivery of a hydraulic pump.

The Lesson Plan

A lesson can range from 15 to 90 minutes with 30 to 40 minutes being the most frequent length. Each entry of subject matter is cross referenced to the visuals or the handouts, or both, as figure 17-1 shows.

Figure 17-1. Lesson plan for calculating hydraulic pump capacity.

ROMEO ENGINE PLANT	TOPIC: *How to Calculate Hydraulic Pump Capacity*		TIME (est.): *25 min.*
	AUTHOR: *SBP*	SOURCES: *Fluid Engineering, chapter 11*	
	UNIT NO: *17*		

OBJECTIVE: Upon completing this topic, the trainee will be able to:

1. *Explain the function of a hydraulic cylinder.*

2. *Calculate the area of a circle and the volume of a cylinder.*

3. *Calculate the required rate of hydraulic pump delivery.*

SUBJECT MATTER: (Course content to be taught in order to produce the terminal behavior outlined above)

1. *Description of hydraulic cylinder and its function (diagram 1).*

2. *Calculation: area (piston head) and volume of cylinder (diagram 2).*

3. *Formula of rate of pump delivery (diagram 3).*

4. *Summarize with quiz (diagram 4).*

5. *Quiz solution (diagram 5).*

METHODS, MEDIA, TECHNIQUES, INSTRUCTIONAL STRATEGIES: (How will content be taught?)

Use overhead transparencies (diagrams 1-5) and handout showing schematic of hydraulic system. Show diagram 5 after they have completed quiz (diagram 4), doing the calculations on their handout.

CRITERION TEST: (How will you know that trainee has met the objective?)

Quiz on diagram 4. Their solution must agree with diagram 5.

Visuals

Five visuals (transparencies in our example) are used in this exercise, as shown in figure 17-2. Numbers one to three are shown as models, with participants making notes on their handout. Number four is the test from which participants calculate the rate of delivery. Number five is the confirmation (correct answer) and is shown after participants have completed the test.

Figure 17-2. Visuals to accompany lesson on hydraulic pump capacity.

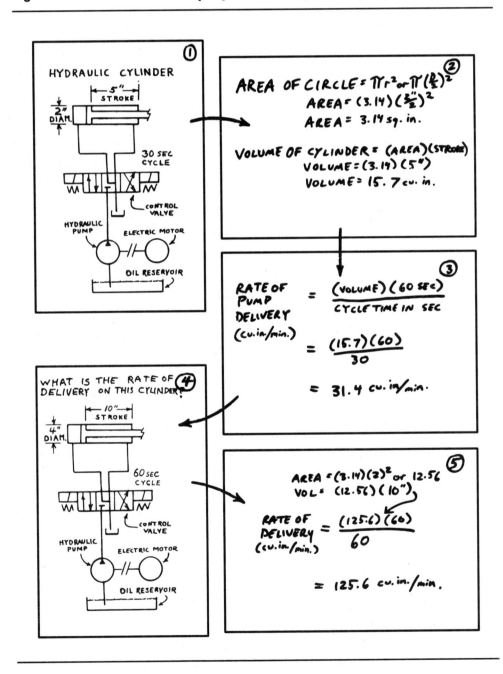

Handout or Page in Notebook

Figure 17-3 is a handout for participants. It summarizes the lesson and gives participants the needed information for subsequent reference (that is, a future resource and job aid).

Figure 17-3. Handout for participants.

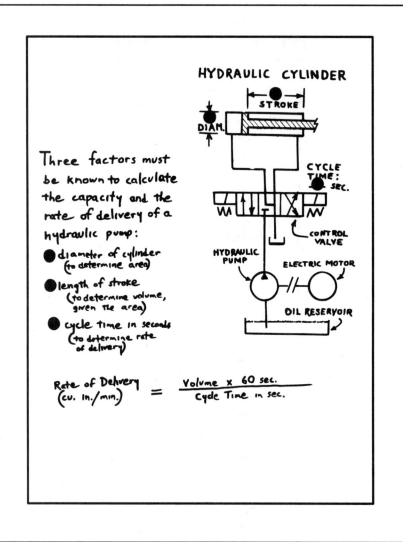

CHAPTER 18
SAMPLE LESSON

This chapter contains four components of a lesson on fire fighting. They are as follows:

- ◆ figure 18-1, sample lesson outline on fire fighting
- ◆ figure 18-2, instructor guidelines on fire fighting
- ◆ figure 18-3, student handout for fire fighting lesson
- ◆ figure 18-4, job aid for fire fighting.

These figures provide an example of the appropriate formats for an instructor-led course. They follow the progression from program design to program development.

Figure 18-1. Sample lesson on fire fighting.

Sample Lesson with Title Page, Instructor Guidelines, and Handouts	TOPIC: Fire Fighting		TIME (est.): 15-20 min.
	AUTHOR: SBP	SOURCES: *Essentials of Fire Fighting,* published by Fire Protection Publications, Oklahoma State University	
	UNIT NO: Environmental Protection		

OBJECTIVE: Upon completing this topic, the trainee will be able to:

◆ Identify the three things needed to cause a fire.

◆ Plan which one(s) to remove to put out different kinds of fire.

◆ Describe the three classifications of fire: Types A, B, C.

◆ Select the best type of extinguisher for each type of fire.

SUBJECT MATTER: (Course content to be taught in order to produce the terminal behavior outlined above):

Why fight a fire yourself? (you versus professionals)

Three components of any fire: the heat-fuel-oxygen triangle.

Examples of each component: which to remove for different fires.

Three kinds of fire (A, B, C) with examples of each.

Major kinds of extinguishers, and what types of fire each is best for.

METHODS, MEDIA, TECHNIQUES, INSTRUCTIONAL STRATEGIES: (How will content be taught?)

Lecture-discussion using deductive method to draw the learning points from the participants. Visuals on flipchart or overhead transparencies. Handout and, if available, fire extinguishers to be examined by the group. Instructor guidelines show how the content will be taught.

CRITERION TEST: (How will you know that trainee has met the objective?)

By trainee's ability to respond correctly to the two exercises on the handout.

Figure 18-2. Instructor guidelines on fire fighting.

Instructor Guidelines: Fire Fighting

Time: 20 minutes

Materials: One handout, one job aid, and different types of extinguishers (if available)

Objectives:
- to identify the three things needed to cause a fire
- to plan which one(s) to remove to put out different kinds of fire
- to describe the three classifications of fire (Types A, B, C)
- to select the best type of extinguisher of each type of fire.

My topic during the next 15 minutes is fire fighting: how to put out a fire. I've got four objectives for this lesson that each of you should be able to meet. Here they are.

Turn to prelettered flipchart page or overhead transparency. Read the four objectives that you've copied from the wording printed above.

Before we learn how to put out fires, we'd better answer a rather basic question: "Why me?"

Why you? After all, we do have a fire department with professionals. Why not phone them or turn in an alarm? In other words, what are some of the reasons why we should tackle a fire when we see one starting?

Call on different participants. Try to get several reasons why we should tackle a fire in its initial stage:
- The fire is much easier to control at the start.
- There will be much more destruction by the time the fire department arrives.
- You may not be able to find a phone or alarm nearby.
- The danger is often greater if you wait (e.g., an explosion).

You've probably all built fires before, perhaps to cook on or to burn trash. So I'm sure you already know the three things needed to have a fire. I'll get you started. One is in the air that surrounds us, so we often take that one for granted. Okay, I'd like you to turn to your neighbor and list the three things needed to create a fire.

(continued on next page)

Figure 18-2. Instructor guidelines on fire fighting. *(continued)*

Indicate who is paired with whom ("You two, you two, you two, etc."). Allow about 15-20 seconds, then reconvene the group. Call on different pairs for their answers until you get the three components of any fire:

◆ oxygen (air, atmosphere, etc.)

◆ fuel (combustible, flammable, etc.)

◆ heat (ignition, flame, spark, etc.)

Turn to the next flipchart page of overhead transparency showing the fire triangle.

We can illustrate these three with a triangle. If any of these components is absent, you won't get a fire. Let's name some of the more common examples of each component.

Oxygen is the easiest one because it is found in the air, in the atmosphere.

Write the words *air* and *atmosphere* beside the right side of the triangle.

Now, what are the most typical things that burn during a fire? Things that can serve as fuel. Just call them out as you think of them, and I'll add them to our diagram.

Under the bottom side of the triangle, write the examples of fuel as they give them to you. Enter them on two lines, so as to prepare the group for the distinction between Type A on your first line and Type B on your second line. Your list will look something like this: (three entries will be enough in each line)

A. paper, wood, cloth, rags, leaves, straw (combustible solids)

B. oil, gas, grease, benzene, tar (liquids)

Okay. This brings us to the third side of the triangle, which is heat. What are some examples of heat, some of the sources of heat that are hot enough to start and to maintain a fire?

To the left of the triangle, write their examples. Your list will probably include things like match, open flame, cigarette, spark, the sun, lightning.

Figure 18-2. Instructor guidelines on fire fighting. *(continued)*

Now here's the good news. If any one of these three components of our triangle is removed, the fire will die. All three are needed to support combustion. Let's prove it. I've got a list describing five different types of fire. For each one, I'd like you and your neighbor to decide which side of the triangle you would remove: the oxygen, the fuel, or the heat. So, go back into pairs and work with your neighbor. Here's the list.

> Distribute the handout. Tell them to ignore the bottom half of the page and to work on only the top half, items one through five. You can circulate to see if anyone needs help and to determine when to bring the group back together.

It looks as if most of you are finished, so let me have you back again. Let's go through the five types of fire and see how you would put out each. Number one is the fire under the hood of your car. Which side of the triangle should be removed?

> Call on different participants for each of the five types of fire. Here are the answers you are looking for, and the reasoning behind each:
>
> 1. Oxygen should be removed. You don't know what is burning (oil, gas, insulation), so you can't remove the fuel. And if the engine block is hot or there's a short in the electrical system, you can't remove the heat (although it would be a good idea to turn the ignition key off).
> 2. Fuel should be removed before the fire spreads. This can be done by wetting the contents (water or soda-acid type extinguisher), thus making them nonflammable, or by carrying the metal basket outside (grasp at bottom, not top) or by pushing it away from drapes, wall, and other flammables. You could also put this fire out by removing oxygen if you had a lid (blanket, sand, CO_2 extinguisher) that would keep air out of the waste basket.
> 3. Oxygen should be removed. A flaming oil drum is too big and too dangerous to attempt to remove the fuel or the heat. Again, a blanket, or CO_2, or anything that might serve as a lid (e.g., sheet of plywood) should cut off air and smother the fire.
> 4. Fuel (the jacket) or oxygen (the air) should be removed. If the jacket can be safely removed, do so. If the flames are advanced, water or soda-acid extinguisher can be used to wet the jacket and make it nonflammable. This removes the fuel. To remove the oxygen, have someone roll slowly on the ground or wrap the person in a blanket, coat, or anything that will smother flames while protecting hands and face from burns.
> 5. There can't be much fuel or oxygen in a closed electrical panel box. The thing to remove is the heat (i.e., the electricity that is feeding the spark or short circuit). Turn off the source of electricity, if possible. If not possible, use CO_2 to cool down the steel box so you can open it and aim the CO_2 inside the box. (Do not use soda acid or any other electrolyte that would feed the sparkling or make the short circuit any worse.)

(continued on next page)

Figure 18-2. Instructor guidelines on fire fighting. *(continued)*

Well, you've done a great job in putting out our five fires. Of course, on a really big fire, like a forest fire, the professionals may attack all three sides of the triangle. You've probably seen films or TV programs on forest fires. Let's look at the three components of a fire and see how they attack each. First comes oxygen, or air. What do they do to remove it, not always, but in some areas where airplanes and helicopters are available? Has anyone seen how they are used to remove oxygen?

> If no one has an answer, provide it yourself: Some types of chemical fog can be sprayed from above to smother a fire by reducing the available oxygen in the air. We can never remove the air (create a vacuum), but we can lower the percentage of oxygen in the air and thus choke a fire.

Next comes fuel. How do firefighters remove the fuel when they fight a forest fire? Got any ideas on this one?

> Answer: By cutting down trees in the path of the fire, by digging trenches or using earth-moving equipment to create a barrier strip of land, by putting water or chemicals on the fuel to make it less flammable or nonflammable.

Finally comes heat. The intense heat of a forest fire will cause dry areas to ignite. What can be done to reduce the heat?

> Answer: By watering down the adjacent tinder and the roofs and siding of buildings in the area, firefighters hope to reduce the heat to a temperature well below the kindling point.

Now, let's begin to wrap this lesson up by putting a label on the three types of fire we've been discussing and the type of extinguisher used on each. They are printed on the bottom half of the handout (figure 18-3) I gave you a few minutes ago. Types A, B, and C are listed at the left, and you've already told me how you would deal with each. On the right side of the page I've shown the type of extinguisher that is often available for fighting a fire. Your job is to draw lines from each extinguisher to the pictures that show what types of fire they should be used on.

> If you can get extinguishers of each type to show to the group, this would be a good time to display them and to put them on the table where the group can see them. Tell the participants that they may come up and examine the labels on the extinguishers during this exercise.

Figure 18-2. Instructor guidelines on fire fighting. *(continued)*

Remember that many types of extinguishers can be used on more than one kind of fire. If you are not sure about any of the types of extinguishers, you can consult your neighbor. This should take you about a minute, so start drawing your connecting lines on the handout.

As participants work, walk around to see that they understand the assignment. When most of them have completed the lines, bring the group together again. Go through each type of extinguisher, asking for each "How many lines did you draw? To which types of fire?" Here are the answers:

◆ Dry chemical ...... A, B, C

◆ Halon (gas) .... B, C (and A if more than 9 pounds)

◆ Carbon dioxide ..... B, C

◆ Water .... A

Well, it looks as if we've met the four objectives that we started with. Let's make sure.

Return to the prelettered flipchart page or overhead transparency of your four objectives. Go through each to show that you have accomplished what you set out to do. Distribute the job aid (figure 18-4) and tell the participants that it can be posted on the bulletin board or next to the fire extinguishers. Thank the group for their active participation in class and adjourn.

Figure 18-3. Student handout for fire fighting lesson.

Heat
flame, lightning,
sun, spark, etc.

Oxygen
(in the air or
atmosphere)

Fuel
A. wood, paper, cloth, leaves, etc.
B. oil, gas, grease, kerosene, etc.

In the table below, you will read a description of five different types of fire. Beside each one, indicate which of the three sides of the triangle should be removed to put the fire out.

Example of Fire	What Should Be Removed?
1. Smoke is billowing out from the hood of your car. Something is on fire. You can't see what it is.	1.
2. You smell smoke and notice that the metal wastebasket in your office has just burst into flames.	2.
3. An oil drum outside the building is in flames.	3.
4. One of your employees has come running to you. His jacket is on fire.	4.
5. The steel electric control box is issuing smoke. You can hear sparking and the sound of a short circuit inside it.	5.

TYPE OF FIRE

Type A:
wood, paper,
cloth, leaves,
straw, etc.

Type B:
oil, gas,
grease,
kerosene, etc.

Type C:
electrical wiring,
motors, etc.

TYPE OF EXTINGUISHER

◆ Dry chemical: monoammonium phosphate, sodium bicarbonate

◆ Halon (gas compressed as a liquid in the extinguisher)

◆ Carbon dioxide: CO_2

◆ Water: pump tank, pressurized, or soda-acid extinguisher

Figure 18-4. Job aid for fire fighting.

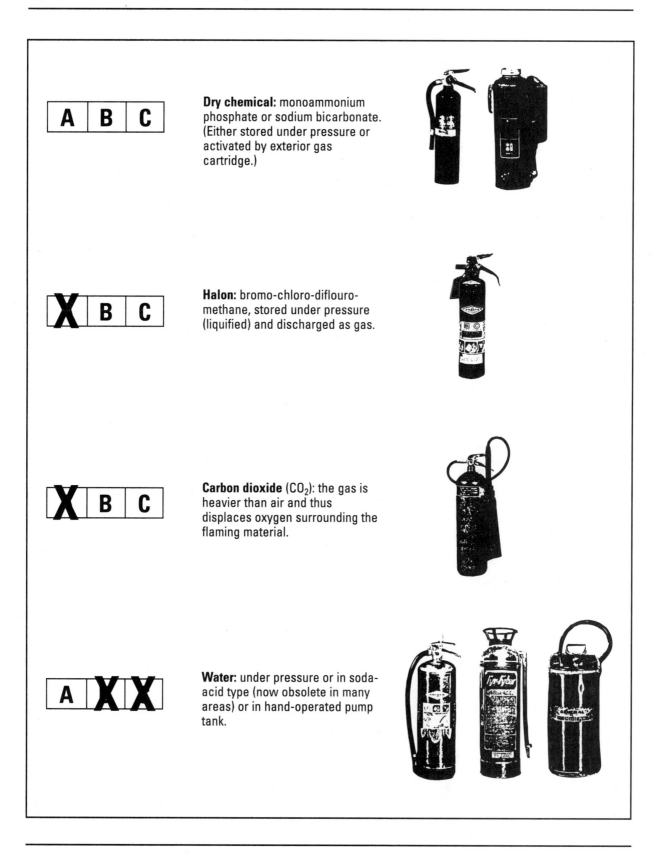

A	B	C

Dry chemical: monoammonium phosphate or sodium bicarbonate. (Either stored under pressure or activated by exterior gas cartridge.)

X	B	C

Halon: bromo-chloro-diflouro-methane, stored under pressure (liquified) and discharged as gas.

X	B	C

Carbon dioxide (CO_2): the gas is heavier than air and thus displaces oxygen surrounding the flaming material.

A	**X**	**X**

Water: under pressure or in soda-acid type (now obsolete in many areas) or in hand-operated pump tank.

SECTION 5

SHARPENING YOUR INSTRUCTIONAL SKILLS

The ASTD Task Force that developed the models for human resource development (HRD) practice came up with 35 competencies that seem to cover the 11 roles HRD practitioners fill. The role of instructor or facilitator requires more competencies than do the roles of program designer or materials developer.

Another way to look at it is that courses might win awards for the quality of their design and the development of the course materials, but they will still fall short of achieving their objectives unless they are delivered by an instructor whose facilitation skills can bring the course to life and maintain a high level of participation and buy-in from the learners.

Sections 5, 6, and 7 address the skills, tools, and techniques needed to give instruction that is truly of world-class quality. Chapters 19 through 23 cover the following information:

Chapter 19, "Who Needs an Instructor?" examines the role of instructor as a catalyst and facilitator of learning, with a comparison of information-centered and learner-centered instruction on nine factors.

Chapter 20, "Breaking the Big S Into S-R-F Links," applies B.F. Skinner's reinforcement theory to the analysis of a script showing an instructor interacting with his class of first-line supervisors.

Chapter 21, "Some Questions About Questions," discusses the use of questions as an instructor's most valuable tool, with 14 guidelines on how to deal with questions in class.

Chapter 22, "Using Questions Effectively," presents a script depicting a class in which the instructor ended every statement with a question, thereby illustrating 13 different uses (purposes) of questions.

Chapter 23, "Using Subgroups to Improve Learning," examines 15 reasons for breaking a class into subgroups, followed by 20 guidelines on using subgroups to increase participation and improve learning.

Upon completing this section, you should be able to:

◆ explain why instructors can be re-placed but not replaced

◆ state at least two characteristics of a catalyst that apply to instructors

◆ list four differences between information-centered and learner-centered instruction

◆ give three purposes of eliciting responses from learners

◆ describe the S-R-F chaining process as applied to a class

◆ deal with trainees' questions that are irrelevant, wrong, or unclear

◆ make use of questions for purposes not dealt with in the past

◆ identify at least three new reasons (occasions) for using subgroups

◆ apply at least five of 20 guidelines on using subgroups effectively.

CHAPTER 19

WHO NEEDS AN INSTRUCTOR?

A Closer Look at Learning

Can people learn without an instructor? You bet. Most of what you've learned throughout your life was not delivered in class by an instructor. Indeed, every day of your life is filled with new learning.

Perhaps a definition of *learning* would be helpful. Most of the textbooks in introductory psychology agree on a definition that runs something like this: *Learning is any relatively permanent change in behavior not due to maturation or instinct.*

If you want a briefer definition, drop the last clause relating to maturation or instinct. Maturation explains why a six-year-old can do many things that a six-month-old cannot. In other words, people can grow or mature into new behavior without the necessity of learning it. *Instinct* refers to a variety of animal behavior, and explains why a cat or dog will find its way home without a map or any discernible learning.

These definitions bring us to the following: Learning is behavior change (performance improvement). And most of the knowledge, attitudes, and skills that you've acquired during your life—leading to changes in your behavior—was learned without an instructor.

This brings us to another question: Do we need instructors? You bet. Let's look at some of the reasons why we will always need instructors in the fields of training and education:

◆ Role modeling is an important part of new learning for many types of behavior. We want an instructor who exemplifies the values and competencies that learners are expected to acquire.

◆ Participants vary in learning styles and the ability to comprehend and apply new behavior. Instructors can give individual attention and help learners to work through their difficulties.

◆ Not all students are motivated to stay with a course that is totally learner dependent (self-study, CBT, programmed learning, correspondence courses, and the like). Instructors can help learners see a course through to completion.

Notice that none of these reasons mentions the instructor's subject matter expertise. We live in an age of instructional technology that enables us to capture expertise on videotape, audiotape, computer disks, telephone networks, on the Internet, by live transmission via satellite, and so on. Expertise can be captured and preserved in a format that makes it available when the learner needs it (and not when the instructor happens to be giving it).

Does this mean that instructors can be replaced? You bet. But not replaced by electronics and self-study. Rather, instructors can (and must) be re-placed into a much more demanding role than that of imparter of information, or lecturer. The new role is that of catalyst and facilitator of learning.

The Instructor as Catalyst

The term *catalyst* comes from science, where it's used to mean something that produces a reaction and change. In training and education, the word refers to instructors who act as catalysts in producing a reaction called learning. Table 19-1 compares the work of catalysts in both fields.

Reflect for a moment on the teachers you had throughout your education. To what degree were they learner-centered catalysts? Information-centered lecturers?

Table 19-1. Catalysts in the sciences and in training and education.

In the Sciences	In Training and Education
A catalyst is anything that produces a reaction and change.	Instructors produce a reaction called learning.
If the reaction would have taken place anyway, a catalyst can be used to accelerate or control it.	People can learn many things on their own, but an instructor can speed up the learning and can do so in a fail safe environment (class, lab, simulation, for example).
Although the catalyst produces and influences the reaction, it does not take part in it.	Instructors can't ensure that anyone learns anything. They can only arrange learning experiences that increase the probability that people will learn from them.
In a chemical reaction that a catalyst produces, the catalyst is not identified (does not appear) in the chemical equation.	In the drama called learning, the student is center stage as the performer and the instructor is offstage in the wings (learner-centered versus information-centered instruction).

How many of your past courses emphasized reasoning (problem solving, decision making, and analytical thinking) and taught you how to figure things out (learn) on your own? In contrast, how many emphasized memorization and taught you to cram and fill your head with information, at least some of which you didn't understand fully or see as useful?

In short, many of our past instructors have not functioned in the role of catalyst. They have not always modeled the behavior expected of today's instructors. And in fairness to them, subject matter expertise (math, social studies, science) was regarded as more important that instructional facilitation skills. In the debate between content and process, content won.

Indeed, Toffler (1970), Naisbitt (1994), and other futurists remind us that the role of public education for the past century has been to prepare students to take their places as dutiful, unquestioning employees in factories, foundries, offices—the workplace. The relationship between teacher and learner was identical to that of supervisor and subordinate: parent-to-child dependency, respect for authority, lock-step adherence to well-established policy and procedures. The theory X of McGregor was alive and well.

Today's world of work demands vastly different behaviors from employees, as our vocabulary attests. Imagine trying to explain to supervisors and managers of 50 or 100 years ago the meaning (and rationale) of such words as *empowerment consensus, stakeholders, self-directed work groups, quality teams, champions,* and so on. Table 19-2 provides a clear picture of the two styles of instruction we've been discussing.

Today's instructor has a responsibility to function as a catalyst, as an arranger of learning experiences as well as an imparter of information. The reason for doing so is that the learning is often more effective (that is, better comprehension, retention, transfer) and more efficient (in that it requires less time and money for learners to acquire new behaviors).

No less important is the fact that employees are starved for good models of a new way of doing business in which there are employee involvement, participative management, greater autonomy and self-direction, and the like. As instructors, we have a responsibility and an opportunity to demonstrate in class the very same behaviors that are required of supervisors and team leaders in the workplace. We've referred to this role of the instructor as a catalyst, based on this most fundamental law of learning: People learn best not by being told but by experiencing the consequences of their own thoughts and actions.

We have been strongly influenced in our own instructional style by the teachers we have had. By answering the three questions that follow, you should be able to gain insight into your own style and how it has been modeled by your past years of schooling.

1. What percentage of your teachers were information centered? Learner centered?

2. In what kinds of courses would you expect to find the information-centered style? What courses attract a learner-centered style of instruction?

Table 19-2. Two styles of instruction.

Factors	Information Centered	Learner Centered
1. Stated objective	To cover all points; to get a lot of information across; to adhere to the lesson plan.	To change behavior (improve the performance) of the learner.
2. Underlying objectives	To meet instructor's need for recognition as the expert.	To meet learner's needs; to improve performance.
3. Role of instructor	Imparter of information; expert; lecturer.	Arranger of experiences and activities; moderator.
4. Method	Talk; show and tell; instructor does 95% of the talking.	Socratic method—instructor asks questions and does no more than 50% of the talking.
5. Typical question	Do you have any questions? Do you understand?	Why do we do it this way? What would you do if . . . ?
6. Learner's role	Passive—a sponge who absorbs information and periodically repeats it to give the instructor feedback.	Active—learn by doing; learners correct their own behavior because they are experiencing the results of their own actions.
7. Purpose of feedback (or tests)	To see if trainee understands the information; to test the trainee's retention; to see if information should be repeated.	To see if trainee can apply what was just acquired; to see if trainee needs more practice; to provide additional (remedial) instruction.
8. How instructor gets feedback	By asking trainees if they have any questions; by asking trainees to repeat (parrotlike, often rote learning) what instructor has just explained,	By giving trainees tasks or situations in which they must practice and apply their newly acquired skills, concepts, procedures, rules, etc.
9. How instructor controls learner	Reward and punishment (sanctions and embarrassment).	Positive and negative reinforcement (praise and constructive criticism).
10. Instructor's qualifications	The expert who knows more about the procedure, system, rules, etc., than anyone else.	The nondirective counselor type; the moderator and coach who acts as catalyst.
11. Instructor's basic philosophy	"There's so much our trainees have got to know before they'll ever be able to do the job correctly [i.e., before they'll ever know what I know]. Much repetition is necessary."	"We learn, not by being told, but by experiencing the consequences of our own actions. Learning is an experiential process. We learn by doing."

3. As you look through table 19-2, decide what percentage of your own instruction is described by attributes listed in the left column and in the right column. In other words, your style is _____ percent information-centered and _____ percent learner centered.

References

Naisbitt, John. (1994). *Global Paradox*. New York: Avon.
Toffler, Alvin. (1970). *Future Shock*. New York: Bantam.

CHAPTER 20

BREAKING THE BIG S INTO S-R-F LINKS

This chapter will introduce you to the psychology behind learning. It applies B.F. Skinner's reinforcement theory to the analysis of a script showing an instructor interacting with his class of first-line supervisors. Readers who want more information about Skinner's theory will find it in any introductory psychology text.

Stimulus, or S, is the information we give to learners, often in large doses (that is, the big S). These large chunks of information should be broken down into a chain of S-R-F links made up of the following:

Stimulus: Anything that the instructor presents to the learner. The stimulus may be visual (real or a representation) or verbal (spoken or written). In some types of training, the stimulus may appeal to other senses (for example, taste and smell in training for technicians, or touch in training paper or fabric salespersons, printers, and the like). The only way we can ever know if our learner understands our stimuli is by eliciting responses. Thus, in the terminology of learning theory, the purpose of the stimulus is to elicit a response. If you don't expect a learner response, don't waste time presenting the stimulus.

Response: Anything the learner does—whether the learner says, thinks, or performs it—in response to a stimulus or group of stimuli. The response serves three main purposes:

- It gives us feedback on how well our learner understands.
- It gives the learner an opportunity to see how well he or she understands and can apply the new learning.
- It improves retention and transfer because the very act of responding forces the learner to manipulate and internalize new knowledge, skills, and attitudes.

Again, to apply the terminology of learning theory, the response (or a succession of them) is the desired new behavior (or a verbal explanation of it in cases where the behavior expected at work is either inappropriate or impossible to obtain in class).

Feedback: Any information the learner receives that reinforces a response next time the learner is confronted with the same situation (that is, receives the same stimulus or set of stimuli). Sometimes the learner is dependent upon the instructor or other students for feedback, as in the analysis of a role play in which the learner has participated. At other times, the nature of the task is such that the learner's response will generate its own feedback, as in learning to balance a monthly statement from the bank against a checkbook, or in learning how to apply flux to metal to prepare it for soldering. In those cases, if the learner does not respond correctly, the bank statement won't reconcile and the solder won't take hold.

The three components, stimulus (S), response (R), and feedback (F), together make up the smallest element in an instructional sequence. Summarizing, we emerge with the following model:

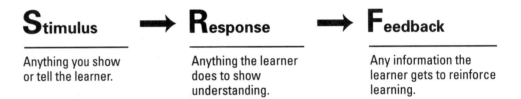

Stimulus	→	**R**esponse	→	**F**eedback
Anything you show or tell the learner.		Anything the learner does to show understanding.		Any information the learner gets to reinforce learning.

Let's examine a script that illustrates the S-R-F chaining process. We have diagnosed the S-R-F links in the instructional chain to show how the instructor is structuring questions (Ss) so as to shape the learners' responses (Rs). The lesson is on performance appraisal, and the trainees are first-line supervisors.

Instructor: On pages 13-14 of the workbook you read a reprint of an article on self-evaluation. The author was pointing out the benefits of getting your subordinates to evaluate themselves on each aspect of their work before you evaluate them. What are some of the benefits of this?
(Pause to wait for hands.) Yes, Bill.
S ↓

Bill: One benefit is that we can find out where our people feel they need help. It's one thing to tell them what we think, but we can do a much better job in training and coaching them if we find out how they see themselves first.
R ↓

Instructor: Right. And as several of you pointed out when we were discussing the Steve and Andrea case study earlier, Andrea missed a real opportunity to find out where Steve felt he needed her help. How about some other benefits of self-evaluation first? Yes, Ted.
F S ↓

Ted: It helps in relaxing the person we've been reviewing to get him or her to do the talking. People feel better telling us their strengths and weaknesses than they do in having us tell them.
R ↓

Instructor: That's true. Often when we evaluate, the other person is on the defensive. That disappears when you have that person do the evaluating. Okay. There are other benefits we could list, but let's move on to a concern I sometimes hear supervisors express, namely that if we invite people to evaluate themselves first, they might give themselves outstanding ratings and show us that they walk on water. This would make our job harder in sharing our perception of their performance. How do you feel about this concern? Betty Jo?

Betty Jo: My boss does my annual review the way that is suggested in the cassette and workbook. He has me evaluate myself first, and then shares his own perceptions of my strengths and weaknesses. And, he is usually more positive about my performance than I am. His ratings are higher than mine.

Bill: Which is what the article in the workbook says. I forget the actual percentages, but in the majority of cases the employee's self-rating was lower than the boss's.

Instructor: In fact, only 19 percent of the time were the employees self-ratings higher than the supervisor's rating. Now, is that good or bad?

Marge: It's good. It enables us to do the listening and find out why most employees assigned a lower rating. As Bill said earlier, this helps us do a better job in coaching and training them.

Instructor: So you're saying that self-evaluation is much more consistent with the true purpose of appraisals, which is to be a coach and not just a judge. Now, what do you think would happen to that 19 percent figure if our employees came into a performance review thinking of it mainly as a salary review?

Frank: They might have a lot more good things to say about themselves since they want to get as big a recommended salary increase as possible.

Instructor: Exactly. The 19 percent who rated themselves higher than the boss did would be a much higher percent. Does that mean that salary shouldn't be discussed?

Ted: If it comes up, I'll discuss it, of course. But I tell the person at the start of the appraisal that this is not a salary review, and that that will occur at another time. The two shouldn't be confused.

Carol: (a supervisor from the personnel department) In fact, that's why we keep salary reviews and performance reviews six months apart. We don't want the performance appraisal to turn into a negotiating session. And most companies do the same.

Instructor: How many of you are already getting your subordinates to rate themselves as part of their preappraisal preparation?

Participants: (show of hands while instructor counts)

Instructor: Eleven of you. That's really good. And how many are not doing it but like the idea and plan to incorporate it into your action plan?

Participants:	(show of hands while instructor counts)	R ↓ F
Instructor:	Very encouraging. Okay. Let's see what information and what forms we want to give to subordinates when we first contact them to schedule a time and place for their review. Then we can pair up with the person next to us for a mini role play in which we give them the instructions we would give a subordinate on how to prepare for a performance appraisal. But before we pair up, let's see if we can agree on what forms or materials we will need. Yes, Derwin.	S ↓
Derwin:	I'd want a copy of the employee's job description since the review should really start by reviewing the job.	R ↓
Instructor:	To see if the duties and responsibilities are still current. Exactly. Let's not talk about performance before we both agree on what it is we're performing. Okay. What other forms and material will we need?	F S ↓
Marge:	Well, we'll certainly want a copy of the last review, notes we made on actions to be taken, areas to be improved, and so on.	R ↓
Instructor:	So that each appraisal is also a progress report on what we've done since the last appraisal. Good. Any other forms needed? Yes, Frank.	F S ↓
Frank:	We might want to give our employee a blank copy of the appraisal form. If we're expecting the person to do a self-appraisal, we'd better give him or her the form to do so.	R ↓
Instructor:	Which means that during the review we can compare comments and ratings on the two respective forms—the employee's self-evaluation and our evaluation.	F

And so on.

In this chapter, we've defined the three elements of an instructional sequence: stimulus, response, and feedback. We've illustrated the instructors' role in creating a chain of S-R-F links.

An analogy might be useful. Think of the instructor as a tennis coach who is teaching a beginner to play the game. The instructor ends each statement, or stimulus, with a question that puts the ball back in the learner's court. The learner then hits the ball back (the response), thus continuing the volley. Like the skilled tennis coach, the instructor structures questions in a way that builds the learning.

It is this ability to ask the right questions in the right sequence that makes an instructor most effective. The next two chapters will focus on questions as one of the instructor's most valuable tools.

CHAPTER 21

SOME QUESTIONS ABOUT QUESTIONS

Instructors are quick to agree that questions are one of their most valuable tools for making a point, for assessing understanding, for arousing interest, for testing, and so on. Yet many instructors are uncomfortable in using questions as a part of the natural flow of a lesson and a means of converting a lecture to a dialogue. Here are the questions that participants in instructional skills workshops frequently ask during the session on asking questions, along with our answers.

1. **Is it better to call on participants by name or ask overhead questions and hope for volunteers?**

   If you are trying to create a free flow of conversation and dialogue between learners and instructor, then it's better not to call on individuals by name. Naming your respondent in advance has several negative effects:

   ◆ The person may be embarrassed.

   ◆ Someone else may be better qualified to answer and thus benefit the group.

   ◆ Others will feel off the hook and not think through their own answers.

   ◆ The climate becomes one of classroom recitation like a parent-to-child series of transactions in which the instructor plays the role of judging parent.

   However, an effective instructor can call on participants by name without encountering any of the negative side effects just noted. One way is to let a person know why you're calling on him or her in particular: "Harry, I know you've had some experience with this problem at your location. What do you feel are some of the..."

The danger of hoping for volunteers, of course, is that you may get none or that the same people will respond, leaving the learners who never volunteer—the silent majority—behind, not contributing and perhaps even resentful. Our next question addresses this.

2. How do I involve those learners who never volunteer, the silent majority who see learning as a passive activity, a spectator sport?

Pareto's 20/80 ratio probably applies to classroom behavior as well as to so many other phenomena. Namely, 80 percent of your volunteered responses come from 20 percent of your learners. In a class of 20 trainees, the same three or four persons may be answering all the time. Since people learn best by being actively involved, you want everyone responding. How can you accomplish this?

There are many ways. After you've posed a question, have your trainees each turn to a neighbor and respond to that person. On short answers, have each person write it on notepaper, and then discuss the responses. On polarized issues, such as yes or no and more or less, ask for a show of hands for each response. Once you've broken the ice with such techniques, your learners will be more willing to volunteer.

3. Is it a good idea to repeat the question to make sure everybody understands it?

In general, yes, although repeating every question can become tiresome. Most questions shouldn't need repeating. But if the question was not worded clearly, or was spoken too softly for everyone to hear, or came from out of the blue, then it's a good idea to repeat it.

4. How should I deal with someone who has just given me a wrong answer, especially if the person has rank or status in the group?

Two issues here. Let's deal with rank or status first. Such persons have no corner on the market when it comes to intelligence or understanding. Everyone in your class is entitled to make mistakes and have misconceptions. But by the same token, everyone is entitled to respect, and it is the instructor's job to save face for everyone.

A wrong answer from someone is an indication that others may also be having difficulty. It's not likely that you picked the only person who did not understand. Thus, you may want to turn to the group after a wrong answer and ask, "How do the rest of you feel about Jackie's response? Is your own answer similar?" This neutral wording will let you know how widespread the problem is and get another person who has an acceptable answer to explain the reasoning behind it to Jackie and anyone else who was having trouble. This relieves you from always being the one to correct wrong answers, and gets your trainees to view one another as a resource.

5. **Sometimes I just don't understand a student's answer enough to know whether it's right or not? What should I do in such cases?**

     You have several possibilities here:

     ◆ Tell the student you don't understand what he or she is saying, and ask the student to put it in different wording if possible.

     ◆ If you think that you understand some of it, try a restatement. The student will step in with clarification as needed.

     ◆ Ask the rest of the group for help: "Do you all understand Tom's response? I'm not sure I do. Can someone interpret it for me?"

6. **What if a student is taking forever to answer, perhaps repeating himself, rambling, or having trouble organizing his thoughts?**

     After you've allowed a student a reasonable time to organize an answer and you see that the person is in trouble and that you're wasting group time, you may want to interrupt and summarize: "Let me see, Bill, if I understand what you're saying. You feel that . . ." Or, if you are at a loss to understand Bill well enough to attempt a summary, you may want to ask the group, "Can someone summarize Bill's response?" Or you might simply interrupt, thank Bill, and say, "I'd like to get answers from several people on this question, since it's a difficult one."

7. **What if no one answers my question?**

     Let's examine some of the possible reasons:

     ◆ The question may have been so obvious or simple that no one wants to look like the class idiot by answering it.

     ◆ You may not have broken the ice yet, in which case some of the techniques discussed under question two apply here.

     ◆ It's possible that no one knows the answer, in which case the question was premature or your prior instruction was inadequate.

     ◆ Perhaps, no one understood the question. You might say, "Do you understand what I'm asking?" Or you might ask why this question seems to be giving them trouble, or you might rephrase the question, which gives them new wording and additional time to think the answer through.

8. **How should I deal with a student who asks irrelevant questions that interfere with the flow of my instruction?**

     If the questions can be answered in a sentence or two, it might be easier to deal with the question rather than with the disruptive behavior. However, if the questions are coming from the same person and are making it hard for other participants and you to keep on track, you might say to the disruptive student, "I'm having trouble relating your question to the point we've been discussing. Maybe I'm missing something." This gives the person a chance to explain the relevance or to drop the question and acknowledge its irrelevance.

Sometimes a student's question may be irrelevant or disruptive to you but of interest to the group, perhaps because it concerns a gripe they all have or a hidden agenda that is now out. The next question addresses this particular type of interruption.

9. **What if a student asks a question that is irrelevant but of great interest to the group? Or a question that you'll be addressing later in the course is premature at this point?**

You might start a course by taping a sheet of flipchart paper to the wall and writing on it the title "To be taken up later." Then, as people ask questions that you'll be dealing with in a subsequent session, you can write a reminder note for all to see. Sometimes participants bring up questions of a policy nature that you'll want to check with someone in authority before answering. The chart buys you time to do so.

If you've shared the schedule and the course objectives with your trainees early, you're less likely to get irrelevant or premature questions. And when you do, you can simply refer to the schedule or to the objectives.

10. **If no one else answers, is there anything wrong with answering my own question?**

If you asked the question to test understanding or to get the group's input, then you're defeating your purpose by answering it yourself. Their failure to answer is a symptom, and you should try to analyze the problem underlying it. Was your question understood? Was it relevant? Do they know the answer?

Many instructors feel embarrassed if no one answers within a few seconds. You may have to wait five to 10 seconds for an answer, especially to a complex question. Rephrase it to increase their understanding of what you want. This also gives them more time to think through their answers. If no one volunteers, ask them to turn to their neighbor and discuss their answers. You can then circulate, listening in on a half-dozen answers to find out where the group had trouble with your initial question.

11. **What if I don't know the answer to a student's question? Doesn't this cause a loss of credibility?**

You'll lose more credibility by trying to bluff an answer than by stating that you don't know the answer but will try to find out before the next class. Or you might ask the group if anyone knows the answer. It's far more important to be a good facilitator than to be the one with all the answers.

12. How should I deal with a student who asks a question that is really a statement of opinion?

One of the most common ways a student will get the floor in order to make a point is by asking a question. Such questions often begin with wording like "Don't you think, sir, that the best way to . . . ?" When you recognize that someone is really expressing his or her opinion or making a point, it's a good idea to throw it back to that person: "That's a good question, Chris. What do you think?" In short, give the questioner the chance to make his or her point. Don't take it away by answering the question yourself or by throwing it to the group.

13. What if a student asks a question about something I covered 10 minutes earlier? Should I take time to answer?

This depends. You might acknowledge for the group's benefit that "we discussed that a little earlier, but evidently you still need some more time before you're ready to accept it. You're questioning whether. . ." Then ask the others if anyone else is having trouble. If no one is, you have good reason to suggest that the student see you during the break "so we don't take up everyone else's time." Of course, if the question can be answered in half a minute or so, it's easier to do so and not make an issue of it.

14. What if the students don't accept my answer and are fighting it? This often happens when I'm teaching company policy or procedures.

Don't take sides by either defending or knocking the company. Simply acknowledge that what you're explaining may not be popular, but that this is the way things are. If you know in advance that you'll be facing resistance, it's well to have the persons responsible present to explain and sell the new things you're teaching. You may jeopardize your effectiveness as an instructor if you question or defend your content.

If the answer is not a matter of policy or procedure but is being met with resistance, you might ask for help from the group. "Has anyone tried the technique I'm describing? Have you found it to work?" Or, you may be able to relate a personal experience in which you found it useful to do what you just described in your answer.

Finally, in certain types of courses it is desirable to state at the start that some of the suggestions and answers you'll be sharing won't be appropriate or acceptable to everyone. Thus, it is the job of each learner to select what is relevant and reject what isn't. Once you've said this, it's easy to deal with students who are fighting you: Simply point out that if your answer isn't relevant, they shouldn't act on it.

Chapter 22

Using Questions Effectively

Questions are probably an instructor's single most useful tool. Instructors can use them to arouse learners' interest, to confirm understanding, and to lead a group of students to discover a principle or work out a solution on their own. Table 22-1 displays a brief dialogue between an instructor and a group of students in class to illustrate some of the uses to which questions can be put.

Table 22-1. Examples of questions and description of their purpose.

Speaker	Dialogue	Purpose of Question
Instructor	Have you added up the points and gotten your scores on the communication response style exercise? Does anyone need more time?	to keep the group together (manage time effectively)
Participants	(No verbal response, but participants look up. No one is doing calculations, so instructor continues.)	
Instructor	Who wants to take a guess on how you came out as a group? What would you guess your highest and next highest styles might be?	to arouse interest (whet the appetite for what is coming)
Participants	(Several participants take guesses.)	
Instructor	Okay. I'd like you to raise your hand when I mention your highest score. How many had *searching* as the highest score? (Hands) How many had *critical?* (Hands) *Empathic?* (Hands) And *advising?* (Hands)	to get information about the group (assess entering behavior)

(continued on next page)

Table 22-1. Examples of questions and description of their purpose. *(continued)*

Speaker	Dialogue	Purpose of Question
Participant	I had a tie between my two highest scores. How should I handle that?	
Instructor	How did you handle it?	to help participants answer their own questions (deductive teaching method)
Participant	I raised my hand twice.	
Instructor	Good thinking. Now, if I counted your hands correctly, it looks as if searching is the big one, and advising came in second. How many remember from your assignment last night the two types of interpersonal relationships that these four response styles illustrate? Let's see hands, please.	to find out whether the homework got done, so as to build on it or not (class management)
Participants	(More than half raise their hands, so instructor continues.)	
Instructor	I'd like you to turn to your neighbor and answer this question: Which two styles are parent to child by nature? And which two are adult to adult? Take half a minute to compare answers.	to confirm understanding (feedback to instructor, reinforcement to participants)
Participants	(Working in pairs, participants answer to their neighbors while instructor circulates to listen in on a number of answers and decide whom to call on.)	
Instructor	Okay. May I have your attention again, please. Let's reconvene, please. Marge, what did you and Joe say were the two response styles that are adult to adult by nature?	to use participants as a resource (to elicit the learning points from the group)
Participant (Marge)	We said that the *searching* and the *empathic* responses are adult responses.	
Instructor	Which means the *critical* and *advising* responses are parent to child by nature. Do you all agree with that? Did anyone come out differently?	to confirm understanding (feedback to instructor, reinforcement to learners)
Participant (Harry)	Tom and I had trouble deciding whether the empathic response is adult or parent. Marge called it adult, but I see a lot of parents showering their kids with empathy and sometimes mothering them to death.	
Instructor	Let's address Harry's concern. What's the difference between empathy and sympathy? Can anyone help us here? Yes, Cindy.	to get participants to help one another (deductive teaching method)

Table 22-1. Examples of questions and description of their purpose. *(continued)*

Speaker	Dialogue	Purpose of Question
Participant (Cindy)	Well, empathy is showing feeling for someone or being sensitive to how people feel, and sympathy is being sorry for them or showing pity for them.	
Instructor	Well put. Empathy says, "I want to understand how you feel," or "I think I see where you're coming from." Whereas sympathy says, "You poor thing. I feel sorry for you." Now then, is sympathy a parent-to-child response or an adult-to-adult response? Anyone?	to draw a conclusion and reach closure (summary point)
Participants	Parent to child.	
Instructor	And is empathy a parent-to-child response or an adult-to-adult response?	(same as above)
Participants	Adult to adult.	
Instructor	Exactly. Sympathy is judgmental, and can mess up your objectivity. But empathy is nonjudgmental. You can still be objective and respond to a person with empathy in a rational unemotional way. Now, Harry, you and Tom weren't sure whether empathy was a parent response or an adult one because you've seen a lot of parents showering their kids with empathy and mothering them. Was that an example of empathy or sympathy?	to lead a learner to correct a misconception (remedial instruction)
Participant (Harry)	Okay. I see the problem. We were confusing the two. Sympathy is a parent-type response, but empathy is adult.	
Instructor	You got it! Now when I asked for a show of hands a few minutes ago, *searching* came in first. And *searching* is an adult response. But *advising,* which came in as your second most common way of responding, is a parent-to-child response. Does that bother anyone? Isn't it desirable to avoid parent-type responses?	to see if learners understand the pitfalls of advising (needs analysis)
Participant	They're not always bad, are they?	
Instructor	Good question. What do you think?	to let a learner make a point (give student the floor)
Participant	Sometimes it's necessary to give criticism or advice, isn't it?	

(continued on next page)

Table 22-1. Examples of questions and description of their purpose. *(continued)*

Speaker	Dialogue	Purpose of Question
Instructor	Sometimes, yes. But in most cases, no. And it's sometimes hard to resist giving advice. People you work with often turn to you for it. What's wrong with giving advice? Take a piece of paper and write down one or two things that can happen when you give a person advice. This should only take you 20 seconds or so.	to get information about the group (assess entering behavior)
Participants	(While participants write, instructor circulates to look over the responses. Instructor then reconvenes the group.)	
Instructor	As I looked over your responses, I saw a lot of good thinking on the pitfalls or dangers of giving advice. In fact, let me record your responses on the flipchart. Who wants to start me off with something you wrote?	to use participants as a resource (to elicit the learning points from the group)
Participants	(Responses from different participants include the following: ◆ People depend on you instead of themselves. ◆ If your advice doesn't work, you get blamed. ◆ There's no commitment if there's no authorship. ◆ People learn best by solving their own problems.)	

The instructor continued, drawing the conclusion that two response styles maintain adult interactions: searching, or getting more information, and empathic, or showing concern for the thoughts and feelings of others. These develop I'm-okay-You're okay-style relationships. The other two response styles, critical and advising, perpetuate parent-to-child interactions and thus tend to develop I'm-okay-You're-not-okay-style relationships.

The course could have been for supervisors, salespersons, or any other group that is concerned with improved communication skills. For our purposes, the process is important, not the content. Our focus is on the use of questions, which are often more effective than statements in influencing the thoughts and actions of others.

The purpose of a question is to get information. The purpose of a screwdriver is to turn a screw. But tools can be used for many purposes. Without much effort, most people can think of at least a half dozen other uses to which you have put screwdrivers. If questions are to be our most useful tool as instructors, we should be adept at applying them in as many ways as they will effectively serve us. Here are some of the more common ways:

◆ **To test understanding:** Use when you need to get a reading on the level of comprehension of your learners. Example: "What would happen if...?"

- **To make a point:** Use to influence your learners to think in a certain way. Example: "Do you think the average employee is only interested in pay?"

- **To lead learners to discover:** Use when teaching deductively (Socratic method). Example: "What are some of the pitfalls of giving advice when someone asks for it?"

- **To stimulate creative thinking:** Use when brainstorming. Example: "How can we get greater employee involvement in our work group meetings?"

- **To assess needs of the learners:** Use when deciding how much or how deep to teach. Example: "How many of you have ever had to...?"

- **To arouse interest in the topic:** Use to elicit a guess. Example: "What percentage of your time is spent listening in a typical day at work?"

- **To get introspection:** Use to help participants analyze their behavior. Example: "What qualities do you possess that have helped you as a project manager?"

- **To ventilate:** Use to address and dispel negative attitudes. Example: "What kinds of flack might we expect from our employees when we announce...?"

- **To poll the group:** Use to reach consensus, get feedback, "test the water." Example: "How many of you feel that we should...?"

- **To rephrase a learner's question:** Use when the group doesn't understand a learner's question. Example: "Are you asking whether we should...?"

- **To steer group:** Use when participants are going astray or not managing time effectively. Example: "How much more time do you want to spend on this issue?"

- **To get a learner to answer his or her own question:** Use when participant was really making a point via a question. Example: "Good question. What do you think?"

- **To summarize and get closure:** Use to wrap up a class. Example: "Now let's summarize. What are the four ways of dealing with a problem?"

CHAPTER 23

USING SUBGROUPS TO IMPROVE LEARNING

Learning is not a spectator sport. The learning process is more effective and more enjoyable when your learners are active in class, doing things and interacting with others. Experience is, indeed, the best teacher. As instructors, we must find ways that will help our learners to experience and internalize the concepts, procedures, and learning points that make up our course content.

Some instructional methods require a high degree of interaction between the learner and the material. Computer-based training, programmed instruction, interactive television, games, and simulations all require a high level of learner involvement and are, accordingly, relatively effective.

Other instructional methods are less demanding and can lead students into a somewhat passive state that is not conducive to effective learning. Methods associated with group instruction are the prime examples, such as lecture, video, and slide presentations. Here the burden is on the instructor to maintain a level of interaction that keeps learners busy, such as thinking, questioning, responding, applying, and internalizing.

Subgroups for Interaction

Breaking the class into subgroups is an effective way to accomplish this. A subgroup can be as small as two persons: ("Now I'd like you to turn to your neighbor and spend a half minute answering this question...."). Or it can be as big as a half dozen or more participants: ("Now I'd like you to work in five subgroups, each of you dealing with a different assignment that you'll report on when we come back from the breakout rooms in a half hour.")

You could, of course, pose questions to the full group and wait for volunteers to respond. However, the 80/20 rule would probably be at work (that is, 80 percent of your responses coming from 20 percent of your learners), so that the same people would respond all the time. Because you want all your learners to be active, the subgroup would give you an opportunity to get responses from everyone and not just from the verbal minority.

There's another principle of group dynamics at work here that instructors must work to overcome. Most people feel comfortable in a small group and will ask or answer a question without embarrassment. In a large group, say an auditorium with 100 or more people in it, most people are embarrassed if called on to speak. Each of us has some threshold of comfort (that is, a certain group size below which we're ready to participate and above which we would rather be a passive observer and maintain low visibility). By having learners work in subgroups, you can operate well within everyone's threshold of comfort and thus make it easy for each person to participate in a supportive, low-risk environment.

A favorite issue of instructors is class size. Typical questions include: What is the ideal group size? When is a class too big or too small? These questions diminish in importance when we realize that a class of 60 participants can be broken into 12 groups of five learners just as easily as a class of 15 can be broken into three groups of five. And within each class, the learning is the same.

Reasons for Creating Small Groups

Following is a list of 15 reasons for breaking your class into subgroups. It shows occasions when it makes sense to divide and conquer, along with the benefits of doing so.

1. Learning (retention) is better because learners are responding actively. That is, the instructor is breaking the large chunks of information into small stimulus-response-feedback (S-R-F) links.

2. Interaction increases synergism. There is better thinking when participants discuss their responses with one another; ideas beget ideas.

3. The instructor gets more feedback. Responses are coming from all participants, and the instructor can circulate and collect a broader sample of responses.

4. Learning is accelerated. It's quicker to reach consensus with three to five people than with 15 to 20. Participants are thinking more quickly.

5. Learners can discover and work things out for themselves. The emphasis is on deductive not inductive learning.

6. Emphasis is on adult-to-adult learning (andragogy) rather than on parent-to-child learning (pedagogy); we thus avoid dependence on the teacher.

7. Subgroups help to vary the pace, break up a lecture, and increase the level of activity and interest (for example, as a pickup in the midafternoon slump).

8. The instructor can pair up experienced and inexperienced participants.

9. When time is short, the class can be broken into task forces with different assignments. Each group then reports back to the full class.

10. The instructor might need three to five minutes of free time to make a phone call, study the lesson plan, and the like. A spontaneous subgroup assignment buys time.

11. If there are some participants who are not responding or contributing, the instructor can listen to their subgroup and get feedback to see if they are in tune with the group.

12. One purpose of many workshops is team building. By working in different subgroups, participants get to know one another better.

13. Listening skills are improved as participants learn how to summarize, restate, separate fact from opinion, evaluate relevance, seek consensus, and the like.

14. Participants have higher interest and commitment to the lesson when they have authorship and can buy in through the process of subgrouping.

15. Learning is fun when all participants share the responsibility for the success of a class.

Guidelines on Using Subgroups

Following is a list of 20 guidelines for using subgroups effectively. These are dos and don'ts of handling such assignments smoothly. As you read this list, place a check mark in front of the guidelines you plan to incorporate into your own instruction. Select those guidelines that best fit the courses and the participants with whom you deal.

1. The ideal size of subgroups is from three to six persons. The minimum number is two, and the suggested maximum is eight.

2. Define the subgroup's task in very specific terms. Spell out the assignment on a handout, chalkboard, flipchart, or overhead projector.

3. Tell the groups how long they have on each assignment. Give guidelines on how they should budget and apportion the time on subtasks (for example, "Plan to spend about five minutes on the first question, then about three minutes on each of the other questions").

4. To help pace the group on longer assignments (30 minutes or more), have each group appoint a time watcher to keep the group on schedule. Or make announcements from time to time (for example, "It looks as if most of you are on question three or four by now").

5. If the members of a subgroup have not worked together before and you want them to appoint a spokesperson, do not tell them this until they have had several minutes to get organized and are beginning to tackle the assignment. Then interrupt just long enough to ask them to pick

someone who will take notes and report for the subgroup when the class reconvenes.

6. If you want reports from each group, hop around and call on a different group for each subtask. In other words, don't let the first group you call on steal everyone else's thunder and lead to subsequent reports that are repetitive or apologetic.

7. If you do not want reports from each subgroup, tell them this in advance so they do not waste time selecting a spokesperson or agreeing on a report.

8. On assignments that benefit from a visual summary, give each subgroup a flipchart or several sheets of chart paper and masking tape to affix it to the easel or wall. Or give them acetate sheets and special markers if you're using an overhead projector.

9. Limit reading assignments to five to 10 minutes of group time (one to two pages of handout as maximum). Give longer assignments in advance as premeeting work. Otherwise, valuable group time is wasted, fast readers finish early and must wait, and slow readers feel pressured or embarrassed.

10. Don't call on group members to read aloud. Many have poor reading skills and will waste time, show embarrassment, stammer, and so forth. Have them work from notes or flipchart sheets.

11. Have subgroups that are preparing outlines or lists on flipchart paper post their papers on the walls when they reconvene. Then allow 10 to 15 minutes for everyone to circulate, reading all the flipchart sheets and making notes before you begin the discussion or reports.

12. Form differently configured subgroups by seating participants differently each day or half day. Keep a seating chart of each arrangement so as not to repeat pairs. Your objective is to have everyone work with everyone else at least once by the end of the workshop.

13. Tell groups at the end of the first day that "one objective of this course is to get to know people who can help you (or you them) after this course. With this in mind, please pick up your name card and notebook right now, and move to a different seat so that you will have new neighbors when you arrive tomorrow."

14. Set up room so that participants can go into subgroups immediately without lost time or movement. If seated at a U-shaped table, put a colored sticker on each person's name tent card to indicate which group that person belongs to (blue group, green group, and so on). Have circular tables so members can see and hear everyone else equally well when they break out into subgroup work.

15. Instructors should circulate but not participate. Listen unobtrusively but do not join in unless the participants are off track or don't understand the assignment. Listen for examples, illustrations, and other points that you can use in the summary or closure statement with which you end the exercise.

16. In general, keep your own wrap-up or summary short. If you've structured the group work correctly, participants have already come to their conclusions in the group and don't want to drag the exercise out. It may not be necessary to have a lengthy discussion in the full group if the subgroups have met your learning objectives.

17. The first subgroup to report to the full group sets the stage for the other groups' reports. Give them feedback that will help others who have not yet reported. For example, if the report was too long or too detailed, say, "Well, your group certainly did a thorough job. I'm glad you went to that degree of detail in your group work, although it may be more than we need in the reports." Similarly, a report that is superficial or too short might lead you to ask a few probing questions to draw the spokesperson out and to let others know what you're looking for.

18. Use a larger subgroup of four to eight persons if the assignment will be richer for the input of more participants. For example, more people would be advantageous in discussing a case study or brainstorming. But when the response you want requires no great depth of thought and can be discussed fully in a minute or less, use subgroups of two or three people.

19. When using small subgroups, there is no need for participants to leave their seats. Simply make the assignment or pose the question, then tell people you'd like them to work with their neighbors. Then indicate who will work with whom: "You three...you three...you three..." and so on.

20. The easiest and quickest subgroup to use is two persons. A lecture or one-way presentation can be made dynamic and interactive simply by throwing a question to participants every five to 10 minutes. Example: "Now, based on what I've just covered, let me pose a question that I'd like you to take half a minute to discuss with your neighbor...." There is no group too large for this kind of subgrouping. It can keep an audience of hundreds actively thinking, responding to your message, and internalizing it.

If you follow some of these suggestions for using subgroups during your courses, you will discover that the higher levels of participation that result will improve participants' learning, retention, and end-of-course ratings.

SECTION 6

TEACHING INDUCTIVELY AND DEDUCTIVELY

The basic training given to new recruits in all branches of the military is inductive. Instructors tell the trainees what they must know. In contrast, senior officers who attend courses on strategy and tactics are taught deductively. Here the instructor's role is to describe situations and pose questions that lead the officers to deduce the appropriate military responses.

The lecture method is inductive: The instructor is inducing information into the learners. The case method is deductive: The instructor is giving learners the opportunity to deduce the key points of the lesson through their analysis of the case. Effective instructors are comfortable in both modes. They know when and how to teach inductively and deductively.

The chapters in this section describe inductive and deductive methods of instruction and provide you with a chance to revise inductive lectures to the deductive format. Following are descriptions of what each chapter covers:

Chapter 24, "Observations on the Lecture Method," presents 12 characteristics of lectures, along with five ways an instructor can use questions to break up the lecture and elicit relevant responses. Included is an exercise comparing the advantages of text and of lecture (that is, the written versus the spoken word).

Chapter 25, "A Comparison of Two Instructional Strategies," examines the when, why, and how of teaching inductively and deductively, with scripted examples of each and illustrations of the types of questions used in each mode.

Chapter 26, "The Deductive Lecture," contains a script of three different inductive lectures on the topics of goal setting, listening effectively, and time management. Your job is to select one of the three, identify the key learning points, and construct questions that will elicit these points from your trainees by teaching the topic deductively. The chapter contains a script of the same three lectures taught deductively, with the key learning points printed in bold type preceded by the question or assignment the instructor used to elicit the desired responses.

Upon completing this section, you should be able to:

◆ list at least six limitations of the lecture method

◆ describe five ways of using questions to break up a lecture

◆ state at least six advantages of text over lecture

◆ identify courses where inductive teaching is better; same for deductive

◆ name four factors that determine whether inductive or deductive is better

◆ give two examples of inductive questions; of deductive questions

◆ describe the process of converting course content to a deductive lecture.

CHAPTER 24

OBSERVATIONS ON THE LECTURE METHOD

12 Characteristics

Following is a list of 12 characteristics of lectures. As you read the list, think about the degree to which the items apply to the lecture courses you've attended or given.

1. Very few lecturers identify the behavior changes they expect from their listeners. In fact, most lectures aren't intended to change behavior. The lecture's "objectives" (when there are any) are often stated in teacher-centered terms (for example, "I want to *cover* the main..., I will *stress* the importance of...," and so forth) rather than in learner-centered, behavioral terms (for example, After this lecture, the learner will be able to...).

2. One of the easiest ways to teach is by the lecture method. Comparatively speaking, it takes less time to develop a lecture on a given topic than it does to create virtually any other teaching approach to the same topic.

3. Lectures tend to make audiences passive. That is, most of the time, some attendees listen dutifully, some take notes, others daydream, and so on. Except for interruptions (if permitted), or at question-and-answer periods at the end, audiences are less involved than with most other teaching methods.

4. Lectures are generally void of useful feedback to the speaker as to how well the listeners are learning. Except for the occasional "I don't understand your last point," most of the time lecturers aren't sure what their audience is learning, if anything.

5. Conversely, listeners aren't certain what they are learning. It is very easy for listeners to think they understand and can apply what is being taught, only to find out at a later time (perhaps on the job or

during an exam) that they have been wrong. Listeners' passive role during a lecture contributes to their false sense of understanding.

6. Lectures are generally less threatening to the instructor because the speaker gets involved in a comparatively limited give-and-take with the audience and, therefore, the audience has less opportunity to challenge what is said.

7. By and large, lectures are far more reinforcing for the lecturer than the listener. In other words, the "what's in it for me?" favors the speaker more than the listener. This is one reason why audience members often consider lectures ego trips for the lecturer.

8. Lectures are a poor way to make use of human beings. People are brought together to listen to a speaker at a central location. Most of the time, the speaker could be replaced by a tape player, and the audience by a tape recorder, without diluting the overall communication process very much.

9. The major criticism of lectures is not so much their use, but rather the illusion that it is a complete method. To put it another way, if lectures were seen as only a part of the instructional process, and a small part at that, one would have little to complain about. Unfortunately, too often it turns out to be the only method used.

10. In a diversified training program such as management development, the same instructor is usually not an expert on each of the topics covered. Thus, the lecture method places a burden on the instructor and trainees alike.

11. Lecturers assume that the trainees have low entering behavior and are dependent on the instructor. This may be true in teaching adolescents. But in programs for adults (management development, sales training, and the like), the trainees bring a wealth of experience that should be shared.

12. The lecture method continues to foster the notion that telling is teaching. Unfortunately, teaching requires a lot more than telling, and we must add to our instructional arsenal methods that are consistent with one of the most basic principles of human behavior: People learn best, not by being told, but by experiencing the consequences of their actions.

Breaking Up the Lecture

Although the lecture method can be an efficient means of imparting information, its limitation lies in the fact that most lecturers regard the method as a one-way communication. They provide their learners with no opportunity to think things through for themselves or to experience the consequences of their own thoughts and actions.

The material that a lecturer presents, whether by telling or showing or both, might be thought of as the **stimulus.** In fact, every major point (whether a concept, principle, technique, procedure, or something else) that is dealt with in a lecture is a separate stimulus. If it's important enough that we want the learner to remember it, then it's necessary for the lecturer to get a **response** from all the learners (not just one or two). Why? Because people learn best not by being told, but by experiencing the consequences of their thoughts and actions. In short, a good lecturer is an arranger of experiences and not merely an imparter of information.

Questions are the main tool a lecturer has for breaking the big S (all Stimuli) down into a chain of S-R-F links (Stimulus-Response-Feedback). There are many occasions or opportunities for asking questions. Following are some of the more frequent:

- ◆ to get learners to take a guess that will whet their appetite and arouse interest before introducing a new topic, an important fact, a major concept

- ◆ to assess the needs of learners by determining their existing level of understanding, familiarity with the subject, entering behavior, and the like

- ◆ to elicit examples and experiences from learners to illustrate and bring to life a concept, procedure, skill, principle, or the like

- ◆ to measure understanding by seeing if learners can apply (manipulate, utilize, transfer, and so forth) what they were just told

- ◆ to teach deductively by asking a sequence of questions designed to enable learners to discover for themselves (that is, via the Socratic method).

Consider a lecture that lasts 45 minutes and deals with eight to 10 major learning points, such as concepts, procedures, principles, rules, or steps in a process. At the end of each learning point, the lecturer should have a planned question that will give the learners an opportunity to respond. This **response** can be thought of as a sales receipt in that it tells both the instructor and the learners four things: that they (a) heard, (b) understood, (c) accepted, and (d) can apply the new learning point. In preparing an effective lecture, the instructor usually must spend more time identifying the desired responses and planning how to elicit them than in arranging the stimulus material. This requirement spotlights the difference between teaching (that is, imparting information) and learning (that is, improving competencies). If your objective is to cause learning to take place, it may be necessary to tell learners less in order to have more time to elicit responses.

Text and Lecture

There are two major ways to impart information to your learners during the first stage of the three-stage learning model, which is made up of acquisition, demonstration, and application. They are through the printed word (for example, text) and the spoken word (for example, lecture). Illustrations should be used to increase understanding and retention with either the printed word or the spoken word.

Review the advantages of text in table 24-1. Then create a similar list to show the advantages of lectures. We can then make better decisions as

Table 24-1. Advantages of text and lecture.

Advantages of Text	Advantages of Lecture
It's permanent; available when the learner needs it for reference.	
Learners study and learn at their own rate (rather than at the instructor's rate).	
Reading is two to four times faster than listening to a lecture.	
It's portable and can be made available wherever it's needed (i.e., the instruction comes to the learner rather than vice versa).	
Learners can underline, make marginal notes, and tailor the material to their own needs and level of understanding.	
It can be reproduced and distributed without dependence on hardware or facilities.	
Quality control is excellent. The message, flow, examples are the same every time it is used.	
The cost of training is less with each new learner who goes through the text.	
No confusion of sound and sight. The learner either reads or studies visual material; never has to take in both simultaneously.	
Learner does not need to waste valuable time going to a group meeting held at the convenience of the instructor.	

to when to use lecture, when to use text, and how to use either method to its best advantage.

Text and lecture are the two most popular methods a trainer has for imparting information. The written word has permanence but may be difficult to modify. The spoken word lacks permanence but can be easily modified to meet the varied needs of different audiences. The effective instructor uses both text and lecture, drawing on the advantages of each. By so doing, you can avoid some of the drawbacks of the lecture method that were noted in our list of 12 characteristics at the start of this chapter.

CHAPTER 25

A COMPARISON OF TWO INSTRUCTIONAL STRATEGIES

A Need for Both

Think about this proverb: If you give a man a fish, you've fed him for a day, but if you teach a man how to fish, you've fed him for a lifetime. This proverb is the essence of the difference between inductive, or imparting, instruction and deductive, or Socratic, instruction.

The inductive instructor presents new information to learners, whereas the deductive instructor asks questions and draws new information—whether insights, new relationships, new ways of applying existing knowledge, or the like—from learners.

In some situations, the inductive strategy is clearly superior. If the instructor is teaching concepts or procedures that are unfamiliar and have no precedent in the learners' experience, then the instructor must impart a lot of information and tell the learners what they need to know. Student responses are output—feedback that lets the instructor know how well the students understand.

The inductive strategy is necessary in teaching such information as computer language to programmers, personnel policies and procedures (for example, how to calculate one's retirement pay), and technical manipulations on a new piece of equipment.

In other situations, the deductive strategy is clearly superior. If the learners are already somewhat familiar with the subject matter or if the content has an internal logic that enables learners to figure things out for themselves, then the instructor can use the learners as a resource, asking questions and posing situations that lead them to discover the learning points (concepts, procedures, rules, and so forth) for themselves. In this type of instruction, students' responses consist largely of input to the learning process.

The deductive strategy is useful in teaching such information as the following:

◆ problem solving or decision making via case method and personal experience

◆ statistics and quality control

◆ communication skills to supervisors

◆ selling skills to salespersons

◆ concepts and skills to managers for things they've been doing a long time, such as time management, performance appraisal, setting goals and standards, selection interviewing, counseling and coaching.

Up to now, we've examined the nature of the course content and the learners' familiarity with it as the major factors affecting instructors' decisions to use an inductive or deductive instructional strategy. Instructors should also consider the behavior they are looking for in their learners. If they want people to perform routine, well-defined procedures that require little thought, then the inductive method will prepare them for the job very nicely.

Conversely, the deductive strategy is more appropriate if they want learners to think for themselves, work out alternative ways of getting a job done, and engage in troubleshooting and problem solving when conventional ways of doing things don't work. In short, the deductive strategy is best for teaching people how to fish.

The Performance Appraisal Workshop: Inductive Example

Following is the transcript of an inductive lecture that deals with one aspect of performance appraisals: having subordinates evaluate their own performance and comparing it with the supervisor's appraisal. Please study this transcript, so that you can compare it with its deductive counterpart on the pages that follow.

Instructor: In the preworkshop assignment you read a reprint of an article on self-evaluation. The author was pointing out the benefits of getting your subordinates to evaluate themselves on each aspect of the work before you evaluate them. There are three major benefits of doing this.

First, you can find out much more about your people: how they feel they're progressing and where they need your help. It's one thing to tell them what we think, but we can learn a lot more if we listen to them before sharing our perceptions of their strengths and weaknesses.

Second, people will be more relaxed and less defensive. They feel better telling you their strengths and weaknesses than in having you tell them, which is likely to put them on guard.

And third, they are the ones responsible for improving the performance. They must first accept the need to change before improvement will take place. By getting them to spell out to you the nature and scope of their need, you are setting the stage for having them accept responsibility for their growth and improvement over the coming review period.

Some supervisors are concerned that if they ask their subordinates to evaluate themselves, they may give themselves outstanding ratings, and this might make the performance appraisal meeting even more difficult because you then have to be the bad guy and show them that they don't walk on water. Well, according to the study that you read in your workbook, employees rated themselves higher than their supervisor did only 19 percent of the time. They were in agreement 30 percent of the time, and the subordinate's rating was lower than the supervisor's 51 percent of the time.

Having your people evaluate themselves before coming to an appraisal and then sharing these ratings with you during the appraisal is much more consistent with the true purpose of an appraisal, which is for you to serve as coach rather than as judge. It's time to take inventory and plan for growth and development. It's not a time for salary review. If employees approached the performance review as a time to get a salary increase, then you would not get honest self-appraisals. That's one reason we keep salary reviews and performance appraisals six months apart—so that the appraisal can focus on performance and not become a negotiating session.

Many supervisors are already getting their people to do a self-evaluation as part of their performance appraisal. I expect a number of you may want to do so on the next appraisal you conduct. Here are three things you should make sure subordinates have in advance, to prepare for the review.

First, make sure they have a copy of their job description. They should review it to see if the duties and responsibilities have changed since the last review. It's helpful to tell them, "Let's not discuss performance until we both agree on what it is we are performing."

Second, make sure they have a copy of their last review—notes that were made on actions to be taken, areas to be improved, and the like—so they can see the degree to which these expectations have been met.

And third, employees will need a blank copy of the appraisal form to complete prior to meeting with you. Of course, you are also filling out this form before the appraisal so that when you meet you can compare comments and ratings from the two respective forms.

Table 25-1 compares the inductive and deductive strategies. Read it before you study the transcript of the deductive example of the same lecture.

The Performance Appraisal Workshop: Deductive Example

The following script should be familiar. You saw it in chapter 20, where it illustrated the instructional process as a chain of stimulus-response-feedback links. Here it illustrates how the deductive instructor

Table 25-1. A comparison of two instructional strategies.

	Inductive	Deductive
Description	The instructor presents (induces) new information to the learner via lecture or visuals, or both. Instructor is usually talking at least 90% of the time.	The instructor asks questions and helps the learner to discover (deduce) new concepts, principles, insights. Instructor is in 50-50 dialogue with learners.
Purpose	To impart knowledge and procedures that are black and white and lacking an internal logic; to tell learners what they need to know.	To develop thinking and reasoning skills or effect attitude change, or both; to lead the learners to figure things out for themselves.
Assumptions Underlying This Strategy	Learners are dependent on the instructor to tell them what they need to know. They are unlikely to figure things out for themselves.	Learners already have some knowledge of the topic and bring a lot of experience to the table. Their knowledge and experience can be pooled and processed to produce new learning.
Teacher-Learner Relationships	Parent-to-child; superior-subordinate; dependency on teacher (instructor centered).	Adult-to-adult; equal partners in learning; dependency on one another (learner centered).
Use of Questions	Questions are to test for understanding (that is, questions get output so as to measure learning).	Questions are to elicit new information and insights (that is, to get input so as to create learning).
Advantages	◆ Takes less class time to impart a lot of information. ◆ Less risky because instructor has greater control over what happens in class. ◆ Easier and less time needed to prepare for class. ◆ Useful when instructor's purpose is to give an overview, such as an orientation or briefing, with no further behavior expected of the learner. ◆ Easier for instructor to prepare visuals in advance of class and arrange them in the best sequence.	◆ Learner develops thinking and reasoning skills more fully. Learners are better able to function on their own after training without depending on the instructor, supervisor, or the like. ◆ Learners understand and remember better because they discovered it for themselves. ◆ The class is more interactive, lively, interesting. ◆ Learners buy in and accept responsibility for meeting the learning objectives. ◆ Useful when the subject has an internal logic and lends itself to deductive thinking (that is, problem solving, decision making, and the like).

can use questions to lead the learners to deduce, or discover, the key learning points for themselves. The learning points are the same ones the inductive instruction made earlier in this chapter.

Instructor: In the preworkshop assignment, you read a reprint of an article on self-evaluation. The author was pointing out the benefits of getting your subordinates to evaluate themselves on each aspect of their work before you evaluate them. What are some of the benefits of this? (Pause to wait for hands.) Yes, Bill.

Bill: One benefit is that we can find out where our people feel they need help. It's one thing to tell them what we think, but we can do a much better job in training and coaching them if we find out how they see themselves first.

Instructor: Right. And as several of you pointed out when we were discussing the Steve and Andrea case study earlier, Andrea missed a real opportunity to find out where Steve felt he needed her help. How about some other benefits of self-evaluation first? Yes, Ted.

Ted: It helps in relaxing the person we've been reviewing to get him or her to do the talking. People feel better telling us their strengths and weaknesses than they do in having us tell them.

Instructor: That's true. Often when we evaluate, the other person is on the defensive. That disappears when you have that person do the evaluating. Okay. There are other benefits we could list, but let's move on to a concern I sometimes hear supervisors express, namely that if we invite people to evaluate themselves first, they might give themselves outstanding ratings and show us that they walk on water. This would make our job harder in sharing our perception of their performance. How do you feel about this concern? Betty Jo?

Betty Jo: My boss does my annual review the way that is suggested in the preworkshop assignment. He has me evaluate myself first, and then shares his own perceptions of my strengths and weaknesses. And he is usually more positive about my performance than I am. His ratings are higher than mine.

Bill: . . . which is what the article in the workbook says. I forget the actual percentages, but in the majority of cases the employee's self-rating was lower than the boss's.

Instructor: In fact, only 19 percent of the time were the employee's self-ratings higher than the supervisor's rating. Now, is that good or bad?

Marge: It's good. It enables us to do the listening and find out why employees assigned the lower rating. As Bill said earlier, this helps us do a better job in coaching and training.

Instructor: So you're saying that self-evaluation is much more consistent with the true purpose of appraisals, which is to be a coach and not a judge. Now, what do you think would happen to that 19 percent figure if our employees came into a performance review thinking of it as a salary review?

Frank: They might have a lot more good things to say about themselves since they want to get as big a recommended salary increase as possible.

Instructor: Exactly. The 19 percent who rated themselves higher than the boss did would go up. Does that mean that the salary shouldn't be discussed?

Ted: If it comes up, I'll discuss it, of course. But I tell the person at the start of the appraisal that this is not a salary review, and that that will occur at another time. The two shouldn't be confused.

Carol: In fact, I think that's why we keep salary review and performance reviews six months apart. We don't want the performance appraisal to turn into a negotiating session. And most companies do the same.

Instructor: How many of you are already getting your subordinates to rate themselves as part of their preappraisal preparation?

Participants: (show of hands while instructor counts)

Instructor: Eleven of you. That's really good. And how many are not doing it but like the idea and plan to incorporate it into your action plan?

Participants: (show of hands while instructor counts)

Instructor: Very encouraging. Okay. Let's see what information and what forms we want to give to subordinates when we first contact them to schedule a time and place for their review. Then we can pair up with the person next to us for a mini role-play in which we give them the instructions we would give a subordinate on how to prepare for a performance appraisal. But before we pair up, let's see if we can agree on what forms or materials we will need. Yes, Derwin.

Derwin: I'd want a copy of the employee's job description since the review should really start by reviewing the job.

Instructor: To see if the duties and responsibilities are still current. Exactly. Let's not talk about performance before we both agree on what it is we're performing. Okay. What other forms and material will we need?

Marge: Well, we'll certainly want a copy of the last review, notes we made on actions to be taken, areas to be improved, and so on.

Instructor: So that each appraisal is also a progress report on what we've done since the last appraisal. Good. Any other forms we need? Yes, Frank.

Frank: We might want to give our employee a blank copy of the appraisal form. If we're expecting the person to do a self-appraisal, we'd better give him or her the form to do so.

Instructor: Which means that during the review we can compare comments and ratings on the two respective forms—the employee's self-evaluation and our evaluation of them.

And so on.

Summary

Although we've presented the two instructional strategies in sharp contrast in our two-column comparison and our transcripts, the effective instructor rarely sticks to one strategy exclusively. Rather, a blend of inductive and deductive methods will usually go farthest in shaping learners' behavior.

At times you must cover information that is unfamiliar and not related to the learners' experience. Teach it inductively. Then, as the learners begin to understand, switch to the deductive mode and elicit examples of situations that show how well they can apply the new information. When you see that learners can provide wind in your sails, take advantage of this and let the group power the boat. When the wind dies down, you must provide the power to keep the boat moving.

The deductive strategy requires more patience, more flexibility, and more skill in asking questions than the inductive mode. Patience and flexibility are personality traits, but skill in asking question can be developed. Instructors must develop that skill if the deductive mode is to succeed. Most instructors use questions to test for understanding. Such questions come naturally and are the instructor's way of finding out if learners understand what was just presented inductively.

When teaching deductively, instructors use questions to elicit new information and insights. Such questions also serve to test, but instructors are testing for application, not acquisition. Instructors are looking for the learners' analytical skill and not for immediate recall. The intent behind the questions distinguishes the two strategies from each other. To illustrate the point, here are some typical inductive questions:

◆ Can you describe the four steps in our procedure for...?

◆ Who can tell me the three parts to a...?

◆ What's the name of the component that...?

◆ Which access code would you use to retrieve this file...?

Following are some typical deductive questions:

◆ Can you think of some advantage of doing...?

◆ Under what circumstances would you and wouldn't you...?

◆ What problems might we face when we try to...?

◆ Since A is bigger than B, what happens if...?

Inductive instruction is designed in response to the question, What information do I want my learners to have, and how well must they know it? Deductive instruction is designed in response to the question, What kind of problems (whether decisions, analyses, or something else) must my learners deal with in their work, and how can I ask questions that will stimulate these thought processes in the class?

Phrasing and sequencing of questions are important to the success of the deductive process. To ensure they will be effective, it's a good idea to write out the questions you plan to use as you prepare for the class and to indicate on your lesson plan where you'll use them. Then, as you develop skill and confidence over time, good deductive questions will come to you more and more naturally without writing them out in advance.

Table 25-2 will help you to summarize the distinction between inductive and deductive instruction. The decision as to which is appropriate depends on the variables shown in the left column.

The effective instructor is comfortable and skilled in both methods, inductive and deductive. Table 25-2 should be helpful in deciding when to use each. Table 25-3 enables you to compare your entries with ours.

Table 25-2. Guide to summarizing inductive and deductive instruction.

	Use inductive method if:	Use deductive method if:
The learner's entering behavior (existing knowledge and experience) is		
The desired terminal behavior (course objectives) are to		
The instructor displays strength in these skills and traits		
Use the words *shorter* and *longer* in the following six boxes:		
The time available to prepare for class is		
The time available to teach in class is		
The retention by the learner is		

Table 25-3. Possible distinctions between inductive and deductive instruction.

	Use inductive method if:	Use deductive method if:
The learner's entering behavior (existing knowledge and experience) is	low or 0.	relatively high or unknown.
The desired terminal behavior (course objectives) are to	know concepts and procedures that are black and white, no deviation and no easily apparent logic (e.g., rules, regulations, memorization).	reason and think for oneself; figure things out where there is logic and some familiarity (e.g., problem solving, supervisory skills).
The instructor displays strength in these skills and traits	good speaker; able to hold attention; well organized; good flow; uses questions to test for understanding.	good listener; able to ask questions that lead learners to discover and to reason things through.
Use the words *shorter* and *longer* in the following six boxes:		
The time available to prepare for class is	shorter; consists of planning flow of Ss (stimulus, or information).	longer; consists of planning the sequence of responses, then determining what Ss will elicit these Rs.
The time available to teach in class is	shorter; instructor is in control of time.	longer; instructor is responsive to learners' rate of discovery.
The retention by the learner is	shorter because much of the information is like water off a duck's back.	longer because the learners coinvent (that is, deduce) the learning points.

CHAPTER 26

THE DEDUCTIVE LECTURE

This chapter contains scripts for three lectures that were delivered inductively. Your job is to select one of them and prepare an outline for teaching it deductively. Your choices are lectures on setting goals and standards, listening effectively, and time management. Select any one of the three on the basis of your level of interest. Then write out the questions you will ask your class, listing them in sequence and indicating the answers you hope to elicit. Compare your questions and desired responses with ours at the end of the chapter.

Remember that the inductive lecture is characterized by statements and one-way communication, whereas the deductive lecture makes heavy use of questions and two-way communication, or dialogue. The questions you'll be writing should serve two main purposes:

◆ **Discovery and "aha":** Questions can help learners think things through for themselves, discover underlying concepts and relationships, and experience the "aha" of personal insight. This approach is always a more powerful form of learning than one in which the instructor delivers information as a fait accompli that requires little thought and provides no challenge. It provides deeper understanding, better retention, and broader transfer.

◆ **Feedback and buying in:** Instructors can use questions to draw examples, analogies, and illustrations from participants rather than provide them themselves. This use of questions helps participants to buy in to the lesson, and it gives the instructor feedback on how well they are following the train of thought that leads to their next discovery and aha. Put another way, questions help instructors assess the group's repertoire of knowledge, skill, and attitude (entering behavior) on which they are building when they teach deductively.

The inductive lecture focuses on the stimulus (S), which includes the things instructors want to show or tell the learner. The deductive lecture focuses on the response (R), which includes the key points, insights, relationships, and concepts they want the learner to discover. Working backwards from these Rs, instructors then depict situations and draft questions (Ss) that will elicit the desired responses (Rs).

On a separate sheet of paper, write out a script for one of the three lessons that follow. Try to limit each bit of information that you give to your learners to no more than 30 seconds, ending each bit with a question for the learners. You'll probably need to pose four or five questions to teach the lesson deductively.

Lecture A: Setting Goals and Standards

Most of us are quite accustomed to setting goals and objectives at home: to have the lawn mowed by noon on Saturday, to get the basement renovated by September, to raise fresh fruit and vegetables, and so on.

However, panic sets in when employees are called upon to write down their goals for the next six months or for any other review period. There are many reasons for this reaction: fear of the unknown ("I don't know what barriers I'll run into..."), fear of the consequences ("What if I don't meet the goals...?"), fear of hidden agendas ("Hasn't my work been good so far? Then why must I write out my goals now?").

Several facts need to be understood if an organization is to achieve its mission:

◆ Goal setting is natural.

◆ The only way organizations achieve goals is by having employees achieve them.

◆ Playing the game—even if the game is work—is much more fun if there are goals, and the players and their coaches are keeping score. The fun comes about because it provides opportunities for challenges and growth.

To begin with, let's agree on what a goal is and what it isn't. Goals are statements of outcome that describe certain conditions to be met within a specified time frame. They are measurable and observable.

Goals are not the same as activities or wishes. Consider these three statements (writing on flipchart): During the next three months, I plan to:

1. conduct a study to determine ways of reducing customer complaints

2. put customer relations back on a healthy footing

3. reduce customer complaints by at least 50 percent over the prior three months' figure.

Notice that the first statement describes an activity, the second one describes a wish, and the third one describes a goal. Only the third meets the criteria for a goal.

Goals are usually a one-time thing. Once they have been met, there is not much excitement or challenge in going back and meeting them again.

Correcting a problem or achieving a new level of performance is not to be repeated once it has been achieved, at least not in the same form.

In contrast, standards are expectations that must be met on a regular, repetitive, ongoing basis. Answering the office phone within three rings is a standard, not a goal. Maintaining sufficient inventory so that orders can be filled within five working days is also a standard.

Sometimes, a standard may begin as a goal. For example, if our service people had never determined how many service calls were reasonable to make during the day, they might begin by setting a goal of, say, seven calls per day. Once this had been achieved, the number might then become a standard, to be maintained on a regular basis.

Each of you should examine your own jobs and identify the one-time goals you are working on and the ongoing standards you are expected to meet. You might also consider what kind of jobs lend themselves to standards and what kind to goals.

Lecture B: Listening Effectively

Most people spend the majority of their time at work—over 80 percent—communicating with others. Of the four skills they use—reading, writing, listening, and speaking—the most frequently used is listening. People spend 45 percent of their communicating time at work listening. Speaking came in at 30 percent, reading at 16 percent and writing at 9 percent. This is especially interesting in light of the heavy emphasis placed on reading and writing by the public schools, to the almost total exclusion of listening and speaking.

Focusing on listening and speaking, one might expect these two communication skills to have equal time. However, not all our interactions with others are one on one. Attendance at a meeting or a class, for example, requires a lot more listening than speaking. And when more than two persons are interacting, the proportion of time spent listening will rise relative to the time that the other persons spend speaking.

Most college graduates can read at 500 to 600 words per minute, whereas the average person speaks at 125 to 150 words per minute. Thus, listening gives the mind more idle time than does reading. As a consequence, it's easy for the mind to wander, to daydream, or to go off on tangents because it isn't being sufficiently challenged.

One thing we as listeners can do is use this slack time to organize the message, summarizing mentally from time to time, analyzing content in terms of main points and supporting detail, determining the speaker's intent as well as content, looking for messages that are implied but not stated, evaluating the logic and factual basis of the message, avoiding barriers of an emotional or semantic or physical type, and giving the speaker feedback that keeps both of you active, such as questions, points of clarification, and summary statements.

For example, an effective listener is able to summarize and catalog a message while receiving it. This is done by representing each new point by a key word or phrase. If you were not doing this a moment ago, you will now find it impossible to recall the seven bits of advice I just gave you on how to use the slack time you have when listening. In fact, you probably can't recall more than three or four of my suggestions.

Here's how you might have used key words or phrases to organize my advice (instructor writes the following outline on the flipchart):

1. Summarize while receiving.
2. Main versus support.
3. Intent as well as content.
4. Implied versus stated.
5. Logic.
6. Barriers (3).
7. Interact.

Studies have shown that our skills as listeners are weak, yielding a listening efficiency of about 25 percent. By practicing these guidelines, you should be able to raise this to a 60 to 70 percent efficiency.

Lecture C: Time Management

The most precious resource you will ever manage is your own time. Viewed in its full perspective, your time is your life—the number of minutes you will spend on earth. Viewed in its narrowest perspective, your time is either being invested in meeting goals or spent on activities that may not have been worthy of your time.

Managers spend too much time worrying about doing things right, and too little time thinking about doing the right things. In short, time management is concerned with using our time smarter, not harder or quicker.

Time management begins by examining the major goals and accomplishments that must be met during the coming months. Once these are spelled out and agreed to by employees and their managers, it is appropriate to answer two questions: How have I been spending my time? and How should I be spending my time? The first question is best answered by keeping a weekly time log and analyzing, minute by minute, how your time was spent during a typical week. The second question is answered by preparing a daily to-do list, establishing priorities, and following the list throughout the day.

Each new day should begin with a revision of the prior day's to-do list. Yesterday's "B" priorities—the midlevel priorities—that didn't get done are today's "A" priorities (critical) or "C" priorities (perhaps they'll go away if you wait another day or so).

Some activities should be held until you have a batch and can deal with them all at once (for example, returning phone calls, correspondence, and sharpening tools).

Some activities are not worth your time and should be delegated or declined.

Some activities require a heavy block of uninterrupted time and should be done with the door closed and by having someone else or voice mail handle telephone calls. If this is not possible, find a free conference room or arrange to work at home.

Some people don't know how to end a communication. They phone you, drop into your office, call meetings, and waste your time. Learn how to set limits at the start. It is then much easier to wrap things up yourself, by saying: "I'm sorry to have to run now, but I do have that prior commitment I mentioned earlier."

Ineffective time management is often the result of ineffective communication, ineffective problem solving that deals with symptoms rather than root causes, or ineffective team building and supervision. We can free up much of our time by taking time to communicate, to address problems before they get out of hand, and to invest in people.

Although there are many concepts and skills associated with time management, in the final analysis, how you manage your time is largely a matter of attitude. If you believe that everyone else is entitled to your time, that every request that comes your way is important, that every phone call must be taken as it comes in, then time is managing you rather than the other way around. Only when you accept your goals as more important than anything else will you be ready to manage your time effectively.

The Deductive Lecture—Some Models

Now you have a chance to read deductive approaches to the three lectures written in the familiar inductive style.

On the enclosed scripts, the bold type indicates learners' responses to the instructors' questions. The type changes should help you to analyze the script in terms of what the instructor says and does (the stimulus, or S), and how the instructor elicits responses from the group (the response, or R). Compare this with your own scripted outline.

There is no one right way of preparing or presenting a deductive lecture, of course. Our examples will differ from your own outline and should serve mainly to stimulate ideas and provide sample questions in those areas where you had difficulty knowing what response you wanted to elicit or how best to get it.

The questions used in a deductive lecture can serve to draw examples, analogies, and illustrations from participants and can lead learners to think things through for themselves, following a train of thought that you've planned in advance. You might find it useful to examine your own treatment of the deductive lecture to see if you made good use of both types of questions because they serve different but equally important purposes.

Because the emphasis in a deductive lecture is on the response (R), the stimulus (S) should be lean and focused on eliciting the next response. Examine your outline to see if this is, indeed, the case. Also, determine if you gave enough thought to how you would elicit your responses. Did you, for example, consider the wording of the questions you would ask and situations you would pose? Or did you leave too much to chance and the spur of the moment? If so, you might find it useful to select another one of the remaining two lectures and underline the key bits of information that you'd like to get—that is, deduce—from your learners. Then decide what information and what questions you'll need to give your learners to elicit these responses. Next, write out the script of your deductive lecture, indicating everything that you will say and that you expect your students to say.

In short, a deductive lesson is response driven. The information (stimulus) that you give to your learners is there to elicit the desired responses.

Following are the three lectures in a deductive format.

Lecture A: Setting Goals and Standards

Today we're going to be discussing goals and standards, how they differ, and how we use each at work. To get started, let me ask you for some examples of goals that some of you are working on at home or in connection with your family. Who can give me some examples?

Mowing lawn this weekend, sending kids to college, renovation...

Great. Goal setting seems to come naturally to most of us, at least in our personal lives. Yet, when managers ask their employees to write down their goals for the next review period, there is often panic, or at least a degree of resistance. What do you think are some of the reasons employees resist setting goals and putting time or money limits on their activities at work?

Fear of the unknown, things I can't control, fear of hidden agendas, fear of the consequences if I don't meet my goals...

Sometimes these fears are valid. Often the reason is that employees have failed to distinguish between wishes, activities, and goals. Employees think they have set a goal, but in reality it's a wish or an activity. (Instructor writes the three words on a flipchart.) Do you think you know the difference? Let's find out by looking at a few examples. (Instructor uses handout or overhead transparency to present the following examples.)

During the next three months, I plan to:

- conduct a study to determine ways of reducing customer complaints
- put customer relations back on a healthy footing
- reduce customer complaints by at least 50 percent over those of the prior three months.

Now, which of these is the goal? Which the activity? Which the wish? Please turn to your neighbor and see if you can agree on which is which.

After the participants agree on a definition of goal, activity, and wish, the instructor has several of them give their answers, along with the reasons why.

As we've just seen, goals are a one-time thing, not likely to be set again once they've been achieved. Wishes sound nice but have no built-in measures to let you know when or how they've been met. And activities are open ended and could last an hour, a week, or forever.

Now, what is a standard? Who can help us on this one?

An expectation, a quality or quantity to be maintained....

Good. Can you and your neighbor come up with a few examples of standards to be met by employees around here. I'll give an example: Our switchboard operators have a standard of answering within four rings. Now, see what you come up with.

In manufacturing, tolerances, scrap, rejects; in sales, calls per day, paperwork in by Friday.

Lecture B: Listening Effectively

Our topic today is communication. It's a big one, covering reading, writing, listening, and speaking. In fact, I'd like you to write these four words on your notepaper and put a percentage beside each to reflect the proportion of time you spend on each. Make sure the four percentages add up to 100. Reading, writing, listening, and speaking.

Participants write down their estimates on paper.

Now what do you think the percentages of each were in a study? Which of the four communication activities got the highest rating? The next highest? And so on.

Participants guess on each of the four. Then instructor writes as follows:

Listening is most frequently used: 45 percent. Speaking came in at 30 percent, reading at 16 percent, and writing at 9 percent.

Now, where was the emphasis placed back in grade school and high school? Which of these four did your teachers spend most time on?

Reading and writing...

Now, did some of you give listening and speaking an equal percentage, or feel that they are closely related? Who did? (**Show of hands.**) Thank you. Well, if all our interactions were one on one, they might be more nearly equal. However, consider all the situations where you are in a group, like this class. What proportion of this class do you spend listening and speaking?

Guesses, leading to understanding of why listening was 45 percent and speaking 30 percent.

Most college graduates can read at a rate of—Does anyone know?— 500 to 600 words per minute, whereas the average person speaks at 125 to 150 words per minute. This means the mind is more idle when listening than when reading. What are some of the things we can do with this idle time to improve our listening skills? I'd like you to work in threes and see how many ideas you can come up with—you three, you three, you three (and so on). Take a couple of minutes on this.

The instructor reconvenes the group and goes around the room, getting one idea from each subgroup until a number of ideas have been recorded on the flipchart: Organize, evaluate, ask questions, outline....

One technique to improve your listening skill is to summarize periodically what has been said by picking key words or phrases to help you remember. For example, I'd like you to outline what I've said so far, using short phrases of a word or so. Do this on notepaper. I'll start you with a first entry: Four percentages, listening highest. Now complete your outline, and then show it to a neighbor.

The participants outline the lecture, and the instructor asks several of them to share it with the group.

Studies have shown that people have an average listening efficiency of 25 percent. By applying the guidelines you generated and the outlining of key words, you should be able to raise this to a 60 percent to 70 percent efficiency.

Lecture C: Time Management

Our topic today is time management. We are talking about the most precious resource you will ever manage, since in the final analysis your time is your life. Each of us has the option of either spending time or investing it. Incidentally, what's the difference between spending and investing time? Can you think of an example of each that relates to your work?

Participants volunteer examples of time spent and time invested.

Our focus is on the effective use of time, not on efficiency or working faster; on using our time smarter, not harder or quicker. The process starts by examining our major goals for the coming period. Why is that the best place to start a program of effective time management?

Because that's what we're being paid to accomplish, because if you have no goals, then it really doesn't matter how you spend your time....

How have you been spending your time? A weekly time log is useful in answering this question. How should you spend your time? A daily to-do list is useful here. How many of you keep a daily to-do list?

The instructor asks those who raised their hands to describe how they do it: when (start or end of day), what format, how well it works, and so on. The instructor uses this discussion to establish the importance of setting A, B, C priorities and of upgrading or downgrading the prior day's carryovers.

Now, I'd like each of you to take a piece of notepaper and write down the three biggest time wasters you face in your work, the things that keep you from getting the really important work done. Then compare your list with your neighbor's and see what entries you have in common.

The instructor waits half a minute and then cruises the room to see what responses are coming up again and again, such as telephone interruptions and people who drop in to chat. The instructor lists the common ones on the flipchart.

Okay. Now that we've identified some of the common time robbers, let's see what ideas some of you have for getting better control of our time. I'd like you to work in groups of four persons each, listing all the ideas you can generate for managing your time more effectively. You'll need three or four minutes on this.

The instructor reconvenes the group after five minutes, and then calls on each subgroup to share its members' ideas. The instructor lists the ideas on the flipchart: batching similar work, delegating, declining unimportant jobs, escaping to a conference room to avoid interruptions, setting limits at the start of meetings and phone calls, communicating effectively the first time, addressing problems before they get out of hand....

This is a great list you've come up with. Each of you should be able to find a few new ideas that you aren't already applying. Whether you do or don't make better use of your time as a result of today's meeting is not a matter of knowledge. You've got to believe in the importance of your time—and your life, since time is life.

Summary

This exercise illustrates the fact that many learning points can be elicited from the learners deductively rather than delivered inductively. What the instructor requires is skill in depicting situations (such as analogies or illustrations) and skill in asking questions that lead learners to recall or discover the desired learning points.

Don't expect the questions you outlined to agree with ours. Rather, the issue is whether you were able to draft five or six questions that should draw out the key learning points from your learners. If you did so, congratulations. If you had difficulty, you may want some further practice by selecting one of the other two inductive lectures and converting it to the deductive method.

SECTION 7

USING TRAINING TOOLS EFFECTIVELY

Flipcharts and overhead projectors are the tools found most often in corporate classrooms. Both can be used either to give or to get information. We've included a chapter on each. PowerPoint and other forms of computer-generated graphics have made the use of flipcharts and overhead transparencies much simpler as presentation devices. Their value as recording devices rests in their ready availability and their user-friendly operation.

Our discussion of tools also addresses the three most popular instructional methods used in teaching soft skills courses: role play, case method, and games and simulations.

Many training tools can be used either to give or to get information. For example, flipcharts and overhead transparencies can be used by the instructor to give information (stimulus, input) or by learners to record their thoughts or actions (response, output). Similarly, the experiential learning methods of chapters 29-32 can be designed to present the learning points or to give learners practice in applying the learning that they have just acquired. Following is a description of the chapters in section 7:

Chapter 27, "Introductions, Icebreakers, and Mixers," describes the three most common ways of dealing with participant introductions and six exercises to break the ice and get participants relaxed and comfortable with one another.

Chapter 28, "Flipcharts and Overhead Transparencies," lists 18 characteristics and benefits of flipcharts, followed by 24 guidelines for using them effectively. It also describes the features of overhead projectors, their advantages over the flipchart, and 15 suggestions for preparing and using transparencies.

Chapter 29, "Using Games and Simulations," contains four examples of common games: The Construction Game for team building; The Personnel Game, which is an in-basket exercise; The Maze, for goal setting and achievement; and The Bingo Game, an icebreaker.

Chapter 30, "Preparing Role Plays," includes guidelines for writing and revising a role play, along with a discussion of the two major purposes of a role play: application of skills taught previously and discovery of one's style, values, perceptions, and patterns of behavior.

Chapter 31, "Using Role Play in Class," discusses three roles: critical, foil, and observer. It shows a sample observer rating sheet, along with an eight-step procedure for conducting a role play and a discussion of five alternate techniques for getting all participants into the role plays.

Chapter 32, "Using the Case Method," describes the sources of case studies and includes examples of the two major types of cases: documentary and script for analysis.

Upon completing this section, you should be able to:

◆ describe three types of participant introductions

◆ identify at least three icebreakers and mixers

◆ state at least 10 guidelines for using flipcharts effectively

◆ list at least 12 dos and don'ts for using overhead transparencies

◆ describe two games or simulations and the purpose of each

◆ prepare or critique a role play and rating sheet

◆ identify the steps in conducting a role play

◆ describe the two major types of case study and when to use each.

CHAPTER 27

INTRODUCTIONS, ICEBREAKERS, AND MIXERS

When you're starting a course in which the participants do not know everyone else present, it's important to take time for introductions and perhaps an exercise that serves as an icebreaker or mixer (that is, an exercise that gets participants to mix and thereby meet a number of other participants). Your purpose is to get people at ease, reduce nervousness—yours and theirs—and set the stage for a healthy level of participation.

If most of the participants know one another and you are the outsider, it might be better to have the program manager (whether the client, course administrator, or someone else) draw up a seating chart for your benefit, with everyone's name and department, or you might use name tent cards and tell the participants that this will help you get to know them better.

Introductions

Three possible approaches to introductions are to have participants introduce themselves, introduce one another, and introduce themselves to members of subgroups. Following are descriptions of each method:

◆ **Participants introduce themselves:** In some courses where the ability to speak with poise and levity is an integral part of the course design, there's an advantage in having participants present themselves. This approach gives the instructor a needs analysis overview of each participant. Courses in which this method is appropriate include programs on making presentations, on running meetings, on selling skills, and instructional skills. If you have a roster of participants as a handout, distribute it and announce that you'd like people to introduce themselves in the order that their names appear on the roster. Ask them to mention any errors in spelling, address, or phone number so that participants can correct their copies. This is your easiest way of taking attendance. It also enables participants to add information to the roster as participants introduce themselves and describe their work.

◆ **Participants introduce one another:** In this method, participants pair up and interview one another for about one minute each. Then the instructor reconvenes the group after two minutes and has each person introduce his or her partner. Instructors might want people to work with their neighbor in pairs, because they probably know one another (assuming you allowed them to sit wherever they wanted). Or you may want them to pair up with someone they don't know and prepare to introduce their new friend. Either way, it's a good idea to give the group some guidelines on the flipchart or overhead projector of what information is appropriate, such as name, department or location, years with the company, something memorable about this person (hobby, travel, an achievement, family).

◆ **Large group introductions:** If there are too many participants (say, 40 or more) to permit the group to spend one or two minutes on individual introductions, you may want to ask people to sit in teams or subgroups of five or six people. They can then introduce themselves within the subgroup. An alternative group introduction exercise that adds some fun to the activity is to have everyone take a piece of notepaper and answer the three *L* questions: "If you had Aladdin's magic lamp and could be granted three wishes, where would you most like to be living, with whom would you most like to be loving, and what would you most like to be learning? Tell the group to cover their answers as they write. After a minute, have them fold the papers and place them in a pile in the center of the table. They should then shuffle and distribute. Taking turns, each person reads a paper, and everyone in the group tries to guess which participant is the author. This process continues until everyone in the subgroup has been introduced.

Exercises as Icebreakers and Mixers

Icebreakers and mixers should meet the following objectives:

◆ setting the participants at ease and melding them as a group
◆ generating excitement, interest, and an expectation that the course will be relevant and fun
◆ giving the participants information that moves them closer to the course objectives

◆ giving the instructor information about the group's present level of knowledge, attitudes, and skills (that is, serving as a needs assessment).

The six examples that follow are icebreakers. The Bingo Card exercise and Matching Exercise are mixers. All six examples can easily be developed to meet all four objectives.

Bingo Card

On a standard sheet of white paper, draw a 5-by-5-inch grid consisting of 25 squares of about 1 inch each. If your class size is under 20 participants, a 4-by-4-inch grid of 16 squares is more appropriate. In each square, write a different attribute of participants, such as has a pet cat, drives a Ford, was born in another country, jogs daily, or loves Chinese food.

Give a copy of the grid to each participant. Announce that they are to circulate among the group to get participants to sign the blocks that they think accurately describe them. A participant can sign each card only once. The first person to fill a card or to get everyone's signature once should shout "bingo." This stops the game. The instructor then verifies the selections on the card by asking each person who signed for confirmation. For example, the instructor might ask, "Joanne Thomas, do you have a pet cat? What's its name? Who's feeding the cat while you're here this week? Bill Jackson, what model Ford do you drive? How's it running?"

Another bingo game uses questions relevant to the course. Instructors would fill the card with a variety of questions, and participants would then try to find another participant with the correct answer. This person then enters his or her answer and initials in the square. For example, in a new employee orientation course, the squares might have questions like these: name of our president, our best-selling product, approximate number of employees, and the company's age.

Subgroup Learning Exercise

Instructors can determine participants' needs before a course by sending them a precourse assignment (case study, self-assessment, or questionnaire) and asking them to return it at least three days prior to the course. As the first exercise of a course, instructors can put participants into subgroups of three or four and have them swap answers. Instructors can then provide feedback either from the platform or in the form of a handout.

If there wasn't sufficient lead time to distribute an assignment prior to the course, then the first exercise of the workshop can serve as an icebreaker if it is done by subgroups of participants. Here are some examples:

◆ a game or simulation that generates excitement, interaction, and insights relevant to the needs of the participants

◆ a self-assessment that identifies the participants' entering behavior (knowledge, attitudes, skills)

◆ a questionnaire or case study that introduces new terms and concepts, and serves as a preview of the issues to be addressed.

On Your Feet

This exercise begins with the instructor's request that everybody stand and not sit down until they hear the statement that best describes them. Some possible statements include the following:

◆ If you've had less than one year of experience, please sit.

◆ From one to three years' experience, please sit.

◆ From three to eight years' experience, please sit.

◆ From eight to 15 year's experience, please sit.

◆ Let's have a hand for the veterans of over 15 years!

There are many issues besides experience that the instructor and the participants might be interested in as a means of getting to know the group better, including the following:

◆ distance traveled to get here (under 10 miles, 10 to 20, 20 to 100, and so on)

◆ number of subordinates in supervisory or managerial training

◆ level of competence (such as totally green or intermediate)

◆ number of years with the organization (under two, from two to five, five to 10, and so on).

An alternative form of this exercise is to make up a series of questions related to the content of the course. For example, to launch a course on wellness (health and fitness), the instructor might get everyone to stand and then announce:

All the miracle drugs and advances in modern medicine have been able to add about two years to our average life expectancy. But there are seven health practices that all of you know quite well and that if you were doing regularly would add about 14 years to your average life expectancy (if you're under 40, and proportionately less as you get older). As I identify each of the seven, remain standing if you're following it and sit down if you're not. All set? Here's the first one.

The instructor then lists seven health practices relating to sleep, exercise, drinking, smoking, and so on. This serves to dramatize the purpose of the course as well as to break the ice. Such an exercise ends with the instructor giving a hand to the last few people who remain standing.

Questions Relevant to the Course

For this exercise, the instructor asks participants to work in subgroups of four to six people. The instructor lists questions on a handout or a flipchart. These questions are ones that everyone in the group should be interested in hearing other participants answer.

In a supervisory training course, for example, the following questions would serve as a good icebreaker:

◆ What's your name and your department or section?

◆ How long have you been a supervisor? How many people are in your group?

◆ What do you like most about being a supervisor, and what do you like least?

◆ What would you most like to get out of this course?

Advise the class that each person should take about a minute to tell the others in the subgroup the answers to these four questions.

The instructor can circulate and listen in on answers, especially to the last two questions. Then, upon reconvening the subgroups, the instructor can make a few summary remarks to show how the course design relates to the group's needs.

Critical Incident Reports

This exercise depends on the use of a brief written assignment that can be sent out with precourse material or given out as participants arrive. The assignment is for each participant to write a paragraph or two in answer to the following question:

Think back over the past few months and recall a situation that you experienced at work that relates to the topic of this workshop and that stands out in your mind as unusual (perhaps because it was especially exciting, frustrating, rewarding, or embarrassing). Describe it in the space below.

The instructor collects these and reads them, selecting whom to call on to relate the incident to the group. For example, in a sales training course for district managers, here are some selections the instructor might make:

Let's hear from Mary Price. Mary was making a sales call in San Francisco during the last earthquake. How did you and your client handle that, Mary? Bob Raskin had a client leave him last year to switch to a competitor. Tell us how you managed to get him back last month?

Because each critical incident is a miniature case study, the instructor can select the reports that best illustrate the learning points to be made during the course. If the participants come up with a number of good critical incidents, this icebreaker can be done in subgroups in which each person takes three to four minutes to report the incident and answer questions about it.

Matching Exercise

If participants are expected to have certain knowledge before attending the course, the instructor might start the class with a exercise in which participants would match a list of items or names with their definitions. One column would contain a sequentially numbered list of items to be known, such as persons, tools, products, procedures, or technical terms, and the other column would be brief definitions that would be identified by letters *a* through *m,* for example.

Each participant would receive the list and instructions like the following:

> Match up as many terms and definitions as possible on your own. Then get help from other participants on the ones you don't know. A participant cannot help you with more than one item. Keep moving until you've completed the exercise. Then call "time" and we'll give you the answers to check your own responses against.

As an example, consider a course for newly hired bank tellers. The bank wants to use an icebreaker that will find out how much these trainees know about checking accounts before they begin teller training school. So the one column of their matching exercise contains entries such terms as *payer, drawer, postdated check, MICR numbers, restricted endorsement,* and *clearinghouse.* The second column contains a brief definition of each of these terms. One of the two columns contains a space for trainees to enter their selection from the other column. A handout contains the correct answers.

Summary

We've just looked at three ways to handle introductions and six examples of icebreaker and mixer exercises. Initial impressions are powerful and often lasting. By starting with a participative exercise, you can take the spotlight off yourself and place it on the participants, thereby establishing that the course will be learner centered and not instructor centered.

CHAPTER 28

FLIPCHARTS AND OVERHEAD TRANSPARENCIES

Flipcharts and overhead transparencies are two visual devices that share many of the same guidelines for their effective use: print large, limit the wording, use dark colors, don't block the view, and so on. A major difference rests with the size group for which each is appropriate. Flipcharts are restricted to classes of 30 or fewer participants. Overhead projectors can be effective with any size group, from two to 2,000. We'll examine the flipchart first and then overhead transparencies.

Benefits of Flipcharts

The flipchart, as shown in figure 28-1, is probably the most useful visual device found in classrooms. Its many features and benefits make it a popular training aid for instructors and participants alike. Some of its advantages are listed below:

- ◆ Easels are portable so they can be carried easily to workshops, breakout rooms, and elsewhere.
- ◆ Their writing surface is cleaner than those of blackboards and whiteboards.
- ◆ They are inexpensive because paper pads and easels are relatively low cost.
- ◆ Instructors can use many colors on them, and the contrast against flat white is good.
- ◆ Instructors can use flipcharts spontaneously or prepare how they'll use them before class.
- ◆ Instructors' use of flipcharts stimulates and reinforces participants' contributions.

Figure 28-1. Notes on user-friendly flipcharts serve as minutes.

- print, don't write
- pretitle sheets before class
- use dark colors to print
- highlight with other colors
- don't block with your body
- abbrev. words like mgmt.
- have participants make entries
- mount key sheets on wall

◆ Flipcharts require no electricity, so instructors can use them outdoors or in remote locations.

◆ Flipcharts are user-friendly, so participants and new instructors can use with comfort.

◆ Instructors' notes on them serve as minutes and documentation of group meetings.

◆ Because they're portable, flipcharts can be moved to good lighting, such as by windows and under spotlights.

◆ The excellent contrast of black against white makes entries very readable.

◆ Flipchart notes can be transcribed and distributed to all participants.

◆ The easels can be moved around classroom as the focal point changes.

- ◆ Sheets can be affixed to walls for reference during workshops.
- ◆ Flipcharts are useful as a stimulus device or response devise to give or get information.
- ◆ Instructors can lay out diagrams, notes, or other material for the pad in light pencil before class.
- ◆ Flipcharts are good in breakout rooms and for small-group instruction.
- ◆ Presentation sheets can be prepared, rolled up, and then taped up.

24 Guidelines for Using Flipcharts Effectively

If you've been using flipcharts—and who hasn't been?—you are already following many of these guidelines. Your role might then be to read through the list and find the half dozen suggestions that you've not been putting to use. You might underline or highlight these less familiar guidelines.

1. Print, don't write. If your script is more legible than your printing, however, write.

2. Use large print. Make up a test sheet and then see if your first participant to arrive can read it from the farthest corner.

3. Place the flipchart in the light. Depending on the room, tilt it toward a window, move it under a ceiling light, or use the overhead projector as a spotlight.

4. Print in dark colors. Black, blue, purple, brown are the most readable. Avoid red or green.

5. Alternate colors. If you have many entries (more than 10) down the page, vary the colors by using black and blue alternately.

6. Highlight key words. Red, green, orange, and lighter colors are good for underlining or circling key words.

7. Pretitle the sheets. Plan your use of the flipchart and enter titles at the top of pages before class.

8. Presketch diagram. To help you use available space effectively, sketch your diagrams in light pencil before class.

9. Make notes to yourself. Small notes in pencil in the upper corner of a flipchart sheet can serve as your reminder of key points.

10. Post sheets on wall. Pushpins, magnets, or masking tape (depending on the wall surface) will hold key sheets for future reference.

11. Index your key sheets. If you want to turn back quickly to earlier material on the flipchart, index key sheets with paper clips or masking tape tabs.

12. Mask preprinted list. If you want to discuss each entry before seeing the next ones, fold the page up and fasten with masking tape.

13. Select a recorder. To speed up class, have a participant who prints neatly serve as your recorder to summarize key ideas. Select different people throughout the workshop. Some may need more help with wording than others.

14. Have participants make entries. On some exercises you may want to get participants to record their ideas on flipcharts. Have several flipcharts to avoid waiting.

15. Use flipcharts side by side. Extend your writing surface. Have questions on one sheet, record answers on another; or list advantages and disadvantages; or features and benefits.

16. Relate new to old. Tie new learning points to prior flipcharts by pointing to them, as visual anchors. This gives continuity and flow to your course.

17. Illustrate spontaneously. A picture, such as a model, diagram, schematic, or flow chart, is worth a thousand words. Illustrate by drawing as you speak.

18. Negotiate wording. The ideas participants offer tend to be wordy. Ask them, "How can I capture that idea up here in a few words?" Don't take away their authorship.

19. Abbreviate and simplify. If a participant's contribution is to say, "request assistance," record it as "get help" (as you repeat "request assistance"). Similarly, change the word *management* to *mgmt.*

20. Stand clear of the flipchart. Don't block the pad as you write. Step aside. Stand sideways as you write.

21. Put notes on the rear of the flipchart. The flipchart is an excellent place to tape your instructor guidelines—on the rear side at your eye level, ready at a glance.

22. Have teams report on the flipchart. When using subgroups, give each team a flipchart or a few sheets of pad paper to outline its report and present to the full class.

23. Put masking tape on the easel. If you're mounting sheets on the wall, tear off a dozen two-inch-by-three-inch strips of tape and put them lightly on a rear leg of the flipchart, so they're ready when you need them for mounting.

24. Reproduce key flipcharts. When participants are proud of contributions and follow-up is desired, take the flipcharts back to the office to be typed up (or reduced) and copied for all.

Advantages of Transparencies

An overhead projector has many of the same advantages as a flipchart and is almost as common a visual device as the flipchart. Here are some of the features they share:

◆ To use the projector, the instructor is in front of the group, facing participants.

◆ The device can be used to present (stimulus) or record (response).

◆ Material prepared in advance is quite portable.

◆ The equipment is readily available and easy to use.

◆ The instructor can highlight, use color, mask, create on the spot, and the like.

Overhead projectors have a number of advantages over flipcharts. Here are the most notable ones:

◆ With a large screen, transparencies can be seen by hundreds of people.

◆ Photographed material can be presented in full color on transparencies.

◆ Overlays enable instructors to build up a complex visual gradually.

◆ Blank acetate over a prepared transparency permits marking up without defacing.

◆ Participants can be given black-and-white copies as handouts or notebook material.

Transparencies can be prepared in four major ways, depending on time, budget, and the nature of the visual you want to project. Here are the four ways:

◆ **By hand:** Felt-tip pens in color enable the instructor to print a message or draw or trace a diagram or any other nonverbal material, or do both.

◆ **By machine:** Most copy machines will take acetate sheets in the paper feeder tray and will reproduce a black-and-white master on acetate as an overhead.

◆ **By PC and laser printer:** Personal computers can generate a variety of typefaces and sizes (usually 18- to 30-point type), which can be printed on acetate by a laser printer.

◆ **By art service:** Many art supply stores will take full-color artwork, photographs, and layouts and copy them on acetate. This service usually costs between $3 and $10, depending on quantity.

It's a good idea for instructors to use cardboard mounting frames to protect transparencies that they expect to use many times, particularly with transparencies they'll use each time they present a course. Following are benefits and uses of the cardboard mounting frames:

◆ Instructors can write guidelines and commentary notes on the frame.

◆ Instructors can number the frames and transparencies to keep them in order.

◆ A black-and-white copy on paper can be hinged with tape on top of each transparency (to protect it, identify it, and mask it until the moment of viewing).

◆ Transparencies are slippery and easily get out of sequence without framing.

◆ Frames keep thumbprints and finger smears off the transparencies.

An increasingly popular alternative to transparencies is the use of PowerPoint. It enables the instructor or graphics designer to generate the message on a PC and then connect the PC to a projector that puts the message onto a screen. Many of the guidelines on the appearance of overheads apply to PowerPoint, but the means of generating the visuals differ greatly.

Suggestions for Preparing Transparencies

As you read this list of suggestions, place a check mark in front of each entry that you plan to apply when you prepare transparencies.

1. Limit the amount of information. Show key points, not entire printed pages or complex diagrams.

2. If transparencies are to be printed by hand, slip a sheet of lined or graph paper under the acetate as a guide.

3. Use template guides, such as stencils, triangle, and French curves, to create smooth lines and a professional appearance.

4. Use desktop publishing software to generate black-and-white originals. Make acetates in the copy machine, then use colored markers to highlight them.

5. Enlarge or reduce original art from texts via the copy machine until the size is correct for a transparency.

6. Enlarge typewritten words via the copy machine or generate words on a PC using type fonts of 18 to 30 points.

7. Use colored acetate sheets for variety in a lengthy presentation; make each section a different color.

8. Prepare visuals horizontally rather than vertically so that they fit the screen more naturally.

9. Start a file of clippings, pictures, cartoons, diagrams, and the like to use in illustrating your visuals. Art stores have collections of these on many topics.

10. Build from simple to complex diagrams (models, schematics, flow charts) by preparing up to four overlays (one hinged on each side of the cardboard frame).

11. Add color with felt marking pens, colored pressure-sensitive acetate sheets (available in art supply stores), or via the use of a colored printer.

12. Add masks to cover areas you don't want participants to see right away. Make the masks by using strips of cardboard hinged with tape to the frame that can be lifted as each new idea (component, step) is taken up.

13. To focus attention on part of a large diagram, use colored acetate sheets as overlays and cut a window to reveal the part you want to highlight (in other words, frame it).

14. Create diagrams, flow charts, graphs, and the like without labels so that you can get participants to name the parts; then add names as they supply them.

15. Use capital letters for titles and lowercase letters for phrases and text. This lettering improves appearance and readability.

Suggestions for Using the Overhead Projector

As you read this list, place a check mark in front of those suggestions that you have not applied in the past but plan to use in future classes.

1. Check the projector before the class. Make sure it's in focus with large images and check a transparency with small print from the rear of the room.

2. Correct for the keystone effect (that is, one in which the image is a trapezoid rather than a rectangle) by tilting the screen or the projector.

3. Set up the projector so that you can stand beside it (not behind or in front) with table surface to hold two piles of transparencies (used and unused).

4. Turn off projector when you're not referring to transparencies because the strong light is distracting.

5. Don't project a visual until you're ready to discuss it. Otherwise participants will be reading it instead of listening to you.

6. On diagrams, charts, and complex material, allow five to 10 seconds for participants to acquaint themselves with the visual before you discuss it.

7. Give participants copies of key visuals so they can make notes (and not be preoccupied copying everything you're projecting).

8. When pointing, use a hexagonal pencil that won't roll on the surface of the projector; do not point to the screen itself.

9. Place a sheet of white paper over a transparency to mask a list of items; you can then slide it down to reveal each new item as you discuss it.

10. Some projectors have a roll feed of transparent film. Slip prepared transparencies under the film so you can write on them without marking them.

11. When recording ideas that participants are giving you, negotiate the short wording that you'll write on the transparency by asking them something like, "Is it okay to say...?"

12. When recording ideas or creating a visual in class, place a sheet of paper over the bottom half of the transparency to rest your hand on as you write or draw.

13. If a screen is not available, tape sheets of flipchart paper to the wall and project on this surface (or directly onto a white or light wall).

14. Do not project onto a whiteboard (that takes felt markers) because the glare and "bounce back" will make viewing difficult for some people.

15. Check to make sure that the upper lens and reflector aren't blocking parts of the screen for some participants; throw image higher on screen.

Some Questions for Follow-Up

How well prepared are you to make and use overhead transparencies? These questions should help you to take inventory and evaluate your readiness.

1. Do you know what supplies you have on hand and who is available to help you prepare professional overhead transparencies? Do you have each of the following:

    ◆ typesetting and lettering

    ◆ colored acetate overlays

    ◆ stock artwork and line drawings

    ◆ pressure sensitive graphic tape in various widths

    ◆ colored marking pens

    ◆ copy machine that makes transparencies from black-and-white artwork

    ◆ copy machine that enlarges and reduces black-and-white artwork

    ◆ frames to mount and protect transparencies

    ◆ PowerPoint to prepare transparencies.

2. What supplies would you like to order or purchase from an art supply store or stationery store to give you the resources you need to prepare professional transparencies? (List each item and its cost. You may want to phone some stores.)

3. Which of the 15 suggestions for preparing transparencies do you plan to apply in creating visual support for your classes? (Indicate by number.)

4. Which of the 15 suggestions for using the overhead projector do you plan to apply in your workshops? Specify things you've not done before but are going to try in future classes. (Indicate by number.)

CHAPTER 29
USING GAMES AND SIMULATIONS

People learn best from experience. An excellent way that trainers provide hands-on learning is through the use of games and simulations. Hundreds are available for the human resource development market, and thousands have been developed by instructional designers. These forms of experiential learning enable participants to practice and apply specific concepts and skills, from simple board games to complex computerized simulations. This chapter provides examples of four games and simulations:

◆ The Construction Game, for team building, goal setting, leadership, productivity

◆ The Personnel Game, in-basket for clarifying personnel policy and procedures

◆ The Maze, for goal setting, motivation, competition, achievement

◆ The Bingo Game, an icebreaker and to measure HRD knowledge.

The Maze and the Bingo Game are designed for use at the start of a class, whereas the other two exercises can be used as either a game or a simulation. What's the difference? A game is played mainly for fun at the start of a class. Participants have little or no awareness of any learning points. These come out following play during the discussion and analysis of the behavior that emerged.

In contrast, a simulation comes after participants have been given the key learning points and are expected to apply them and use their new concepts and skills. Simulations occur during the application stage of learning, whereas games are played during the acquisition stage of learning. Computers are sometimes used with simulations that present learners with many options or are complicated to score, or both.

The Construction Game

Your firm is hereby invited to bid on the construction of Warehouse No. 724, shown in figure 29-1. You will be allowed five minutes to prepare and submit a sealed bid. This will be a folded paper containing three items of information:

1. the name of your firm's president (team leader), who must turn in the bid

2. the time required by your firm to build Warehouse No. 724 (in minutes)

3. the method of construction (what parts will be built first, second, and so forth).

The bids will be opened immediately, and the winning firm or firms will be selected. Performance during the period of construction will be judged solely on the basis of how well the contract holder meets his or her time estimate and completes the job as bid, along with maintaining harmonious relations with the employees involved. In short, your fulfillment of the contract will be based on your ability to maintain a high level of productivity throughout construction and maintain a harmonious work team.

When the teams have completed their construction, the instructor announces which teams are the winners. Each team member receives a handout with 10 questions to discuss with other team members. The questions address the following topics:

◆ Did all team members participate?

◆ Did each member estimate his or her own time needed?

◆ Did members function as a team or as a group of individuals?

◆ Did your team check on other teams' progress?

◆ Did anyone serve as timekeeper, and did your team submit its work to the quality control test?

◆ Did your leader check each member's contribution?

◆ Were assignments made on the basis of players' different abilities, and during play were some players given other responsibilities?

◆ Was any thought given to modifying your method during the playing of the game?

◆ Did your team share leadership?

◆ In what ways was your team a leader?
   — by having the most realistic time estimate?
   — by completing the construction in the least amount of time?
   — by having the best quality construction?
   — by enjoying the experience?
   — by applying teamwork most effectively?
   — by learning the most from the experience?

Team leaders then report on what key learning points emerged in their team.

Figure 29-1. Warehouse no. 724 for construction.

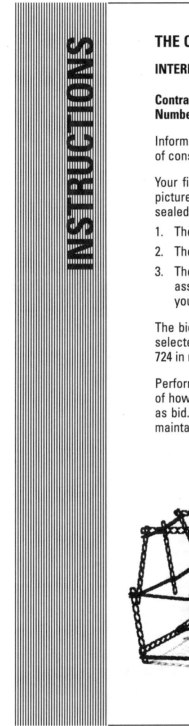

THE CONSTRUCTION GAME

INTERNATIONAL CORP.

Contract Specifications: Warehouse No. 724
Number of Parts: 112 extruded high-tensile Interlocking steel members

Information required in sealed bid: time required to build warehouse and method of construction

Your firm is hereby invited to bid on the construction of Warehouse No. 724, pictured below. You will be allowed five (5) minutes to prepare and submit a sealed bid. This will be a folded paper containing three items of information:

1. The name of your firm's president (team leader), who must turn in the bid.

2. The time required by your firm to build Warehouse No. 724 (in minutes).

3. The method of construction (a sentence or two describing how you plan to assemble the structure: what parts will be built first, second, etc., and who in your organization will be responsible for assembling which components).

The bids will be opened immediately, and the firm(s) with the best bids will be selected. Since International Corp. requires the construction of Warehouse No. 724 in more than one location, more than one firm may be selected.

Performance during the period of construction will be judged solely on the basis of how well the contract holder meets the time estimate and completes the job as bid. In short, your fulfillment of the contract will be based on your ability to maintain a high level of productivity and quality throughout construction.

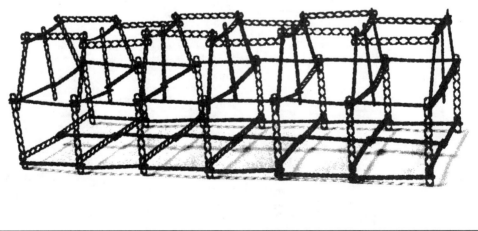

The Personnel Game

You are Sandy McMaster, a supervisor. Figure 29-2 shows five items in your in-basket from Debbie Burk, the departmental secretary. Each item is from or about members of your work group. For each, decide what you'll do, whom you'll talk to, and what you'll say. Record your proposed actions on the Action Report Form. There are 20 items to be processed, and you must leave for the airport in 30 minutes.

Figure 29-2. In-basket items requiring action.

1

INTER-OFFICE MEMORANDUM

Sandy McMaster:

Joe Carson's wife called last Tuesday around 7:30 PM to see if he was here. I saw him leave around 5:30 PM and get into a car driven by Sue Tiegler, Mr. Austin's secretary. I know it's none of my business, but they have been seeing a lot of each other, and Carson's wife is now getting suspicious. This is the second time she has called after hours.

Just thought you should know.

Harry Bannerman
Manager, Night Security

cc: J.P. Kreitz, V.P.

2

from the desk of
D. R. Burk

Sandy:

You had a call last week from a Mr. Ted Rosen at Inforomex. Seems George Jackson, whom we let go three or four months ago, was applying for a job and Mr. Rosen was calling us for a reference.

I verified the dates of employment and told him that Jackson was a conscientious and good worker who was over his head in the kind of work we had him doing here. (I explained the nature of the work, and Jackson's weakness in math.)

Debbie

3

INTER-OFFICE MEMORANDUM

To: Sandy McMaster

From: Helge Lindstrom

I've been here for almost six years, and am being paid almost the same as Mary Dawson, who just joined us last year.

Now I'm sure Mary Jane deserves it and she is a good employee. But I don't feel it's fair for new people to come in and get salaries that are about the same as those who have been holding the same job for years.

Doesn't experience count too?

The present system almost encourages us to quit and come back in again at a higher level. I realize this sounds foolish, but that's the only way to get any kind of decent salary increase . . . to jump companies or jobs.

4

SANDY:

WHILE YOU WERE GONE, DEBBIE KNOCKED HERSELF OUT WORKING ON THE MATHIS PROJECT WITH ME. THE TYPING LOAD WAS EXTRA HEAVY, AND SHE STAYED LATE SEVERAL NIGHTS TO HELP ME GET THE THING DONE.

I'D LIKE TO DO SOMETHING TO SAY THANKS, AND WAS THINKING OF A CHECK (OR CASH) FOR $30 FOR HER AND HER HUSBAND TO GO OUT FOR DINNER ON US AS A WAY OF SHOWING OUR APPRECIATION.

DO YOU AGREE? AND CAN YOU GET A CHECK WHITHOUT DEBBIE KNOWING ABOUT IT?

BOB UMBERTO

5

Sandy:
I'm going to be taking a course for the next eight weeks at the University's extension program. We meet at 4:30 every Tuesday and Thursday, which means I must leave here by 3:45. I can make up the time by skipping lunch or by working until 5:30 the other nights. What do you think?

Mary Jane Dawson

We've reproduced five of the 20 items in McMaster's in-basket. As participants complete the exercise, the instructor distributes scoring guidelines (five points maximum for each item, with 100 being a perfect score).

Guidelines for Scoring

1. The question here is a familiar one: At what point does the supervisor become involved in the personal business of employees? The answer is straightforward: when employees' actions begin to affect performance on the job, the company's image, or the safety or welfare of other employees. We have no evidence that any of these have been adversely affected. Moreover, we have no reason to assume that Joe Carson is doing anything wrong. Harry Bannerman obviously thinks he is, but that is mere conjecture. And phrases like "Carson's wife is now getting suspicious" and "seeing a lot of each other" tell us more about Bannerman than about the situation.

   Thus, we feel that Sandy McMaster should not talk to Joe Carson. If McMaster does talk to Carson, he should only tell Carson that his wife called in around 7:30 looking for him. He should not mention Sue Tiegler.

   McMaster might thank Bannerman for informing him, and perhaps find out why he felt it necessary to send a copy to J.P. Kreitz because this presents Kreitz with only one side of the situation and gives Carson no chance to explain. There are many possible legitimate explanations. For example, Joe Carson and Sue Tiegler may be going to night school every Tuesday and sharing the ride.

   Give yourself one point for thanking Bannerman, two points for saying nothing to Carson, one point for recognizing that Carson may have a legitimate reason for seeing Tiegler, and one point for expressing concern that Kreitz received the information. *Total:* five points. Enter your score.

2. Most organizations require that inquiries to verify employment and get a reference check be directed to the personnel department. Lawsuits have occurred when supervisors have responded, giving information that the former employee felt was unfair or false. (Remember: In a lawsuit, it doesn't always matter who was right. Indeed, this is often impossible to determine when plaintiff and defendant each claim to be right.) Personnel departments know how to verify that a request is legitimate and what information should and should not be shared. Given the possible legal repercussions of reference checks, Sandy McMaster should explain to Debbie Burk that such inquiries should be directed to the personnel department (two points). McMaster should also get any additional information that Burk has relating to the inquiry. For example, is Ted Rosen the personnel director or George Jackson's supervisor? Did Burk say anything else about Jackson's performance (one point)? Then McMaster should call personnel to tell about the inquiry and Burk's response (one point). Personnel may want to put an official verification of employment into writing just to have it on record. *Total:* five points. Enter your score.

3. A common problem in periods of double-digit inflation: Employees who receive cost-of-living adjustments will naturally perceive them as raises and will be annoyed to see a new hire make the same money. There are two issues here. First, Sandy McMaster has to deal with Helge Lindstrom, who is disgruntled. Second, McMaster should verify the current earnings and past record of salary increases for Lindstrom and Mary Jane Dawson. It makes sense to check the record first so that McMaster will be armed for the talk with Lindstrom (two points). This will mean talking with personnel, unless McMaster keeps complete wage and salary records on the group. Then McMaster should talk with Lindstrom, explaining how cost-of-living increases occur in almost all companies. It would be appropriate to say something like the following: "While your salary was increasing here, Helge, so was Mary Jane's at her last place of employment. We had to match her level when she came on board, in the same way that if you were to go elsewhere, your new employer would have to match your present earnings" (three points). McMaster should not get into a discussion that compares Lindstrom and Dawson's relative worth, even if it turn outs that Dawson is a better performer and has gotten better merit increases. *Total:* five points. Enter your score.

4. The issues here are whether an individual can request company funds to pay a bonus for outstanding work and where the money comes from. A manager should have money in the budget to take an employee to lunch or dinner, or in this case, to give an employee a bonus to recognize outstanding performance. The manager should have the prerogative to decide how the money might best be used since the manager is in the best position to determine what type of bonus will have the best effect (for example, dinner with spouse, dinner with boss, a dozen roses delivered at home with a note of thanks). You should have Sandy McMaster tell Bob Umberto what your policy is on giving an individual a bonus (three points) and where the money comes from (two points). *Total:* five points. Enter your score.

5. Would you allow an employee to leave early for class? Would you require the employee to make up the time, and if yes, when? These are the questions Sandy McMaster must answer before getting back to Mary Jane Dawson. Most organizations encourage people to continue their education and would then allow an employee to leave early for class (two points). Answer the question about making up time according to your organization's policy (three points). If you have no policy on this (that is, if it's left up to the supervisor), give yourself credit for whatever you had McMaster tell Dawson. *Total:* five points. Enter your score.

Summary

The Personnel Game enables supervisors to clarify their understanding of 20 human resource issues affecting their work group and to recognize their responsibility in administering personnel policies and procedures as issues arise.

The Maze

Eight different mazes are printed in figure 29-3. Without taking time to study them, quickly select one that you think you can complete in 60 seconds. Time yourself, tracing the paths from each numbered box on the left to its terminal blank box on the right. Enter the path number in each blank box.

Based on your first experience, repeat the task on another maze that you feel you can complete in 60 seconds. Again, time yourself, enter path numbers in the blank boxes, and compare your performance on the two trials.

Summary

When faced with the need to set goals or estimate the time required to complete an unfamiliar task, managers are influenced by two conflicting

Figure 29-3. Mazes to follow.

needs: challenge (high risk) and security (low risk). The postgame discussion focuses on how players felt when they selected mazes that were too easy or too difficult and how their performance on this task compares with their ability to set challenging but achievable goals at work.

The Bingo Game

The objective of the Bingo Game, shown in figure 29-4, is to complete the five squares in a column (down), or a row (across), or a diagonal as in the game of bingo. You must circulate and find a different person to provide the information for each square of a winning entry. Enter the answer on the first line of the box. You must get the name of each of your source persons and find out something unusual or unique about them. Enter this information on the second and third line (bottom) of the box. Shout "bingo" when you've met the objective. You will then be asked to read off your five entries and to introduce your five source persons.

Summary

The Bingo Game is useful as an icebreaker and mixer, as described in chapter 27. Figure 29-4 shows an additional purpose. The 25 items relate to information that should be familiar to trainers. Thus, the game serves as a preview or review of course content in a train-the-trainer workshop.

Figure 29-4. Bingo by completing the boxes.

1. Title of a book by Peter Drucker:	6. Gives orientation to new employees:	11. Author of *Preparing Instructional Objectives:*	16. Meaning of CBT (CAI), CRI, and CPR (any two):	21. Went to workshop by Bob Pike:
2. Has taught supervisory training:	7. Name of executive director of ASTD:	12. Who was Pygmalion? So what?	17. Gets Creative Training Techniques:	22. Teaches the longest course of anyone here:
3. Has used an opaque projector:	8. Has taught time management:	13. B.F. Skinner's contribution to HRD:	18. McClelland, Maslow, McGregor have this in common:	23. How fast (wpm) the average H.S. graduate reads:
4. Can give brief definition of OD:	9. Reads two monthly HRD magazines:	14. Has taught in three other countries:	19. How many watts in projector bulbs?	24. Malcolm Knowles' contribution to HRD:
5. Two suppliers of courses based on behavior modeling:	10. How fast (wpm) trainers talk (average):	15. Number of slides in standard carousel:	20. Has taught selling skills:	25. Name of a Lakewood editor:

CHAPTER 30

PREPARING ROLE PLAYS

There are two major purposes for role plays in a workshop: application and discovery. Application is present whenever learners have an opportunity to apply certain functions or behave in certain situations they have already learned. Discovery is present whenever the players have an opportunity to gain insights into their own values, style, perceptions, and patterns of behavior.

These two purposes are not mutually exclusive. In fact, some element of discovery is present in every role play that is conducted effectively. The feature that distinguishes the two purposes is not the presence or absence of self-discovery, but the presence or absence of prior instruction.

Putting it another way, the first aim of role playing, learning by application, is primarily concerned with practicing the use of new knowledge and skills, whereas the second, learning by discovery, is primarily concerned with insight and the modification of attitudes. Again, let's emphasize the word *primarily*, because the elements of knowledge, skills, and attitudes are present in any learning situation.

Because role plays are primarily to provide learners with an opportunity to apply the knowledge and skills that they have just acquired, the selection or writing of role plays must focus on the creation of realistic situations in which learners can apply their new skills.

The first time you use a new role play in class, you should think of it as a field test in which you determine whether the information given to the players produces the desired behavior. It is not uncommon for writers to expect their directions to cause players to focus on a particular issue, only to discover that the players concentrated on a different issue and missed the writer's main point altogether. (Sometimes players focus on a minor detail that the writers included only to give reality to the assignment.) If other trainees in subsequent training sessions with the same directions have the same results, writers have clear evidence that revision is necessary.

In creating role plays, the critical incident technique is often helpful. Let's illustrate this with an example. Suppose you are responsible for training the sales managers in your organization. Periodically you bring them together for training and for briefings on new policy, changes in the product line, and so on. At these training meetings you would like to use role playing to help them develop skill in supervising their salespersons. You could, of course, sit down and write several role plays dealing with different aspects of the sales manager's relationship with salespeople, but you frankly have not been in touch with field operations for several years and are quick to admit that you don't really know the kinds of day-to-day problems that your sales managers are encountering. How do you find out? By requesting critical incident information from regional sales managers. Figure 30-1 shows one way to solicit that information.

Figure 30-1. Example of a critical incident questionnaire.

MEMO TO: Regional Sales Managers

FROM: Director of Sales Training

SUBJECT: Preparation for Sales Meeting
on November 27

To help us prepare for our meeting next month, I would like you to recall the events of the last few months and select an incident that occurred between you and one of your salespeople that you feel is unusual and that taught you a lesson (either a how-to-do-it success story or a how-not-to-do-it failure story). The incident you select may be used to develop a case history or role play for our forthcoming meeting; all names will be changed.

You will probably need several paragraphs to describe the incident or series of incidents. Please indicate what made the situation critical. That is, describe how this situation is different from the usual, and what you learned from it.

Please have this back to me by November 15.

Armed with the replies from this request, you should have the information you need to prepare realistic role plays for your meeting. Another advantage of the critical incident technique is that there will probably be greater interest and ego involvement by your trainees at the November 27 meeting because they have previously given some thought to the problems that they'll be dealing with. The workshop becomes theirs, thanks to their contributions.

One way to view a role-play assignment is to compare it with a jigsaw puzzle two people want to complete. Most puzzles come in boxes that display a picture of the completed puzzle on the cover. The picture helps the players lay out the pieces in their approximate positions. In role playing, each player has some of the pieces required to construct the entire picture. Neither can do it alone. Each must interact with the other, finding out what pieces the other person has, indicating what pieces are missing, and together constructing the picture. The observers are usually given both assignments. By equipping them with the picture on the puzzle box cover, we enable them to analyze how effective the players are in putting their pieces together and emerging with the correct picture. (And here the analogy breaks down, for in role playing there is usually no single correct picture, but rather a number of acceptable solutions, or appropriate actions.)

Writing the Role Plays

In writing role plays, your job is to set the stage rather than to prepare the script. Role playing is not a theatrical exercise for trainees to show their dramatic talent. Rather, our objective is for the players to be themselves and to act naturally. This means, for one thing, that the situations you create must be realistic. That is, the situation you describe in the assignment that goes to the players must lie well within their framework of experience as something that has happened or might easily happen.

Your write-up of each role should avoid telling players how to act. For example, suppose you are teaching customer courtesy to bank tellers and are creating role-play assignments for the teller and the customer. It would not be appropriate to tell the customer to be angry or to tell the teller that Mr. Smith is a very finicky customer who has made you angry on previous occasions. Instead, your job is to set the stage in such a way that the opportunity for anger is strongly present. You might, for example, tell the customer that you have been waiting in line for 10 minutes, during which time other persons who arrived long after were helped at the other teller windows.

A role play is successful to the degree to which it promotes interaction between the two players. One of the shortcomings of role-play assignments prepared by novice writers is that they let the players off easily. That is, the players reach a mutually satisfactory solution with a minimum of interaction. Often this is the result of giving one of the players most of the pieces of the puzzle, so that very little interaction was needed to get the remaining pieces from the other player. Consider the role play in figure 30-2, for example.

This assignment requires very little interaction because there are very few facts given to either player and the only acceptable solution to this role play is for the supervisor to give Sally enough time off to go to the dentist. No negotiation. No problem solving. No interaction. Now let's rewrite this role play in a way that will produce much more interaction, thus giving the players a much better opportunity to practice and apply the skills they have learned. Figure 30-3 presents an alternative role play.

Before assigning parts and distributing role plays, you must make sure that the members of the group are in agreement on what constitutes

Figure 30-2. Role play with inadequate interaction.

> **ROLE:** Sally, Administrative Assistant   **PLACE:** Supervisor's Desk
>
> **SITUATION:** You have just called your dentist for an appointment. He has told you that the best time for you to come would be tomorrow at 3:00 p.m. You have agreed to come at that time.
>
> You realize that you must ask Ms. Watkins, your supervisor, for time off tomorrow to go to the dentist. The dentist's office is about 45 minutes away from work, so you'll probably need to be gone the entire afternoon, at least from 2:00 p.m. on. You find your supervisor at her desk and ask her.
>
> **ROLE:** Ms. Watkins, Supervisor   **PLACE:** Your Desk
>
> **SITUATION:** You are seated at your desk doing some administrative work when Sally, one of your workers, approaches you.

Figure 30-3. Role play with good interaction.

> **ROLE:** Sally, Administrative Assistant   **PLACE:** Supervisor's Desk
>
> **SITUATION:** You've been having a toothache for the past three days. Last night it was really acting up, so you've just called the dentist for an appointment. The earliest he can see you is tomorrow at 3:00 p.m. In fact, you got this appointment only because another of his patients had canceled. (He's a busy dentist who gets booked up at least three weeks in advance.)
>
> You realize that you must ask Ms. Watkins, your supervisor, for time off tomorrow to go to the dentist. The dentist's office is about a 45-minute bus ride away from work, so you'll probably need to be gone the entire afternoon, at least from 2:00 p.m. on. You find Ms. Watkins at her desk and ask her.
>
> **ROLE:** Ms. Watkins, Supervisor   **PLACE:** Your Desk
>
> **SITUATION:** Your boss just called. The project he wanted from you by next Monday has been moved up, and now he wants it tomorrow by 5:00! You are going to need everyone in the department. In fact, you might need some overtime. You are seated at your desk, trying to figure how to get the work by tomorrow at 5:00, when Sally, one of your best administrative assistants, approaches. You are counting on Sally to oversee and coordinate the work of the others to ensure completion of the project by 5:00.

---

appropriate and inappropriate behavior in the kinds of situations that will be enacted. This includes knowledge of the company's policy and procedures, plus skill in establishing a positive climate, listening and summarizing, probing to get needed information, and so on.

One of the most effective ways of reviewing the knowledge and skills that should emerge during a role play is to create a checklist of questions or criteria that will guide the discussion following enactment. Figure 30-4 shows such a checklist. This handout helps to focus the observer's attention on the player's performance. Some instructors prefer to distribute an observer rating sheet before the role play, spending 10 minutes or so on a discussion of the items to make sure that the group understands what each one means and agrees that each is important. During this discussion, the participants may elect to add items to the list or to delete an item or two that they feel is unimportant.

An alternative approach is to have the group develop its own list of criteria for evaluating the player's performance. Using a flipchart or chalkboard, the instructor will lead the group in developing a list that can then remain in full view of the group throughout the role play and subsequent discussion. If you want each observer to rate the players against each criterion on the list, simply number the items and ask participants to put the same numbers on a sheet of notepaper and indicate their ratings beside each.

Figure 30-4. Questions for postenactment discussion.

	Good	Average	Weak
How effective was Ms. Watkins, the supervisor, in:			
1. listening to Sally and summarizing her request to confirm understanding?	___	___	___
2. showing empathy that let Sally know that her supervisor wanted to find a mutually beneficial outcome?	___	___	___
3. winning Sally's acceptance of a course of action that both parties will support? ..	___	___	___
How effective was Sally, the administrative assistant, in:			
4. letting Ms. Watkins know that she wants to see the project completed by 5:00 tomorrow?	___	___	___
5. volunteering to work overtime this evening or early tomorrow morning in exchange for the time off?	___	___	___
6. offering to phone Ms. Watkins as soon as the dentist is finished and taking a taxi back to the office if necessary?	___	___	___

CHAPTER 31

USING ROLE PLAY IN CLASS

When using role play with a group that is new to the technique, begin the session with a discussion of what role playing is and isn't. Namely, it is an opportunity to apply the concepts and skills we've been learning. It is not acting or drama. Whereas an actor's efforts are aimed at making an impact on an audience, participants in role plays direct their efforts to one another, concentrating on applying the skills they have learned and are developing. The situation they role-play is taken from the real world. The idea behind role plays is that a situation that has happened before could easily happen to you.

Often trainees new to role plays will object to it on the grounds that it is an artificial situation calling forth behavior that would not actually occur in real life. They argue by saying, "If this were a real situation, I would have behaved differently." The implication is always that they would behave correctly if they were interacting with their workers and did not have a bunch of colleagues looking on. The evidence does not support this objection. Research and field studies indicate that once the initial artificiality of the first half minute or so of a role play is past, the players tend to behave in much the same way that they would on the job.

Before assigning parts and distributing role plays, make sure that participants are in agreement on what constitutes appropriate and inappropriate behavior in the kinds of situations that will be enacted. In other words, don't put participants into a role play prematurely. To do so is to invite improvisation and hamming it up, a symptom of their uneasiness.

Reviewing Learning From Role Plays

An effective way of reviewing the knowledge and skills that should emerge during role plays is through the use of an observer rating sheet like that in figure 31-1. This sheet serves as a checklist to help focus observers' attention on the player's performance.

Figure 31-1. Example of an observer rating sheet for role plays on presenting and selling.

Stages of Presentation	What kind of job did the presenter do in:	Excellent	Very Good	Good	Fair
Opening	1. Defining the need and the objective clearly in opening statements	___	___	___	___
	2. Presenting the objective in terms of how it would benefit the other person	___	___	___	___
Presenting	3. Establishing a friendly climate	___	___	___	___
	4. Presenting one idea at a time, using evidence or an example to bring it to life	___	___	___	___
	5. Stating the facts and features (especially dollars) as benefits	___	___	___	___
	6. Giving costs of not doing it (if appropriate)*	___	___	___	___
	7. Emphasizing by relating to the other person's interests	___	___	___	___
	8. Involving the other person(s) by asking questions	___	___	___	___
	9. Listening attentively	___	___	___	___
	10. Giving feedback to show understanding	___	___	___	___
Handling Objections	11. Restating benefits	___	___	___	___
	12. Probing with questions to get real reason for objection, if appropriate*	___	___	___	___
	13. Using questions to clarify buyer's concerns	___	___	___	___
	14. Referring to past success (sale) or experience, if appropriate*	___	___	___	___
Actions	15. Giving an outline for implementation, explaining who will do what, and when	___	___	___	___
	16. Outlining plans for follow-up, along with who, what, and when	___	___	___	___
Closing	17. Asking appropriate questions to get commitment or desired action	___	___	___	___
	18. Restating advantages and disadvantages	___	___	___	___
	19. Seeking a course of action that was beneficial to both parties	___	___	___	___
	20. Closing the sale or agreeing on next action	___	___	___	___
	Total number of checks				
	Multiply by	4	3	2	1
	To get				

Directions for Scoring:

Allow four points for every check mark in the "Excellent" column, three points for every "Very Good," two points for every "Good," and one point for "Fair." A perfect score is 80 points.

*If these steps are not appropriate, award the presenter an "Excellent."

The observer rating sheet has a number of advantages:

- It is a useful way of reviewing the knowledge and skills that should emerge during role play.
- It gives the instructor a tool to help structure or focus the discussion.
- It takes the observer's ratings out of the realm of the subjective and into the area of concrete, objective evaluations.
- The numerical scores at the bottom of each sheet give the instructor feedback that indicates whether the group was ready for the role play or whether further review is first necessary. (A wide range of total scores indicates that further instruction is needed, whereas a narrow range indicates that group members agree on the relative effectiveness of the role play.)

In most role plays, one person is in the critical role (that is, the role we are training everyone in the group to fill), while the other person is in the foil role (the role of the person with whom the participants typically interact in their everyday work). A third role is that of the observer. The observer is responsible for analyzing the interaction and leading the critique that follows the enactment. Observers should take notes during the role play. You may want to break the class into three-person groups so that the role plays can be enacted simultaneously. This gives more chance for practice to more participants. Indeed, if you have three three-person role plays, every participant can fill each role once—critical role, foil role, and observer. You should suggest the location of each three-person group (for example, in the corners of the classroom) so as to minimize distraction and noise.

Generally speaking, the following should occur in a successful role play:

- The person in the critical role and the person in the foil role should agree to what the problem is.
- There should be mutual exploration of possible solutions to the problem.
- There should be mutual agreement on a solution.

These points are implied in the various criteria that might be stated in the Observer Rating Sheet. However, explicit mention of them will help to further structure the observers' attention during the role play and follow-up discussion.

Steps for Conducting a Role Play

The following steps apply when you have one person in the critical role and one person in the foil role. There are many variations to this approach. Five alternatives are outlined in the descriptions that follow the list.

1. If participants are new to role plays, explain what they are and what they aren't. You might ask "How many people have ever been in a role play?" and get them to explain their experience with it.

2. Review the dos and don'ts (desired behavior of the players) that should emerge during the enactment of the role plays. If you're using an observer rating sheet, print these criteria on it.

3. Make the assignments so that all participants know their roles. If you are enacting the role play simultaneously in subgroups, get the persons who were given the foil role to meet and discuss their role, objectives, strategy, and alternatives (that is, what they should do if ... happens). Do the same for those in the critical role and for your observers. These discussions can occur simultaneously in three corners of the room. Observers should be given both roles to read.

4. Visit each group of players and check them out with questions like the following: "Why are you meeting with your boss? What do you hope will happen? What reaction do you anticipate? What alternatives do you see as appropriate?"

5. Visit the observers. Give them enough copies of the observer rating sheet or other discussion guidelines (such as questions or checklists) to distribute to each member of their group. Remind the observers of the importance of their role: to make notes during the role play of actions to be discussed following the enactment, to distribute the observer rating sheet or discussion guidelines after the enactment, and to lead the critique.

6. The postenactment discussion might follow this sequence:

   ◆ What objectives did the person in the critical role have? How well were they met?

   ◆ What objectives did the person in the foil role have? How well were they met?

   ◆ Are these two objectives in conflict? Is a win-win outcome possible? Explain.

   ◆ What behaviors did either party display that helped the two meet their objectives? That hindered the process?

   ◆ What notes and comments can the observers add that haven't been brought up by the players?

7. If the role play was enacted in a large group, allow time for participants to complete the observer rating sheets and turn them over to the person in the critical role because this is the role that participants will fill back on the job. In small group enactments, it's usually sufficient to discuss the issues and not take time to complete the form.

8. If you're using small groups and simultaneous enactments, circulate and listen in on the role plays, so that you can give closure to the exercise with summary comments when you reconvene the group.

Variations on the Spotlight Approach to Role Plays

All too often, role plays are conducted as a spectator sport in which two less-than-willing participants are selected to perform at the front of the room. That room may feel to them a bit like the ancient Roman coliseum where Christians were fed to the lions! Here are five alternative approaches that will give greater opportunity for everyone to experience the benefits of role playing.

◆ **Technique one, Baseball:** In playing baseball, many batters take their turn against one pitcher. Applied to role playing, you can have one person play the foil role (preferably an outsider to the group whom you've briefed on how to play the role), and let many participants take their turn at bat against the foil. You can interrupt every few minutes, sending in another participant to carry on where the last person left off. You might want to discuss and analyze each interaction before sending the next person in, or you might want to preserve continuity and wait until the role play has come to its end before discussing all participants' performances.

◆ **Technique two, E Pluribus Unum:** This Latin phrase that graces the coins in your pocket means "From many, one." In role playing it is sometimes appropriate to assign many to the same role and ask them to act as one. That is, anyone can speak and pick up the ball at any time. It is useful when using this technique to add another rule: Anyone who isn't pleased with the way things are going can call "time" and stop the action. This forces the player in the foil role to leave the group so that the many players in the critical role can analyze how the interaction is going and what they should do differently. Then, when the person calls "time in," the foil player returns. They then tell the foil whether they are starting over, picking up where they left off, or backing up to an earlier point.

◆ **Technique three, The Eternal Triangle:** In some role plays, the person in the critical role is competing with other parties for business. The role may be, for example, that of a salesperson bidding against competitors, a bank officer of one bank determining the rates and conditions of a loan to a customer who is also exploring two other banks. In these three-way, or triangular relationships, you might find it useful to create a role play that has two parties filling the critical role and competing against each other to win over the foil role. They take turns presenting their terms to the buyer until the person in the foil role reaches a decision, terminates the role play, and informs the "loser" why the "winner" made the sale.

◆ **Technique four, Round Robin:** To give everyone an equal chance to perform, you might create three equivalent role plays and select three players to serve as critical role, foil role, and observer. After going through the first role play, you then rotate the players (whoever played the critical role now serves in the foil role, the foil player now becomes observer, and the observer now fills the critical role). By going round robin over the three role plays, each person will have served in all three capacities.

◆ **Technique five, Multiple Roles:** When you are teaching skills and concepts that can best be practiced in a group setting (such as team building or how to run a meeting), you may want to create a role play that has a number of different roles to be filled, usually four or five. You can thus create hidden agendas and differences in perception among the players, and greatly increase the opportunities for interaction. This technique is especially appropriate in courses dealing with conflict resolution, team building, meeting leadership, group decision making, and so on.

CHAPTER 32

USING THE CASE METHOD

Characteristics of the Case Method

Case study refers to the process of providing learners with a situation that they must analyze and discuss, thereby applying the concepts and skills they have been learning. Thus, case method provides the following:

◆ a vicarious way of experiencing real situations in class

◆ a personal and immediate opportunity to apply new learning

◆ a compression of time and documentation (since many case situations took months or years to evolve and reams of memos to describe)

◆ a fail-safe environment in which learners can get immediate feedback and experience the consequences of their thoughts and actions.

No wonder case method is a mainstay in the teaching of law, medicine, business, education, social work, and military training.

The following three elements are present in the case method:

◆ **Case report:** a history of the situation (actual or fabricated), presented to learners in writing, film or video, or via a live presentation. The report can be in many forms, such as a documentary or a script showing interaction. It may be open ended or may show the case as finished business.

◆ **Analysis:** Learners analyze the case, evaluating the actions taken, identifying assumptions and shaky reasoning, and proposing alternatives. This can be done individually as a written analysis or in a group discussion.

◆ **Feedback:** Learners evaluate their analysis of the case on the basis of guidelines or a model provided by the instructor, or both.

In every case study, two types of learning are occurring simultaneously. Learners are developing content knowledge and process skills. Cases are selected or written because they illustrate certain concepts and principles at work, such as marketing, finance, administration, or human. These are macro topics for case reports. There are also the micro topics. Under human, for example, there are hundreds of subtopics, such as insubordination, reverse discrimination, competition versus cooperation, and self-directed teams. The case report should contain enough material to enable learners to dig in and apply their knowledge of the content. That content may include facts, policy, law, concepts, and resources. The analysis of a case report will typically focus on issues relating to content knowledge.

A second benefit of the case method is that it develops process skills, such as reasoning, analyzing, identifying objectives, evaluating evidence, questioning assumptions, separating fact from opinion, exploring alternatives, solving problems, and making decisions. It also develops the skills of communicating, such as listening, probing, reading analytically, questioning, restating, sharing, selling, articulating, summarizing, and testing for agreement. These activities of thinking and communicating are process skills that fill most of the hours your learners spend at work.

Writers and instructors often focus on content knowledge or process skills and overlook the other. The questions, guidelines, and feedback that learners receive should strike a balance between content knowledge and process skills. Both are essential to the learner's success.

Make or Buy?

Can case reports be purchased, or must they be home grown and written from information the course designer collects? Both possibilities exist. Thousands of cases exist for courses that focus on such familiar topics as supervision, sales, project management, and self-directed work teams. The suppliers of such courses usually provide case material with their programs.

Harvard Business School has compiled the largest collection of case material, and its cases are for sale. A number of catalogs deal with different macro topics such as marketing, production, finance, controls, and human. These catalogs and the cases they describe are available from the Intercollegiate Case Clearing House of the Harvard Business School, Soldiers Field, Boston.

Many of the case reports in the Harvard collection are longer and more complex than is appropriate in training programs that can only devote an hour or so to the presentation, analysis, and feedback on a given case. You may, therefore, want to develop your own case material.

The critical incident technique, popular as a tool of needs analysis, is an excellent source of material that can be easily converted into a format appropriate to case method. This technique is a form of survey research in which the respondents (whether trainees, job holders, customers, or someone else) are asked to describe in writing a recent situation that they experienced or witnessed at work that illustrates a problem relating to the micro topic that will be the focus of the course (whether time management, delegation, performance appraisals, or something else). Respondents are asked to report their situations by answering these four questions:

1. What was the problem or situation? (in several sentences)
2. What factor or factors caused or contributed to the situation?
3. What was the outcome? Is this desirable?
4. Could the incident or problem have been avoided?

Figure 32-1 is an example of a critical incident that a respondent submitted for possible use in a course on supervisory skills. The individual turned it in during the needs analysis that preceded the design of a training program on dealing with problem employees.

After receiving this critical incident, the instructor called the supervisor to get permission to turn it into a case study and to change the names.

Figure 32-1. Critical incident for class on dealing with problem employees.

What was the problem or situation?

   I supervise the accounts payable section where Gretchen, one of my most experienced (22 years) assistants, was discourteous over the phone with our printer who wanted payment on a bill that was 45 days old. Gretchen told him that:

   - *other bills were 60 days old and would be paid first*
   - *it wouldn't do any good to talk with her manager since rules are rules.*

What factors contributed to the situation?

   Gretchen is dependable, knowledgeable, bossy, and set in her ways. I can't afford to lose her or to take her off the phones because everyone has responsibility for certain accounts. She takes pride in knowing the company's policies and procedures and in rigidly enforcing them. She has questioned me on several occasions where I bent the rules to speed up payment of a favored supplier who was in financial straits.

What was the outcome? Is this desirable?

   I decided that Gretchen's good qualities outweigh her shortcomings and that I might make matters worse by talking to her about the complaint I got from our printer. Gretchen is set in her ways and is not likely to change. You've got to accept people for what they are, play up their strengths, and accept their weaknesses.

(continued on next page)

Figure 32-1. Critical incident for class on dealing with problem employees.
(continued)

Could the incident or problems have been avoided?

Gretchen was hired before I joined the company. Whether she was this rigid 22 years ago, I don't know. If so, she shouldn't have been put in a job that requires a lot of phone contact with suppliers and customers.

"I already changed the names to protect the woman I called Gretchen," explained the supervisor, whose real name is Harry Boscow. "You're certainly welcome to use the case. Incidentally, I'm scheduled to attend the course in two months, but I certainly won't reveal that I'm the source of the case study."

Given this permission and some additional information that Harry volunteered, the instructor prepared the case study in figure 32-2.

Figure 32-2. The case of Steve Trub.

Case Report: Teaching Old Dogs New Tricks

"Oh, and one more thing, Steve. That woman who answers the phone when you're not there . . . she's something else! When I tried to reach you yesterday, she wanted to know what it was about. I said that it was a personal matter, and she then proceeded to tell me that personal business shouldn't be conducted on company time and over company phones. Now there's a woman with style!"

Steve thanked Larry, promised to do something about it, and hung up. The complaint was not a new one. Last month Rumson Press, one of the company's major suppliers, had called the accounting department (where Steve supervises the accounts payable section), and had talked with Gretchen, the woman in question. The supplier wanted payment of a bill that was 45 days old. Gretchen explained that other bills were 60 days old and would have to be paid first and that Rumson would get paid when its turn came. The bookkeeper at Rumson then asked if the manager was around. Gretchen replied that he wasn't, but that it wouldn't do any good talking to him even if he were around, since bills are paid in the order in which they are received. (Steve had learned all this from the Rumson salesperson on his visit a few days later.)

Steve was faced with a dilemma, for Gretchen was one of his best workers. She had been with the company for 22 years, and knew the accounting system backwards and forwards. Moreover, she was carrying out company policy in the case of Rumson Press. It's a hard-and-fast rule to pay accounts in order and not show preference simply because one firm is putting on more pressure than another. Steve knew that Gretchen would point this out if he tried to correct her. She would consider any correction an injustice and would be likely to tell Steve (and the other women in the section) that "this is what I get for trying to carry out orders."

Figure 32-2. The case of Steve Trub. *(continued)*

Nor was it simply a matter of keeping Gretchen off the phone because the physical arrangement of the section was such that every person had responsibility for certain accounts. A transfer out of the department was out of the question; Gretchen was a dependable worker and served as Steve's lead worker in his absence, answering questions of procedure for the other people in the section.

"I guess the problem is one of trying to teach an old dog new tricks," Steve mused. "You simply can't do it. She's set in her ways, and is not likely to change. Besides, what with living with her mother and having no interests outside of her work, I might do a lot more harm than good if I talk to her. It isn't worth the risk. Everybody's got faults mixed in with their good qualities. You've got to accept people for what they are, play up their strengths and accept their weaknesses."

Some Questions

1. Do you agree with the assumptions Steve has made about Gretchen? Why?
2. How would you describe Steve's style of management?
3. What would you do if you were in Steve's shoes?

The instructor who converted Harry Boscow's critical incident into the case study realized that other trainers would also be giving the course on supervisory skills and would welcome a set of discussion guidelines. Accordingly, the instructor prepared the material in figure 32-3.

Figure 32-3. Instructor guidelines for the case of Steve Trub.

Case Analysis: Teaching Old Dogs New Tricks

Gretchen is an experienced, dependable worker who knows company policy to the letter of the law and delights in carrying it out. What more could any supervisor want of an employee?

Tact, sensitivity to the needs of others, and flexibility—that's what! At least that is what Steve would like to see Gretchen develop. However, he has concluded that she is set in her ways and is not likely to change. "You can't teach an old dog new tricks," he believes.

1. We do not agree with Steve's assumption about Gretchen. We believe that one is never too old to learn. We suspect that Gretchen's problem is one of attitude (and not a deficiency in knowledge or skills). Through patient coaching by Steve, she can be led to realize the possible effects of her handling of suppliers and vendors. His counseling may or may not work. But he owes it to Gretchen and the organization to give it his best try.

In short, the effective supervisor should assume (until the results prove otherwise) that an employee wants to improve, wants to do things that help the company meet its goals, wants feedback on strengths and deficiencies, and wants help in becoming a better, more valuable employee.

(continued on next page)

Figure 32-3. Instructor guidelines for the case of Steve Trub. *(continued)*

2. Steve sees Gretchen as wrapped up in her job, more concerned with the task than with the feelings of people. Perhaps he is guilty of the same thing. That is, Steve might be concerned with the work flow and afraid that Gretchen's output will suffer if he tries to work with her: "It might do a lot more harm than good if I talk to her. It isn't worth the risk."

   In short, we see Steve as job centered (making theory X, parent-to-child assumptions) rather than as employee centered. This is a common behavior of theory X managers. They complain that employees are not developing the way they should or that you just can't teach them some things. The real problem is that theory X managers do not want to invest in people because they believe that the investment won't pay off.

3. If we were in Steve's shoes, we would give her the benefit of the doubt. We would assume that she does want to improve and increase her value as an employee. She thinks she is acting in the best interest of the company. She needs to see the effect of her actions on others. We would spend time with her, tell her the many good qualities she displays in her work, and build on these strengths in pointing out the need for improved relations with suppliers. This can be done in a theory Y, adult-to-adult manner. We would also like to see Steve take the time to inspect what he expects by listening from time to time to Gretchen in her interactions with others, so that he can find opportunities to praise her for her improved handling of people.

Consider the four components that go into the design and delivery of a case study.

1. **Needs analysis:** Critical incidents were collected as a means of identifying the kinds of situations that supervisors face in dealing with problem employees.

2. **Stimulus:** The instructor generates a case study on the basis of the critical incident and other information obtained by phone from the source.

3. **Response:** The instructor prepares questions that will focus the analysis of the case on the desired responses, or key learning points.

4. **Feedback:** The instructor creates guidelines that will give trainers and trainees alike the feedback that confirms that they understand the key learning points.

The Steve Trub case study illustrates the documentary, or narrative, form of writing in which the person preparing the case describes actions and thoughts. Now examine a scripted case study in which the interaction between two or more people is constructed verbatim. Scripted cases are especially useful in the training of people whose jobs require interpersonal communication skills—interviewers, salespersons, customer service reps, employees in hotels, restaurants, airlines, hospitals, and so on.

Figure 32-4 is a scripted case study dealing with on-the-job training. Tom is a supervisor who is just about to assign Jim to paint some windows in a warehouse. They are up near the ceiling so Jim is going to have to use an extension ladder. Following is the script of the training that Tom gave Jim. Make notes beside the script to indicate what Tom did wrong or failed to do. Refer to Tom's comments by number to save writing.

Figure 32-4. Scripted case study dealing with on-the-job training.

Tom:	1 2	You'll have to use the extension ladder to reach the upper ones, Jim. Do you know how it operates?
Jim:	3	Yeah. I've got an aluminum one at home.
Tom:	4 5 6 7 8 9	Good. Well, set the ladder up so that it's leaning against the window sill at the top and out far enough at the bottom to make an angle of about 70 degrees with the ground. Also, you want it extended far enough so that you can always grip the ladder with one hand while painting with the other. In other words, you should never stand on the top or next to the top rung. If you have to go that high, you should come back down the ladder and extend it farther up. Understand?
Jim:	10	Yeah.
Tom:	11 12	Okay. Let's make sure. Can you name the three things to remember when using an extension ladder.
Jim:	13	Oh, boy. Uh. Let's see. Extend it far enough so that I can hold onto it while painting.
Tom:	14	Good. That's one of them.
Jim:	15	Keep the ladder slanted at a 70 degree angle.
Tom:	16	Two down, only one to go.
Jim:	17	And, uh, are you sure there was a third?
Tom:	18 19	Yes. It's the first one I mentioned. Lean the top of the ladder against the window sill not against the glass or the thin wood separating the panes.
Jim:	20	Oh, yeah.
Tom:	21 22	Okay. Now once you get up there, what are you going to do? What will you paint first?
Jim:	23	The thin wood strips that separate the panes.
Tom:	24 25 26 27 28 29	Nope. You should start with the parts of the window that are farthest away from you—then work your way in toward you. It's a good rule to follow whatever you're painting: First paint the part that is hardest to get to, most inaccessible or remote. Then end up with the parts that show the most. So if you are painting a chair or stool, you would first do the underside and the insides of the legs. The last things to paint are the fronts of the legs and the seat. Do you think you understand?
Jim:	30	Yeah, I think so.
Tom:	31 32	Good. Then go to it. You know where I'll be if you run into any problems. But I'll check back in a half hour or so to see how things are going.
Jim:	33	Okay. I shouldn't have any trouble.

As participants in the workshop complete their critique of Tom's delivery of on-the-job training, the instructor gives them a critique sheet, shown in figure 32-5, so that they can evaluate their own responses.

Figure 32-5. Feedback on Tom's training of Jim.

Critique of Tom

Here are 12 failures we spotted—situations where Tom specifically failed to apply one or more of the learning principles. How many of these failures did you identify:

1. At the very start, Tom should have begun the instruction by explaining what Jim would be able to do when the instruction was over (the terminal behavior, or T.B.): "Jim, you'll be painting the windows today so I'd like to take five minutes to make sure you know how to operate the extension ladder and how to paint the thin strips that separate the panes."

2. In line four, Tom seemed to ignore Jim's response to the question, "Do you know how it operates?" Having one at home is not the same as knowing how it operates. Tom should have asked Jim to set up the ladder and **demonstrate** his understanding of how it operates.

3. In lines four to nine, Tom gives out a lot of information without checking to see if Jim understands. There are three different pieces of information in this paragraph—three **stimuli**. Tom should have stopped after each one to get a relevant **response** from Jim and thereby make sure he understands.

4. In line five, Tom has no idea whether or not Jim can visualize a 70 degree angle. Is he carrying a protractor with him? It would have been better if Tom had asked Jim to show him what a safe angle would be by leaning the ladder against the wall. He could then find out if Jim understands what a safe angle really is.

5. In line nine, "Understand?" is a poor question. Jim is likely to answer yes whether or not he understands. In fact, he may not even **know** whether or not he understands. In other words, the question does not elicit a relevant response because trainees often can't tell whether or not they understand and even if they don't understand they may not want to say so to their instructor for fear of offending or of looking dumb.

6. In line 11, Tom asks Jim to "name the three things to remember when using an extension ladder." Naming them is not the same as doing them. Again, Tom is wasting time. He should have gotten Jim to **do** the three things, and watched him while he did so. Many people are not verbal, especially those in jobs requiring physical skill over mental ability. Such employees are a lot more comfortable **doing** things than talking about them, especially when asked in a manner that is somewhat reminiscent of school days and classes where they had to recite.

7. In lines 18-19, Tom should explain **why** he's giving these instructions. Or it might be better if Tom had asked, "Jim, could you tell me why you'd lean the ladder against the upper sill rather than the lower?" Tom could then find out if Jim understands ladder placement—it can only go against the upper sill, and not against the lower sill, the panes, or the wood between them.

Figure 32-5. Feedback on Tom's training of Jim. *(continued)*

---

8. In line 21, this would normally be a good question. It is trainee centered and shows that Tom wants to find out what Jim already knows before teaching him. However, given Tom's style of instruction up to this point, such a question probably looks like a test to Jim—a test of something he hasn't yet been taught. As such, it is likely to put Jim on the spot. He may be thinking, "Tom must have covered this, but I don't remember it." In short, your style as instructor should be consistent. Switching from the information-centered style to a trainee-centered one may confuse the trainee.

9. In line 24, having just tried to find out what Jim already know, Tom's "Nope" sounds something like, "Gotcha, you idiot." It almost looks as if Tom had tried to set Jim up and trap him. Instead, Tom should have led Jim on and helped him to see the adverse results of painting the thin wood strips first. Tom forgot our first principle: We learn best by experiencing the consequences of our actions, not by being told.

10. In lines 26 and 27, right after saying, "then end up with the parts that show the most," Tom should have thrown the ball to Jim, asking him, "Now, Jim, let's see if you understand. Suppose you were going to paint a chair. How would you go about it? What parts would you paint first?" Any time you have to teach a rule or principle or procedure, it's a good idea to get the trainee to describe an example of it. This is one of the best ways to get feedback and thus complete the SRF link.

11. In line 29, look at the question, "Do you think you understand?" Again, this question is a poor one because it is likely to get an irrelevant response. How does Jim know if he really understands until he **does** it? (The problem is the same as the one we discussed in number five about line nine.)

12. In line 31, Tom ends up with "You know where I'll be if you run into any problems." That's bad. He should remain long enough to check Jim out and give him feedback. By so doing, he can correct poor techniques and reinforce good ones at the start. In the **application** stage of our learning model, the instructor should watch the learner **apply** what has just been acquired. This is the only way to find out if the instruction has been successful.

As in the earlier case dealing with Steve Trub, this scripted case study illustrates the S-R-F model at work:

1. **Stimulus:** the script of the dialogue between Tom and Jim

2. **Response:** the learners' notes on what Tom did wrong or failed to do

3. **Feedback:** the critique that identifies 12 failures on Tom's part.

Although it is not always necessary, some scripted case studies include a rewrite of the script to show the desired behavior, or corrected interaction. Figure 32-6 shows how Tom should have trained Jim. As such, it is another example of feedback.

Figure 32-6. The desired behavior.

How Tom Should Have Trained Jim

Tom: You'll have to use the extension ladder on the upper ones, Jim. Do you know how it operates?

Jim: Yeah. I've got an aluminum one at home.

Tom: Good. Well, let's use this one right here. Why don't you show me where you'd place it to paint that window up there? In other words, show me a safe angle for the ladder.

Jim: Okay. [He sets the ladder against the window sill.] How's this?

Tom: Looks good. What will happen if you pull the base out farther away from the wall?

Jim: The base might begin to slip and shoot out from under me.

Tom: And how about the opposite direction? What if you move the base closer to the wall?

Jim: Then the ladder will be too upright. If I lean back, it could go over backwards.

Tom: Good. I notice that you have the ladder resting on the bottom window sill.

Jim: Yeah. If I put it higher, it will be resting on the glass or the thin framing between the panes. And they're not strong enough.

Tom: True. But how are you going to reach the top of the window?

Jim: I can stand on the top rung of the ladder.

Tom: That's a bit dangerous, isn't it? A safer way to reach the top is to extend the ladder farther up so that it rests on the wall above the window. Why is this safer, Jim?

Jim: Uhh. Because I can hold on to the ladder with one hand while I'm painting with the other.

Tom: Exactly. Now, once you get up there, what are you going to do? What will you paint first?

Jim: The thin wood strips that separate the panes.

Tom: Why are you starting with these?

Jim: Because they are the easiest to reach.

Tom: Yeah, but what's going to happen as you reach out to paint the sides of the window frame and the parts that are harder to reach? You may get your sleeve in the fresh paint.

Jim: Okay, then I guess it would be better if I start by painting the parts that are farthest away and work my way in.

Tom: Much better idea. In fact, that's a good rule to follow whatever you're painting: First paint the part that is hardest to get to. Then end up with the parts that show the most. So if you are painting a chair or stool, what part would you do first?

Jim: Uhh. The underside. And the insides of the legs.

Tom: What part would you save until last?

Jim: The fronts of the legs and the seat.

Tom: Good. I can see that you understand. So, go to it. I'll be at my desk if you run into any problems. But I'll check back in a half hour or so to see how things are going.

Jim: Okay. I shouldn't have any trouble.

SECTION 8

TRANSFERRING BEHAVIOR FROM WORKSHOP TO WORKPLACE

The purpose of training is to teach people how to perform back on the job. If the concepts and skills taught during a training program do not translate into the desired performance in the workplace, then the training has been a failure.

Educators are responsible for delivering instruction. Trainers are responsible for delivering performance. And there's the rub because most of the factors affecting the trainee's performance lie outside the realm of the trainer's influence. In chapter 5 we identified a number of factors that can serve as reinforcers or constraints, helping or hindering trainees as they attempt to apply on the job what they learned during training. In this section, we'll examine the major tools and techniques that instructors can use to strengthen the transfer of training:

Chapter 33, "Ideas for Improved Transfer of Training," examines three major classes of factors affecting transfer (personal, instructional, organizational), describes learning curves and retention curves, and presents a list of 20 ways to improve transfer and maintenance.

Chapter 34, "Transfer of Learning From Class to Job," lists 50 factors relating to transfer and provides a three-point scale for evaluating the strength of each, thus yielding a score that reflects the likelihood of transfer and that pinpoints the factors in greatest need of improvement.

Chapter 35, "Using Action Plans for Transfer of Training," contains the rationale behind action plans, a description of their use, an outline of the manager's briefing for the participants' supervisors, examples of the three kinds of action plan entries (intrapersonal, interpersonal, and work group), a sample completed action plan, and a sample three-way agreement.

Chapter 36, "Using Planning Sheets and Self-Assessments for Transfer of Training," describes the benefit of creating planning sheets and checklists that participants can use as memory aids in the workplace. Self-assessments enable participants to strengthen their relationship with persons who are stakeholders in their growth and development.

Upon completing this section, you should be able to:

- give examples of the three types of factors affecting transfer
- describe three types of performance curves and reasons for each
- list at least four of 20 ways to improve transfer in your courses
- calculate the likelihood of transfer, using the 50-item checklist
- identify at least five benefits of having trainees prepare action plans
- prepare the agenda for a one-hour manager's briefing
- create a sample action plan for the course you teach
- generate a three-way agreement for your trainees and their managers
- develop a planning sheet, a form of job aid, for part of a course you teach.

CHAPTER 33

IDEAS FOR IMPROVING TRANSFER OF TRAINING

Training is an investment. If the learners apply at work what they acquired during their learning, there will be a return-on-investment. If they do not, then the training time was merely spent—and hence wasted—rather than invested.

Why would learners not apply at work what they were taught during their training? Three sets of factors may help or hinder the transfer of learning from class to job: personal, instructional, and organizational. Consider the following examples of each.

◆ **Personal factors:** These include such things as **motivation** (Does the learner want to be in class? Does the learner know it already, or believe he or she knows it? Does the worker enjoy the work and the job?); **ability** (Does the learner have the ability to learn?); **attention** (Can the learner concentrate? Or are weightier matters interfering, such as sickness, a marriage breaking up, and so forth?); **relevance** (Does the learner see the course as relevant to the job and to personal needs?).

◆ **Instructional factors:** These include such things as **course design** (Are methods and media appropriate? Facilities and equipment? Length and objectives?); **emphasis** (How does theory compare with practice? Knowledge with skills? Talking with doing?); **instructor** (Is the instructor credible? Effective?); **follow-up** (Do trainers get feedback on learners' performance after training? Are actions taken accordingly, on the trainee and on the course design?).

◆ **Organizational factors:** These include such things as **climate** (Do the norms, culture, and expectations of fellow employees and managers support the new behaviors that were just learned?); **time and timing** (Does the trainee have time to do things the way they were taught? Was the opportunity to apply new learning fairly immediate or too delayed?); **degree of fit** (Do local procedures, forms, equipment agree with those taught to the learner?).

The first of these three factors is internal to the learner, and there is often little the instructor can do to influence the personal side other than attempt to screen the participants (that is, by assessing their entering behavior prior to the course and then making every attempt to get the right faces in the right places at the right times).

The second and third factors are external to the learner. Instructors, course designers, and management share a responsibility for establishing a maintenance system that will recognize and reinforce the desired behavior of learners as they attempt to apply at work what they learned in class. Later in this chapter, you will find 20 ideas for actions and techniques that address the organizational factors.

Learning Curves

Introductory psychology texts typically contain a chapter or so on learning and remembering. Learning can be plotted as a curve to show how learners' performance improves over the length of the course. Figure 33-1 shows such a curve superimposed on the three-stage learning model.

In the "Instructional System" part of the figure, we take learners through the three stages—acquisition, demonstration, and application—where they develop new behavior patterns and improve performance (that is, closing the gap between the learners' entering behavior and our specified terminal behavior). Our role is to develop a sequence of learning

Figure 33-1. The learning curve and the three-stage learning model.

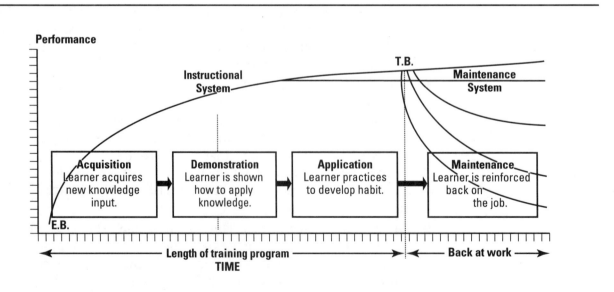

experiences that shapes the learner's behavior in ways determined during the preparation by needs analysis.

In the "Maintenance System" part of the figure, we increase reinforcers and reduce constraints that operate in the work environment and influence the learners' behavior on the job.

Following a course or learning program, the newly acquired knowledge, skills, and attitudes will transfer in one of three ways, as indicated in the retention curves shown in the figure. Following are the reasons for each:

◆ **Continued improvement (curve still climbing):** When skills can be immediately applied and improved through use, performance continues to grow. Some examples of this continued growth include use of computer graphics and the Internet, computer data entry, foreign language, supervisors conducting future performance appraisals, and salespersons on each new presentation.

◆ **Stable performance (curve levels off):** Some types of behavior are binary (that is, learners can do them or they can't, and it's not a matter of degree). Examples of this type of behavior include remembering a concept or theory, spelling a name correctly, recalling a policy, citing a source, performing an operation such as calculating a square root, and recalling a formula, such as converting centigrade to Fahrenheit.

◆ **Declining performance (curve shows rapid decline):** When new learning is not applied, or when attempts to apply it are met with negative consequences, trainees will revert to old habits, wrong behavior, or withdrawal (nonresponse to situations they've been trained to respond to). Some examples of this type of behavior include statements like, "Look. I don't care what they told you in class, you're working for me now. Here's how I want it done."

Trainers have a major responsibility to do whatever they can to keep the retention curve as high as possible (that is, to assure maximum transfer from workshop to workplace). In contrast, educators focus their concern on the learning curve and getting it as high as possible. However, once the course is over and the final grade is determined, there the responsibility ends.

Ways to Improve Transfer and Maintenance

Following are 20 possible ways in which instructors can improve the transfer of training and their maintenance systems. As you read the ideas, place a check mark in the box in front of each one that might be appropriate for the courses you teach. These are the ideas you will want to discuss with your manager or a fellow instructor who shares responsibility for the course. Most of the items will not apply or will take more time than you have to make them work. If you end up implementing three or four of these ideas, the return-on-investment will be well worth it.

1. Each participant completes an action plan that spells out what steps will be taken on the job to apply the newly learned concepts and skills. The participant discusses the plan with the supervisor, and both agree on when and how the plan will be implemented. A copy is filed with the instructor for follow-up.

2. Schedule an alumni day about five to eight weeks after the course, as a time when your participants come together to report (10 to 15 minutes each) on the things they have accomplished by putting to use the concepts and skills they learned in the class. Make this day your graduation. Invite their supervisors.

3. When you teach the entire job to a new hire, have each trainee develop a job description as an ongoing part of the course. Each new procedure or responsibility that you teach gets summarized on the job description in the trainee's own words. This list then becomes a transmittal document that goes with the trainee to the supervisor.

4. Create an association of those who have completed the course—the graduates—who meet once a month for their continued growth and development. They have a program committee to identify areas of interest for further training; you assist by getting speakers or instructors, from within or outside the organization.

5. Develop a newsletter that serves to maintain and reward good performance through recognition: interviews with graduates, success stories, instructive articles, contests, quizzes, case studies for analysis, and so on.

6. Require each learner to send in a critical incident report that summarizes a problem encountered back on the job and that describes how the tools and techniques acquired during the course helped in tackling the problem and resolving it. Make successes public in a newsletter or house organ.

7. In jobs where it is appropriate, such as customer contact jobs, train several surveyors to pose as customers and conduct a shopping survey to see how the graduate is able to handle a number of problems and questions that the shopper poses. Then have your surveyors give immediate feedback and reward, based on performance.

8. Instead of running courses intensively over a short time span, stretch them out and run them extensively, interspersing classroom time with time back on the job. This kind of schedule gives participants time to apply and act on each new set of skills, meet with their supervisors, and address any differences between class and job.

9. Bring your participants' managers or supervisors together before the course starts and, if appropriate, after it is over to brief them on the objectives, content, and format and, most important, on their role as a partner with you in the training of their people. Spell out their responsibilities; give them a letter of agreement that explains the roles and expectations of the three parties: trainer, trainee, trainee's boss.

☐ 10. Schedule people who work in pairs or teams (such as data processing clerks, administrative assistant and supervisor, customer service representatives) to attend training together. Develop your training exercises in a way that strengthens their responsibility to support one another.

☐ 11. Use needs analysis techniques and instruments that can be repeated at some interval after the course to generate data to be fed back to the graduate and the boss. Some examples of these tools are a climate survey, supervisory style inventory, and communication style assessment. Get the parties together to interpret the change.

☐ 12. Make use of planning sheets, flow charts, checklists, and other job aids in the training program, so that trainees can take them back to the workplace and use them on the job. Conduct an audit of the workplace to see how well these job aids are being used; reward and reinforce this behavior.

☐ 13. Set up an assessment lab or a series of modular (independent) self-assessment exercises, and schedule the graduates to come in individually for a free, no-obligation checkup. Give them feedback on strengths and weaknesses, and discuss where they have been able and unable to apply what they learned.

☐ 14. Work with department heads, division managers, and the like to select a training coordinator for each major unit of the organization. Work with these people in scheduling follow-up activities to help each participant as he or she leaves training and returns to the job. Equip these coordinators with checklists and other job aids.

☐ 15. Form a training advisory committee consisting of key managers from your organization's major divisions and departments. Use this group for guidance in developing your courses, and for follow-up in monitoring and reinforcing good performance by graduates.

☐ 16. To ensure that there is an impact on the participants' immediate environment, give surveys and assessments to them and to one or more of the following: the participants' managers, subordinates, customers, or users.

☐ 17. Provide participants and their managers with a list of behaviors to be observed and evaluated back at work following training. Request a copy of this checklist to be returned to the instructor within 30 days following the course.

☐ 18. Create a performance contract in which participants agree to meet the criteria spelled out in the contract in exchange for training. Each participant performs a self-evaluation against these criteria and notifies the training department of fulfillment.

☐ 19. Run training programs for natural work groups, such as departments, branches, or locations, rather than for a mixture that runs across organizational lines. Address specific needs of each homogeneous group rather than a broad group in one-size-fits-all courses for a widely heterogeneous audience.

20. In jobs where productivity can be measured (such as by number of sales made, transactions processed, trucks loaded), schedule a contest for the period immediately following training. Set up a reward schedule so as to have many winners among your graduates.

Estimates by training managers of the amount of learning that transfers from workshop to workplace and can be seen being applied several months after the workshops fall in the range of 20 percent to 25 percent. Such figures reflect a pathetic return on the training investment.

Suppose that by selecting and implementing three or four of these 20 ideas, you could increase a 20 percent transfer to 30 percent. That's a 50 percent improvement in performance.

Trainers often spend thousands of dollars and hundreds of hours designing and delivering courses with little or no investment in the systems needed to recognize and reinforce new behavior back on the job. Transfer of training may well be the new frontier for improving the return on your human resource development efforts.

CHAPTER 34

TRANSFER OF LEARNING FROM CLASS TO JOB

Instruction is effective only to the degree that new learning is converted into performance back at work. This process is known as **transfer.** Many factors influence the degree of transfer and determine the return on the training investment.

Figure 34-1 lists 50 factors that influence transfer of training. They are grouped under the following five major headings:

◆ course design

◆ instructor's skills and values

◆ trainee's abilities and perceptions

◆ workplace environment

◆ role of managers and supervisors.

The list was designed to enable you to evaluate a specific course and the degree to which transfer of training is likely to take place. For each of the 50 factors, your job is to circle the rating that best describes the course, where:

2 = strong; no problem with this factor

1 = moderate; this factor is present, but needs improvement

0 = weak or absent; this factor is negligible or nonexistent.

Consider this example:

47. Are supervisors taking time to recognize and reinforce the trainees' new behaviors back on the job? 2   1   0

In this example, suppose the trainees' supervisors have themselves been through the course or a briefing before the trainees took the course. The supervisors are very supportive, and they encourage their staff to apply the things they learned in class. Thus, you would circle the 2.

Now, suppose the supervisors believe in training but are not very well acquainted with the course and what their staff are learning to do. They give general encouragement but cannot be as specific in their feedback and reinforcement as they should. You would circle the 1.

If the supervisors were too busy to concern themselves with the course and the things their staff learned from it and spent little if any time recognizing and reinforcing new behavior when their trainees returned to their jobs, you would circle the 0.

Figure 34-1. Factors that influence transfer of training.

Course Design

1. How relevant is the content to the trainees' needs? 2   1   0

2. How appropriate are the instructional methods and media? 2   1   0

3. Are there enough job aids, checklists, references, and the like for use on the job? 2   1   0

4. How effective are the learning facilities and equipment? 2   1   0

5. How well do the trainees like the course design? 2   1   0

6. Is the length of the course appropriate to its objectives? 2   1   0

7. Do trainees have enough time in class to practice and refine new skills? 2   1   0

8. How smooth is the flow and transition from one session, topic, or lesson to the next? 2   1   0

9. Do trainees get enough feedback to help them check progress and make corrections? 2   1   0

10. What kind of image does the course have throughout the organization? 2   1   0

Total of circled numbers 1 through 10

Instructor's Skills and Values

11. How well does the instructor know the subject and the trainees' work environment? 2   1   0

12. To what degree does the instructor use language, examples, and analogies that the trainees can relate to? 2   1   0

13. Does the instructor spend additional time when trainees are having trouble learning? 2   1   0

14. To what degree did the instructor teach deductively (the Socratic method) whenever it was appropriate? 2   1   0

15. How effective is the instructor's skill in keeping the class interactive and well paced? 2   1   0

16. Does the instructor have the respect of management and the trainees' supervisors? 2   1   0

17. To what degree does the instructor have learners doing things rather than talking about how to do them? 2   1   0

18. How do trainees rate the instructor on knowledge, credibility, and delivery? 2   1   0

19. Does the instructor follow up after the course to see where trainees can or can't apply what they've learned? 2   1   0

20. To what degree does the instructor prepare trainees to deal with barriers, such as problems and frustrations, that they face at work? 2   1   0

Total of circled numbers 11 through 20

Figure 34-1. Factors that influence training. *(continued)*

Trainees' Abilities and Perceptions

21. How favorable is the trainees' attitude toward the course and the work it prepares one for? 2 1 0

22. To what degree do the trainees possess the necessary prerequisites (that is, entering behavior)? 2 1 0

23. Are members of the trainees' work groups practicing the skills and concepts being taught? 2 1 0

24. How free are trainees of personal handicaps or problems that disrupt their concentration on the course? 2 1 0

25. To what degree do trainees see themselves rather than the instructor as responsible for their learning? 2 1 0

26. How stable are the trainees' job status and personal status, such as marital, health, and the like? 2 1 0

27. How clear are the trainees on the objectives of the course? 2 1 0

28. How committed are trainees to learning and applying new ways of doing things? 2 1 0

29. Do trainees have the courage to stop the instructor when they're lost or can't see relevance? 2 1 0

30. How do the trainees perceive the benefits of applying the new learning back on the job? 2 1 0

Total of circled numbers 21 through 30 ☐

Workplace Environment

31. How well do the workplace norms, expectations, culture, and climate support the new behavior? 2 1 0

32. To what degree did the timing of the training agree with the opportunity to apply it at work? 2 1 0

33. Do the physical conditions in the workplace support the desired behavior? 2 1 0

34. How readily does the course content translate into appropriate behavior on the job? 2 1 0

35. How permanent and resistant to change are the policies, procedures, equipment, and so forth? 2 1 0

36. To what degree do peers and other employees support the trainees' new behavior at work? 2 1 0

37. How frequently do the trainees get to apply on the job what they learned during training? 2 1 0

38. To what degree do trainees receive frequent and specific feedback in the weeks following training? 2 1 0

39. How well understood are the rewards and penalties associated with performance? 2 1 0

40. To what degree does the course have the respect of the trainees' peers and supervisors? 2 1 0

Total of circled numbers 31 through 40

(continued on next page)

Figure 34-1. Factors that influence training. *(continued)*

Role of Managers and Supervisors

41. How strongly do managers and
    supervisors believe in the course
    and those who give it? 2   1   0

42. To what degree do supervisors
    want their trainees doing things
    the way they learned in class? 2   1   0

43. Do supervisors explain the
    value of the course before
    their trainees attend? 2   1   0

44. To what degree are supervisors
    rewarded by their managers for
    coaching? 2   1   0

45. Are assessments made so as to
    give trainees immediate
    opportunities to apply their
    new learning? 2   1   0

46. To what degree do supervisors
    send trainees to the right courses at
    the best time on the basis of need? 2   1   0

47. Are supervisors taking time to
    recognize and reinforce the
    trainees' new behaviors back
    on the job? 2   1   0

48. To what degree are the
    supervisors good role models,
    practicing what is taught in
    the course? 2   1   0

49. How well do supervisors
    understand the objectives
    and content of the course? 2   1   0

50. To what degree do supervisors
    have a development plan for
    each subordinate that includes
    training? 2   1   0

Total of circled numbers 41 through 50   ☐

Total of the five boxes (out of a possible 100)   ☐

With 50 questions and a maximum possible score of two points on each, a perfect score is 100 points. If you get 80 or more points, your trainees should have no trouble in transferring their training from workshop to workplace. Scores between 50 and 80 indicate the likelihood of marginal transfer, and scores below 50 suggest that your efforts should focus heavily on improving the factors that are thwarting your harvest.

The farming analogy is apt. Your classroom is much like a greenhouse where you can plant seeds and control the factors that affect their growth: sunlight, water, temperature, and nutrients in the soil. You can give your trainees an environment that is free of conflicting priorities with enough time to practice and refine their new concepts and skills.

Then comes the moment of truth. Your course is over, and your fragile seedlings are transplanted into the workplace soil where there is no regulation of sunlight, water, temperature, and nutrients. What is worse, your seedlings must contend with rocks, nettles, weeds, and predators committed to killing them. No wonder three quarters of your seedlings do not survive.

The good news is that the 50-item list you just went through can help you to pinpoint the factors that are in greatest need of improvement. Each of the five groups is worth a maximum of 20 points. Any group that got fewer than, say, 16 points is begging for attention, as are the questions that received a rating of zero.

This list of 50 factors can be used again and again on different courses. Think of it as a magnifying glass that you can use to identify in detail the actions that should be taken to maximize the probability of a highly successful transfer of training.

CHAPTER 35

USING ACTION PLANS FOR TRANSFER OF TRAINING

The Action Plan

Participants are not empty vessels waiting to attend class and be filled with new concepts and skills. Rather they are change agents and catalysts who are being equipped with tools and techniques that they will apply back on the job.

One vehicle for accomplishing this is the **action plan.** It is a form that each participant completes at the end of each workshop session. Think of it as a transmittal document that participants take back to their managers and their subordinates for discussion and agreement on how the tools and techniques they acquired in class can best be transplanted and put into action on the job. Action plans work best when classes are scheduled with a week or more between sessions so that participants can meet with their managers. For example, classes can run every Wednesday for five weeks instead of for one week, Monday through Friday.

At the start of each new workshop, participants, working in subgroups of three to four persons each, get out their action plans and discuss the results of their meetings with managers and work group members. These action-plan reviews serve several useful purposes:

- ◆ They provide continuity to the course by reviewing the prior session's content.
- ◆ They place emphasis on applying concepts and skills, not merely acquiring them.
- ◆ They give instructors feedback on where participants need help in putting skills into practice.
- ◆ They enable instructors to follow up with managers who aren't meeting with participants.
- ◆ They reinforce participants for investing the extra time needed outside class.

◆ They give instructors a meaningful means of measuring the impact of the course.

Because participants need time between workshop sessions to refine, discuss, and begin to implement their action plan, we recommend that course sessions be scheduled one to two weeks apart. (This is not possible, of course, when people must travel and be put up overnight.)

Although it is best if participants discuss the action plans with their managers between training sessions, the plans are helpful for participants whether they do or not.

Just as each workshop begins with reports on the prior sessions' action plans and the progress made to date in implementing them, so should each workshop end with a summary of the various actions that different participants plan to take as a result of attending the workshop. This gives instructors feedback on the value of the concepts and techniques just taught. It also serves to help reluctant or uncreative participants whose eyes are opened as they listen to their colleagues share ideas on how they plan to apply their new learning back on the job.

Similarly, we recommend that the final session of the training program be devoted to a summary of the results of the action plans that have been implemented so far. This recap meeting might be scheduled a month or so after the last workshop session. Each participant takes five to 10 minutes to report to the group (and to their managers, seated in the rear) on the results they've obtained in putting their action plans to work. This session then becomes the graduation at which participants receive their end-of-course certificates (and cocktails, wine and cheese, or whatever other recognition might be appropriate).

The Managers' Briefing

The impact of the training is far greater when each participant's manager becomes a partner in his or her development. This partnership is best accomplished by scheduling a managers' briefing several weeks before the program begins. In a word, you cannot train managers' staff **for** them, you can only do it **with** them. Thus, we recommend that two weeks before the first course meeting is held, you conduct a one- or two-hour managers' briefing. The objectives of the meeting would be as follows:

◆ to spell out the course content and purpose

◆ to prepare managers for their role in meeting with participants after each session

◆ to enable managers to explain and sell the course to their staff prior to its launch

◆ to cover administrative details, preclass work, missed meetings, and the like

◆ to win their and your commitment to the partnership concept.

A sixth, and optional, objective is to give managers a hands-on flavor of the course design by showing a sample sequence of instruction and taking them through a typical exercise. This segment would bring the briefing to about two hours. Without it, the meeting lasts about an hour. Here is a suggested agenda for the meeting:

◆ *Why this course:* What we are trying to accomplish in running the program. (Perhaps a senior officer might give this five- to 10-minute introduction.)

◆ *Course content and design:* A bird's-eye-view of the course modules. If appropriate, distribute the brochure, a schedule of workshop dates, a roster of participants, a sample exercise. Time: about 20 minutes.

◆ *Our partnership:* A brief summary of the instructor's role and the role of each manager in meeting with the participants after each class session. How the action plans and course assignments work. Discuss the types of actions that can go in an action plan. (You can use a transparency of table 35-1 if you have an overhead projector available for the briefing.) Distribute a sample completed action plan, like table 35-2.

◆ *A sample of the course (optional).* Show the managers a sample sequence and take them through a typical exercise. Follow the suggestions in your instructor guidelines. Time: about 60 minutes.

An action plan can focus on three different levels of activity: intrapersonal, interpersonal, and work group. Participants can address any or all of these levels as they translate what they've just learned into follow-up actions to be taken in the workplace. Table 35-1 gives examples of actions at each of these three levels, both for everyday situations and for situations that are specific to certain persons or times.

Table 35-2 shows a typical action plan. It is based on the workshop on time management. This example is a useful model to distribute at both the managers' briefing and the first workshop meeting, when you introduce your participants to action plans.

Winning Management Support

Earlier in this chapter, we looked at the objectives for conducting a managers' briefing several weeks before launching a course. Another tool for winning support from each participant's manager is the three-way agreement, as shown in figure 35-1. This form can be distributed and discussed at the managers' briefing, or it can be sent to managers as they or members of their staff enroll in the course.

Some organizations that make use of a three-way agreement treat it as a condition of enrollment. That is, the training department will not accept participants in the course unless their managers have submitted and signed the agreement.

Table 35-1. Examples of action plan entries.

Three Levels of Action	Generic and Ongoing	Specific and Occasional
Intrapersonal (within myself)	Prepare a daily to-do list and assign priorities. Test my thinking for fallacies and faulty reasons. Follow the eight-step problem-solving process in tackling the daily flow of problems that cross my desk.	When preparing my quarterly goals and standards, indicate the relative importance of each via percentages. Make a decision matrix when faced with a major selection (e.g., hiring someone, purchasing something for over $5,000). Prepare a weekly time log every three to six months to analyze how time is being spent and to track improvement.
Interpersonal (someone else and me)	Practice effective listening by summarizing and playing back to the other party what I think he or she said. Ask questions much more often to elicit facts and feelings and to cultivate commitment through increased involvement. Involve my staff in joint goal setting rather than assign goals and standards unilaterally.	Before doing a performance appraisal on Tom next month, I'll meet with him to prepare for the interview. I'll plan for Marge's meeting with me next week (counseling session) by completing the discipline planning sheet. Joanne and I will tackle the problem of high error rate in data entry. We'll work our way through the problem-solving process.
Work Group (for my staff)	Hold weekly staff meeting every Monday morning to review the status of work in process, to establish priorities for the week, to address problems and opportunities, and to foster teamwork. Get each staff member to identify at least one duty (or task, or responsibility) that no one else knows how to do, then select and train one other person in my group to do it. This will give us more flexibility in scheduling to meet the demands on our group.	I plan to conduct a training session on the difference between goals, standards, wishes, and activities, with practice in editing and rewriting them. This will help my staff to be more precise in spelling out their goals for the next quarter. Whenever I hire a new employee in the future, I will schedule that person, as part of the orientation and training in our group, to spend a half day with each member of the group.

Table 35-2. Sample time management action plan for George Brock.

What I Plan to Accomplish	When and How
1. Prepare a to-do list as my first activity of each day so as to determine priorities (A, B, C) and sequence (that is, an agenda for the day).	To be done at my desk over coffee before everyone arrives and the phone starts ringing.
2. Work with Minette and Tom to calculate the actual cost of one hour of their time at work. Then apply this to each activity they do, to see which ones are and which aren't cost-effective. We can then determine which activities should be delegated, shortened, eliminated, and so forth.	Use planning sheet titled "How Much Is an Hour of Your Time Worth." Since they are both at nearly the same salary, I can work with Minette and Tom together. Will try to set this up for the coming week.
3. Set limits on time spent on phone calls, Gang up and batch my placing and my returning of calls. Follow guidelines spelled out in workbook.	Ongoing, beginning tomorrow. I'll see if Mary can take messages for me so as not to interrupt when I'm busy on more pressing matters.
4. Plan how my time in meetings will be spent (both as a leader and participant). Negotiate starting and ending times for myself when others are calling their meetings. Follow guidelines spelled out in the workbook.	Each time a meeting is called, by me or by someone else.

Figure 35-1. Three-way agreement.

Agreement

Between the Training Department and _____ of the _____ Department.

I would like to enroll_____, who reports to me, to attend the Challenge of Management course being held on the following dates: _____. We have discussed the course objectives and content, and agree to make the following commitments so that the training will have maximum impact:

1. The participant named above will attend _____ meetings, one per week, lasting seven hours each. We will work together to arrange work flow and deal with crash projects and crises in such a way as to keep them from interrupting the course.

2. The participant will spend two to three hours in preparation for each class meeting, going through the preworkshop assignments and self-assessments. I agree that these exercises require analysis and discussion by both of us, and I will make time available for us to work together. (Average time: 10-15 minutes per week)

3. During the week following each class meeting, I will meet with the participant to review the action plan that spells out how the concepts and skills covered in the workshop might best be applied on the job. We will agree on how and when the plan might best be implemented. (Average time: 10-15 minutes per week)

4. I will meet with the participant subsequently, as needed, to provide help in carrying out the action plan. And I will plan to attend the executive briefing to be held six to eight weeks after the course is over, at which time my participant and the other participants will each report on the composite results of their action plans as carried out to date.

5. If the participant misses a class meeting or weekly review meeting with me for reasons beyond our control, we will reschedule and make up the loss (for example, in another cycle of the course or a special meeting with the instructor). If we miss two such meetings in a row, we understand that the participant will be discharged and rescheduled, if we so desire, in a subsequent cycle.

The Training Department agrees to meet the following responsibilities:
- to deliver a high-impact program that emphasizes skills development and hands-on learning
- to provide a forum where participants can learn from one another as well as from the instructor
- to avoid embarrassing any individual or department in class
- to maintain confidentiality of any sensitive information that might be brought up in class
- to serve as a liaison between the group and top management on organizational issues
- to make the learning experience enjoyable as well as beneficial.

Participant's manager: _____ Date: _____

Participant: _____ Date: _____

For Training Department: _____ Date: _____

CHAPTER 36

USING PLANNING SHEETS AND SELF-ASSESSMENTS FOR TRANSFER OF TRAINING

Whenever you are teaching procedures, the sequence of steps or phases that make up the procedure can be spelled out on a planning sheet. This should be filled out in class as participants prepare for their role plays, simulations, and other types of practice exercises. Then at the end of class, the instructor can give each participant several copies of the planning sheet for use back on the job.

Planning sheets are especially useful in strengthening the transfer of skills and procedures that may not be required of participants for months after the course is over. Examples include performance appraisals, selection interviewing, and disciplinary counseling, to name but a few.

Figure 36-1 shows an example of a discipline planning sheet, taken from a supervisory training course. Such a form is especially appropriate because discipline is often handled in the emotional heat of the moment where both parties say things they may later regret. Supervisors should use discipline as a tool for restoring desired behavior and not as punishment or a way of getting even. This planning sheet helps in making discipline a positive tool.

Actions that are procedural in nature lend themselves to the use of planning sheets. Planning sheets could be useful in undertaking any of the items on the following list. They have been drawn from courses for managers and supervisors and contain between six and 10 steps per procedure:

- problem solving
- decision making
- delegation
- project management
- career planning
- selection interviewing

Figure 36-1. Discipline planning sheet for a supervisory training course.

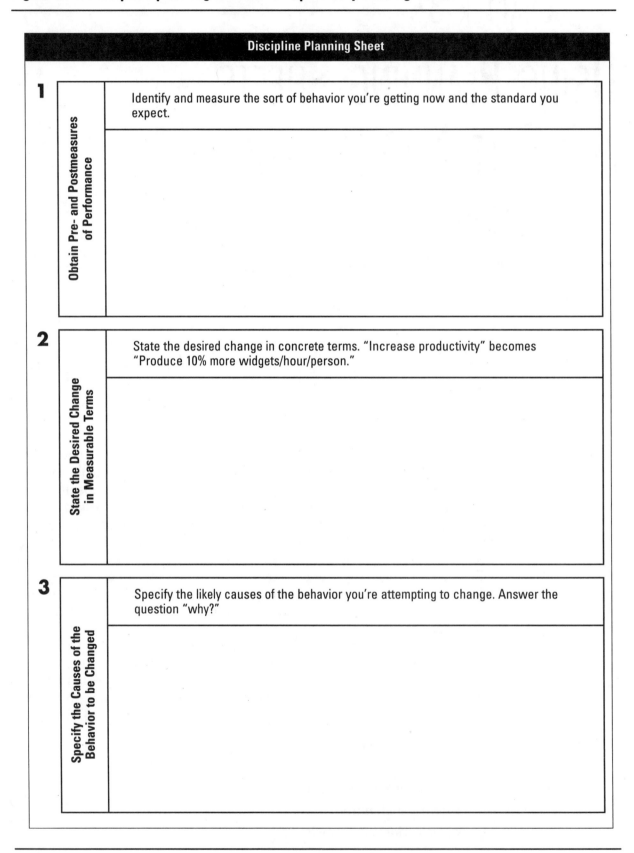

	Discipline Planning Sheet
1 Obtain Pre- and Postmeasures of Performance	Identify and measure the sort of behavior you're getting now and the standard you expect.
2 State the Desired Change in Measurable Terms	State the desired change in concrete terms. "Increase productivity" becomes "Produce 10% more widgets/hour/person."
3 Specify the Causes of the Behavior to be Changed	Specify the likely causes of the behavior you're attempting to change. Answer the question "why?"

Figure 36-1. Discipline planning sheet for a supervisory training course. *(continued)*

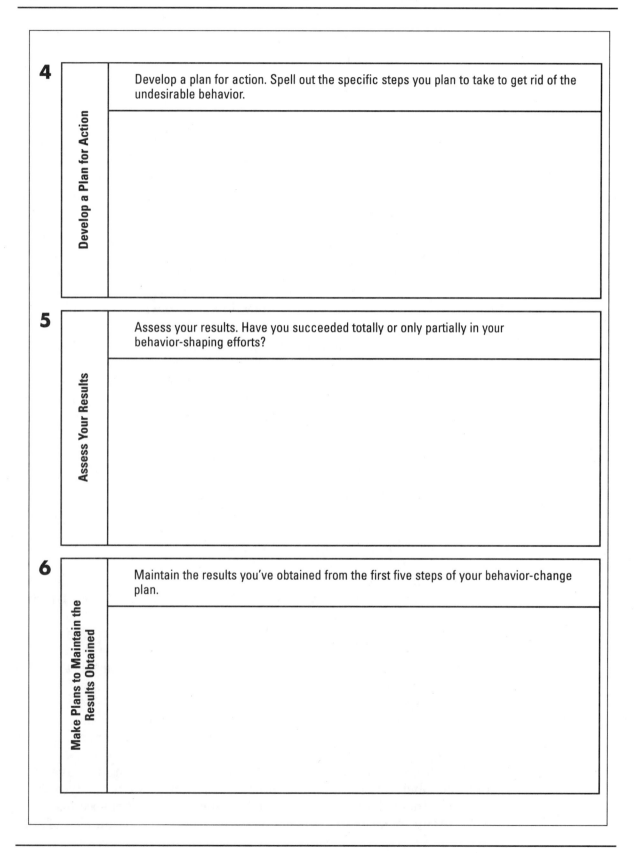

- ◆ coaching and counseling
- ◆ performance appraisal
- ◆ making a presentation
- ◆ on-the-job training
- ◆ planning a meeting
- ◆ disciplining.

How do planning sheets get created? Let's look at an example. Ford Motor Company hired a consultant to design a one-day training program on how to plan and run meetings effectively. During the needs analysis, the consultant discovered that Ford employees had two major areas of complaint about the meetings they attended: premeeting planning and postmeeting follow-up. Here are their complaints:

- ◆ Premeeting planning: The announcements of meetings rarely contained objectives or desired outcomes. Participants often came without knowing their role or what materials to bring. Often the wrong persons attended. The agenda, if any, wasn't clear. Participants didn't know in advance when the meeting would be over.

- ◆ Postmeeting follow-up: The minutes, if any, were distributed long after the meeting was over. Often they failed to indicate who would do what to implement the decisions reached or assignments made. Subsequent meetings would devote time to issues that, presumably, had been put to bed at an earlier meeting.

On the basis of these complaints, the consultant designed two planning sheets to be introduced during the training program and used by its graduates thereafter. Figure 36-2 shows a sample completed copy of the premeeting planning sheet, and figure 36-3 shows the postmeeting planning sheet.

The planning sheets you have examined so far contain a lot of white space for users to enter a description of the actions to be taken. Another form of planning sheet is the checklist, useful when a procedure contains many steps. Figure 36-4 shows the checklist you saw in chapter 13 during the description of making or buying a training program. The course designers enter the estimated dates when planning the entire project, and enter the actual dates as each step takes place. This form enables the designer to see at any given time how far ahead or behind schedule the project is running.

Planning sheets and checklists are tools for improving the transfer of training. Self-assessments are another tool that is useful in building the support of the stakeholders in the growth and development of your trainees.

Hundreds of paper-and-pencil self-scored assessments are available from suppliers of training programs. Trainees are not the only ones to complete them. Trainees can give them to other stakeholders: manager, work group members, customers, spouses, and so on. Examples of self-

Figure 36-2. Premeeting planning sheet.

Meeting Announcement/Agenda	Meeting Leader(s): _Frank_
Subject: _Proposal from Component A_ Today's Date: _Oct. 28, 1999_ Meeting Date/Time: _Nov. 1, 1999/8:30 A.M._ Duration: _Approx. 2 hrs._ Place: _Room 1152_ Confirm by Calling: _Susan on 55432_	Participants: _Tom_ _Sharon_ _Chris_ _Mike_ _Pat_

Desired Outcomes:

- To identify the pros and cons of absorbing workload from component A

- To identify at least two possible alternatives to absorbing the workload directly into our operation

- To develop a list of additional information required before we can respond to Component A's proposal

Background Materials:	Please Bring:
Please read proposal from Component A (attached)	• _Summary of workload/employee_ • _Current overtime schedule_ • _List of pending projects_ • _Projected personnel changes_

Order of Agenda Items	Persons Responsible	Process	Time Allocated
• Factors surrounding Component A's proposal	Frank	Report	10 min.
• Pros and cons of the proposal	Tom	Brainstorm	30 min.
• Alternative actions (at least two)	Chris	Discussion and consensus decision	30 min.
• Additional information/ back-up required	Mike	Rank order from list of pros and cons	40 min.

Figure 36-3. Postmeeting follow-up.

Meeting Recap	Participants:	Frank Tom Sharon Chris Mike

Subject: *Proposal from Component A*

Date of Meeting: *Nov. 1, 1999*

Recap Prepared by: *Sharon*

Additional Copies to: *Pat*

Content Summary: *Frank called a meeting of all department supervisors to discuss the proposal submitted by Component A regarding a workload transfer. After a brainstorming session, numerous issues (both pro and con) were identified. Additionally, two possible alternatives to the current proposal were suggested: to outsource all of the work or to transfer only part of the workload to us. It was determined that more information was required and various group members volunteered to obtain the needed data.*

Actions to Be Taken	By Whom	When
• Determine specific type and amount of work to be transferred	Tom	Nov. 11
• Develop a status report on our department's projected workload and personnel requirements through year end	Sharon	Nov. 15
• Identify cost of outsourcing the work	Chris	Nov. 11
• Determine compatibility of the equipment	Mike	Nov. 4
• Follow up on above and schedule next meeting	Frank	Nov. 10

Figure 36-4. Sample checklist for planning a course design.

New Course Design: Planning Sheet

Course Title: _____   Designer: _____

Client: _____   Date: _____
(individual and organization and department)

		Estimated Dates	Actual Dates
ANALYSIS	1. Prepare Request for Training (feasibility analysis)	_____	_____
	2. Meet to agree on resources, costs, schedule	_____	_____
	3. Conduct needs analysis to identify E.B., T.B., and workplace + and −	_____	_____
	4. Report results and recommend broad objectives	_____	_____
DESIGN	5. Prepare specific course objectives (mediating and terminal behaviors)	_____	_____
	6. Select and sequence content; reference the sources	_____	_____
	7. Determine appropriate instructional methods, both input and output	_____	_____
	8. Select appropriate media and delivery system	_____	_____
	9. Specify how learners' performance will be evaluated (methods and media)	_____	_____
	10. Complete course blueprint and get approval	_____	_____
DEVELOPMENT	11. Review content and intent (objectives) for congruence	_____	_____
	12. Prepare scripts, text, visuals, and hands-on exercises (role plays, case methods, simulations, lab work, etc.), module by module	_____	_____
	13. Seek independent review and edit by writer, subject matter experts, instructional technologists, client	_____	_____
	14. Prepare end-of-course assessment of learners' proficiency	_____	_____
	15. Revise course materials based on input from step 13	_____	_____
	16. Prepare instructor guidelines	_____	_____
	17. Produce tryout edition and run pilot cycle of course	_____	_____
	18. Revise course based on results of tryout	_____	_____
PRODUCTION	19. Conduct briefing and obtain approval to go into production	_____	_____
	20. Produce components of course (videotapes, PC disks, workbooks, etc.)	_____	_____
	21. Announce course availability and dates; promote success story	_____	_____
	22. Assemble and store all components of course	_____	_____
DELIVERY	23. Conduct instructor training workshops, if appropriate	_____	_____
	24. Ship course material as ordered	_____	_____
	25. Monitor course delivery and evaluate impact (step 14)	_____	_____
	26. Prepare success story and cost-benefit analysis, if appropriate	_____	_____

assessments are shown in Table 36-1, which lists a variety of courses and suggests the type of self-assessment that might be appropriate for each.

Since the purpose of these self-assessments is to strengthen the transfer of training, participants should select someone who knows them well and is interested in their growth and development. This stakeholder and the participant can then compare the results of the assessment that they have each completed.

The last entry in table 36-1 mentions an instructor critique sheet. Figure 36-5 shows the sheet that participants can use after the train-the-trainer workshop to evaluate themselves and to have other instructors do likewise.

Table 36-1. Examples of courses and their self-assessments.

Course Title or Topic	Description of Self-Assessment Exercise
Time Management	Participants keep a weekly time log; they review with managers.
Writing Skills	Participants analyze two samples of their writing and share results with their managers.
Supervisory Training	Participants assess their supervisory style and ask their managers to do the same, using two copies of the self-assessment. They then score the instruments and discuss the results.
Sales Training	Salespersons assess their communication style and ask regular customers to do the same. They then compare the results.
Selection Interviewing	Interviewers and their managers assess their personal style (Carl Jung's "psychological types"—sensor, intuitor, thinker, feeler) and compare their scores.
Management Development	Participants distribute multirater 360 assessments of competencies to their managers, peers, and staff, who evaluate them anonymously.
Team Building	Team members complete a climate survey that measures the team's strengths and weaknesses.
Listening Skills	Participants give assessment to their spouse or other family member or close friend, who then evaluates the person against the list of criteria of an effective listener.
Train-the-Trainer	Each participant leaves the workshop with copies of an instructor critique sheet and asks other instructors to sit in on a future class and complete the critique.

Figure 36-5. Instructor critique sheet.

Class given by _____

on the topic: _____

How effective was the instructor in satisfying each of the following criteria? Place an X in the column that applies.

	Excellent	Good	Average	Inadequate	Poor or Omitted
1. Making the topic and objectives (what and why) clear at the start of the class	___	___	___	___	___
2. Establishing the need and the level of understanding (entering behavior) of participants	___	___	___	___	___
3. Breaking up the information input (S) so as to get responses (R) that measure understanding	___	___	___	___	___
4. Eliciting relevant responses from all participants and not just the verbal minority	___	___	___	___	___
5. Giving immediate and sufficient feedback to learners (F) so as to confirm or correct their understanding	___	___	___	___	___
6. Maintaining an appropriate balance between input and output (acquisition-demonstration-application)	___	___	___	___	___
7. Using the flipchart, board, overhead projector, or other audio-visual aids appropriately	___	___	___	___	___
8. Using handouts appropriately (reference materials, job aids, flow charts, hands-on exercises, demonstrations, tests, etc.)	___	___	___	___	___
9. Creating and maintaining student interest via good pacing, wording, analogies, delivery, humor, etc.	___	___	___	___	___
10. Summarizing and giving closure to the class so that it ends on a positive note of high impact and commitment	___	___	___	___	___
11. Managing the time effectively (avoiding spending too much or too little time on parts of the class; sticking to schedule)	___	___	___	___	___
12. Preparing and following an outline that served as an appropriate road map for the journey	___	___	___	___	___
	4	3	2	1	0

Directions for scoring: Add up the number of Xs in each column, then multiply by the value indicated to the right to get the final score in each column. The sum of these five scores indicates the overall effectiveness of the instructor. Out of a possible "perfect" score of 48, this instructor earned a score of . . . . ☐

Additional comments, suggestions, reactions:

Summary

In this chapter, we have examined three types of document that instructors can make or buy to improve the transfer of training from workshop to workplace. They are planning sheets, checklists, and self-assessments that can be shared with the participants' stakeholders after a class or course is over. Some of our examples highlight the fact that today's instructors are in the business of delivering workplace performance and not merely imparting information.

MEASURING THE EFFECTIVENESS OF TRAINING

Top management wants to know what results the organization is getting from the hundreds of thousands of dollars spent annually on training. Instructors and course designers want to know what impact their programs are having on individuals and the organization. Trainees and their supervisors want to know what kind of payoff they can expect from taking time away from productive work to participate in a course.

In short, the evaluation of training's impact is a hot topic. Most organizations evaluate participants' reaction to their courses and how well they learned the material—Kirkpatrick's levels one and two. However, relatively few organizations evaluate the impact of training at levels three and four: Did the participants perform better at work? Did training yield a return-on-investment (ROI)? The chapters that follow address these levels of evaluation:

Chapter 37, "The Case for Value-Added Assessment," presents the Kirkpatrick four-level evaluation model, describes the pros and cons of measuring at levels three and four, cites examples of the value added at each of the four levels, and relates the Kirkpatrick model to the five components of a training system.

Chapter 38, "The Evaluation of Training," identifies three categories of behavior, lists 10 questions to be answered during evaluation, and presents 12 minilessons relating to how evaluation should be conducted.

Chapter 39, "Measuring Training's ROI," lists eight reasons for avoiding level four evaluations and nine reasons for carrying out a cost-benefit analysis, along with a description of four ways of calculating training's ROI, eight observations on conducting a cost-benefit analysis, and four case studies to illustrate cost-benefit analysis in different organizational settings.

Chapter 40, "Conducting a Cost-Benefit Analysis," presents a case study that contains a worksheet for calculating costs of three types (one-time, per offering, and per participant) and benefits at three points of time. Costs appear in seven categories and benefits in four categories. By going though this case study, you will learn how to conduct a cost-benefit analysis.

Upon completing this section, you should be able to:

◆ describe the data to be collected at each of Kirkpatrick's four levels

◆ give examples of when to measure and when to skip levels three and four

◆ cite examples of value added at each of the four levels of evaluation

◆ relate the four stages of evaluation to the five-stage systems model

◆ indicate questions used in formative, summative, and correlative evaluation

◆ describe at least four of the 12 lessons on how to evaluate training

◆ state the four ways to measure ROI on training

◆ list seven categories of training costs and four of benefits.

CHAPTER 37

THE CASE FOR VALUE-ADDED ASSESSMENT

Trainers need to know how they're doing, as figure 37-1 shows. The model in the figure is based on Kirkpatrick's (1998) four levels of evaluation.

Data are easiest to generate at the top of the model and progressively harder to collect and to interpret (that is, attribute to training) as we go down the model. The effects being measured are short range at the top of the model and progressively longer range as we descend (that is, more permanent and more delayed before we can observe and measure them).

Estimates indicate that over 85 percent of all training programs are evaluated at level one. This number drops progressively as we descend, with fewer than 10 percent being measured at level four.

Figure 37-1. Trainers' four levels of evaluation.

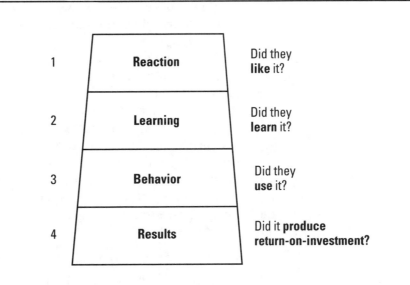

1	Reaction	Did they **like** it?
2	Learning	Did they **learn** it?
3	Behavior	Did they **use** it?
4	Results	Did it **produce return-on-investment?**

These observations should not surprise us. Levels one and two are concerned with the learner's behavior in class or upon completion of the training. Thus, they can usually be measured by relatively simple paper-and-pencil exercises, such as end-of-course evaluation sheets for level one and mastery tests for level two. Such instruments are relatively easy to create and administer and even to interpret, requiring only tallying, scoring, and summarizing.

In contrast, levels three and four are concerned with learners' behavior after the training is over, sometimes long after, as in courses on selection interviewing, performance appraisal, or selling to a multinational client, where it may be months or years before learners have a chance to apply what they learned in class. Although trainers attempt to apply the just-in-time concept and want to offer their programs at a time and place that enables learners to take courses just before they need them, it is virtually impossible to do so in most organizations. Thus, any failure to get satisfactory results when we evaluate at levels three and four may be attributable to the decline in performance due to time lapse (a natural consequence of all training and education) and not to any inadequacy on the part of the learner, the instructor, or the course design.

Self-instructional courses, such as those via computer, text, and interactive video, can help to overcome the delay factor by making training available when the learner needs, not when the instructor and organization offer, it. But self-study has its limits with learners who need the personal touch and with courses that require hands-on learning or interaction with other learners, through role plays, the case method, lab work, and the like.

Workshop Versus Workplace

Just as scientists require an uncontaminated environment in which to limit the factors they evaluate in their experiments, instructors and course designers need one in which to conduct their evaluations. Instructors and course designers have a pure environment in class or self-study to take readings at levels one and two. The learners are captive, relatively free of workplace distractions, and usually motivated to learn—or at least to keep the instructor happy enough to get through the training without hassle or incident.

In contrast, their performance back in the workplace (as measured by levels three and four) is influenced by many variables not addressed in class. They operate in a "contaminated" environment, and no one can control the intervening variables (or even hold them constant or equate for them) so that we might attribute the learners' performance to training alone. Rather, behavior on the job must be attributed to the whole pandemic array of factors influencing how people perform at work, including the following factors:

◆ relevancy of what was taught to what is needed to perform

◆ immediacy of opportunity to apply (discussed earlier)

◆ supportiveness of the learner's immediate supervisor

- ◆ degree to which peers practice what the learner is trying to apply
- ◆ time, money, and resources to support the new behavior
- ◆ rewards and punishments that reinforce behavior (maintaining and correcting)
- ◆ agreement of forms, equipment, procedures between workshop and workplace
- ◆ culture that fosters the learner's long-range performance
- ◆ workplace environment free of distractions, interruptions, and physical constraints
- ◆ immediacy and specificity of feedback that lets employees know how they are doing.

When to Measure at Levels Three and Four

Although the foregoing list might be enough to discourage the staunchest trainer from going beyond the use of smiles sheets and end-of-course tests, there are a number of situations in which the behaviors elicited in class are virtually identical to the performance required on the job. In other words, environmental contamination is minimal. In such cases, level three and four data may be relatively easy to obtain. Courses that deal with the following are examples:

- ◆ safety, drugs, and alcohol (for example, the number of occurrences before and after training)
- ◆ data processing (for example, order entry and inventory control)
- ◆ assembly line procedures (such as soldering, crimping, screwing, and gluing)
- ◆ processing of paperwork (for example, bank tellers and insurance claims processors)
- ◆ customer service (for example, customer service reps behind desk in banks, airports, and hotels).

These jobs are ones where it is possible to measure the quantity and quality of output, number of transactions per hour, number of errors (rejects, overs, shorts, and reworks) per 1,000 units or transactions, and so on.

Level three and four measurements might also be feasible in jobs in which people have a high degree of control over how their time is spent and in which their work is relatively independent of direct supervision or the intervention of other employees. Some examples include:

- ◆ salespersons with accounts and commissions (for example, real estate, manufacturers' representatives, and insurance agents)
- ◆ workers in trades and crafts (such as electricians, plumbers, and carpenters)
- ◆ creative workers (such as computer programmers, designers, writers, and consultants)

- truck deliverypeople (such as route drivers, postal service, messengers, and couriers).

As we look over the types of jobs in which the factors influencing performance are present or absent, we come to several conclusions that can serve as guidelines in deciding whether or not to measure at levels three and four:

- The farther down the organization chart you are training, the easier it is to collect data on performance at work and its impact on the organization's mission and bottom line. Conversely, the farther up you go (that is, to supervisory, managerial, and executive levels), the harder it is to quantify and to observe output.

- The more directly responsible employees are for their own output and the more influence they have over the variables affecting output (that is, line jobs versus staff jobs, producing goods versus services), the easier it is to go to levels three and four.

- The more control employees have over how they spend their time (for example, service repair, taxi driver, consultant), the more accountability they have for demonstrating results and return-on-investment at level four.

- The more direct influence an employee's performance has on earnings (for example, sales commissions, stock options, profit-sharing commissions, bonus, incentives), the greater the likelihood that the employee will work extremely hard at overcoming workplace factors that get in the way of outstanding performance.

When to Skip Levels Three and Four

To the results-oriented manager or owner, there's a certain appeal to the argument that levels one and two don't count. That person might say: "We're not paying employees to like the course or, for that matter, to learn. We're paying them to perform, and training has added no value to the organization until it can demonstrate that it produced improved performance in the workplace and contributed to the attainment of our mission and objective: a return on the investment."

There are several fallacies to this argument, and they are identified by the four facts that follow. When these facts are present in your training programs, it may mean that you should either skip data collection in the workplace or settle for opinions of impact (subjective and soft data) rather than measures of performance (objective and hard data).

- *Fact A: Some workplace behaviors cannot be measured objectively.* We teach supervisors how to do performance appraisals that are constructive, interactive, supportive, focused on performance rather than personality, and legal. But how can the course's impact be measured? We cannot observe our graduates as they conduct appraisals, a rather private affair. Even if both parties agreed willingly to be observed, the presence of an observer would contaminate the appraisal and we would not get a reliable reading. True, we might examine the comments entered on the appraisal form after the review, assuming we get permission. This might show us whether our supervisors have focused on performance rather than personality. But we are still left without any objective measure of the review itself. So we can try for subjective, soft data (for example, by surveying supervisors and their employees, getting their opinions on pre- and posttraining behavior during reviews). Or we can abandon attempts to measure at levels three and four.

◆ *Fact B: Some workplace behaviors may never occur.* Workers may never have to give artificial respiration, operate a fire extinguisher, use karate or jujitsu on an assailant, handle a burglary at a bank, terminate an employee, evacuate a 727 airplane in a water landing, tow a drowning person to shore, or manage a nuclear power plant reactor in a crisis. The ultimate example, of course, is military training. Governments spend billions of dollars annually training the armed services to perform complex operations under combat conditions that, God willing, they will never have to do. In all of these situations, the usual way to assess at level three is to create simulations, a sort of fail-safe approximation of the real thing. But the trainees know it isn't for real, and the emotional response is very different.

◆ *Fact C: Some workplace behaviors cost too much to measure.* We teach supervisors how to do selection interviews. We could follow up by sending a professional evaluator, such as a consultant or psychologist, as a job applicant to each trained supervisor who had a job opening during the three months following training (along with actual applicants, of course, that the personnel department would screen and provide). But this would be expensive, time-consuming, and lead to questions of ethics and appropriateness. What if supervisors found out that they are being shopped, for example? What effect would this have on their level of trust in training and human resource development? To deal with the issue of trust, many companies that shop their graduates will make the practice known during the training. Examples include telephone operators, airline reservationists, and bank tellers.

◆ *Fact D: Most workplace behaviors cannot be attributed to training alone.* Figure 37-2 shows many other factors that influence performance. When behavior is significantly better following a course, trainers are quick to take credit. When it isn't, trainers are quick to cite all the workplace factors that intervened (much like the advertising agency that claims credit for an ad campaign when sales go up, but cites recessionary trends and a flat economy when sales fail to result). The size of

Figure 37-2. Factors affecting performance.

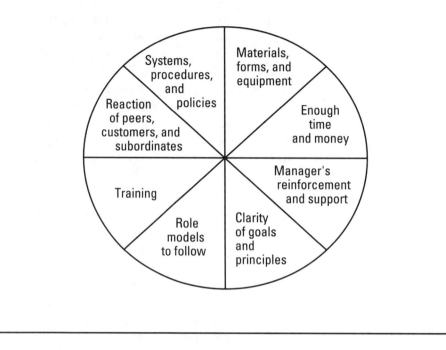

each wedge in the figure differs with each course and each job. The larger the influence of other wedges relative to the size of the training wedge, the harder (and more dangerous) it is for trainers to attribute workplace performance to workshop efforts.

Value-Added Assessment

We have now come to the realization that often the results of training can't be measured (facts A and B), cost too much to measure (fact C), or can't be attributed to training (fact D). This should not lead us to abandon training anymore than the absence of a viable means of measuring the impact of religion on the quality of life (personal and societal) should not lead us to close houses of worship. Although we cannot document the impact of its presence, evaluating the impact of its absence is a far less desirable option. As the saying goes, if you think education is expensive, try ignorance!

But, this act of faith approach avoids evaluation altogether. A different approach borrows the value-added concept from the field of economics and looks at the stages a learner goes through during the course of a training program.

In economics, value is added to a final product or service each time an operation is performed. Consider a loaf of bread on your table. The first value was added when the farmer grew wheat. Then value was added at each of the following stages:

- ◆ when the miller ground the wheat into flour
- ◆ when the baker converted flour and other ingredients into bread
- ◆ when the truck driver delivered the loaf to your home or a store.

In some countries, each contributor pays a value-added tax proportional to the contribution and its impact on final value.

Four Levels of Evaluation

Let's apply this rationale to the evaluation of training each time an operation is performed. Table 37-1 lists four operations in the sequence in which they occur throughout the life of a course. We've identified the value-adding components of each, along with a description of how the value added might be assessed.

A Systems Approach to Evaluation

System is a word we use often. People seem to have a system for almost everything they do, yet most of us would be hard pressed to define the word. (If you don't believe it, close your eyes and try!) That's why we've provided this model of a system, any system.

To prove its universality, consider a heating system and label the components, shown in figure 37-3. Fuel and air are *inputs,* combustion and distribution (radiation, conduction, or convection) are *processes, BTUs* are the *output.* The *goal* is to keep the building within a certain temperature range (say 65-70 degrees F), and the *feedback,* or *control,* is provided by the thermostat. Notice that although the goal appears at the right, defining it is the *first* step in the design of any system. It is also often the most difficult step. How many trainers during a needs analysis have asked managers what behaviors and goals they expect of their trainees and been given answers such as: "I want my people to appreciate the importance of... or to understand why the company... or to know our business better...." Alas, these are wishes, not measurable goals.

In the model, its five parts line up rather neatly with our four levels of evaluation:

- ◆ Input and process correspond with levels one and two and can be measured in class.
- ◆ Output and goals correspond with levels three and four and must be measured in the workplace.

Thus, as we move from left to right on our model, we meet in sequence the four levels of evaluation.

Table 37-1. Value-adding components and assessment of a course.

Four Levels	Operation	Value-Adding Components	How Assessed
Level One Reaction	A course is researched, designed or selected, and presented.	◆ Needs analysis · ◆ Instructional design and development · · ◆ Course materials · · · · · · · · · · · · · · · · · · · ◆ Instructor's delivery skills · · · · · · · · · · · · ◆ Learning facilities · · · · · · · · · · · · · · · · · · · ◆ Program time and timing · · · · · · · · · · · · · ◆ Selection of participants. · · · · · · · · · · · · ·	Evaluation sheets measure learners' reactions to such things as: content relevancy and use format, methods, and media readability, graphics, and image pacing, clarity, and fun comfort, location, and meals when offered and length homogeneity and networking.
Level Two Learning	Subject matter (course content, K-A-S) is delivered to learners.	◆ **K**nowledge is imparted (facts, rules, procedures, policies, concepts, theory, etc.). ◆ **A**ttitudes are shaped (values, perceptions, beliefs, styles, feelings, etc.). ◆ **S**kills are practiced to develop competence (many types of skills, such as perceptual, verbal, cognitive, manual, and psychomotor).	Learners are evaluated throughout training to see how well they are acquiring K-A-S; end-of-course mastery test is used if appropriate.
Level Three Behavior	Learners translate workshop learning into workplace behavior.	Improvement in such individual data as: ◆ Quantity of work ◆ Quality of work ◆ Time to reach competency.	Learners' output is measured; evaluation by self and others; performance in simulations or activities done off line (such as in an assessment lab).
Level Four Results	The organization reaps the harvest of improved workplace performance.	Improvement in such organizational data as: ◆ Overall productivity of plant and department ◆ Market share ◆ Profitability ◆ Work teams without supervision ◆ Reduced cost of lawsuits, insurance claims, lost business, accidents, and turnover.	Cost-benefit analysis or pre- and posttraining comparison of data already in the system (accident rate, new accounts, rejects, absenteeism, and turnover within 90 days).

Figure 37-3. Model of a system.

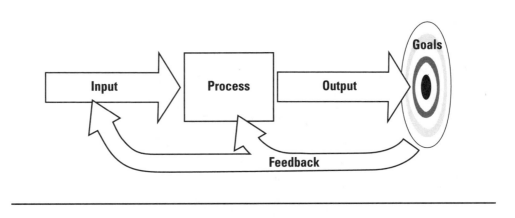

As for feedback, the fifth part of our systems model, this component corresponds to the methods by which we collect data on the effectiveness of training and translate it into modifications in the inputs or the instructional process.

This brings us to the primal question: Why evaluate training? This question is similar to asking, "Why have a thermostat on a heating system?" Without it, a building would alternate between being too hot and too cold, and there would be no way to make the performance of the system better over time. The evaluation of training enables instructors, course designers, participants, their managers, and anyone concerned with improved performance at work to have data that enable them to fine-tune and constantly strengthen the impact of training.

Reference

Kirkpatrick, D.L. (1998). *Evaluating Training Programs*. San Francisco: Berrett-Koehler.

CHAPTER 38

THE EVALUATION OF TRAINING

Trainers require feedback. They need to know how well they are meeting their course objectives, how well their trainees are acquiring the course content, how relevant the content is to their job and their needs outside the classroom, how the trainees are reacting to the course (subject matter, instructional methods, pacing, length, and the like), and what organizational performance improvement can be attributed to training.

Senior management also wants to know what return they are getting on the training investment. Firms like GM, IBM, and AT&T spend close to a billion dollars annually on training. Dozens of other organizations count their costs of employee training in millions of dollars. Human resource development (HRD) management is evolving into a technology in which the costs and the benefits of training are scrutinized by the same steely eyes that allocate funds to other investments of the organization's time and resources. They measure worth by looking at the return on each investment.

There are three categories of behavior to be measured when evaluating training: formative, summative, and correlative. Every trainer must decide which of these is important, and collect data accordingly. Following is a description of each:

◆ **Formative evaluation:** Here we are measuring the learner's progress and the degree to which our learning objectives are and aren't being met. The focus here is on mediating behavior and the attainment of new knowledge, attitudes, and skills that can be shaped and observed during training. These measures are of primary value to the trainee and the instructor as input to their efficient management of the learning process. Formative evaluations are conducted before training (to establish bench levels of the learner's entering behavior) and during training (to diagnose needs) and at the end of training (to document the acquisition of new knowledge, attitudes, and skills).

◆ **Summative Evaluation:** Here we are measuring the learner's performance after training and the degree to which the behavior back at work meets the expectations that prompted the training. The focus here is on job standards, performance criteria, productivity measures, the attainment of organizational objectives, and so on. These behaviors must be observed and measured in the workplace, where many reinforcers and constraints are influencing the trainee's performance. Thus we are measuring transfer of training and not simply acquisition. These measures are of primary value to line managers and those responsible for the allocation of training resources. Conscientious instructors are also concerned with summative evaluation.

◆ **Correlative Evaluation:** Here we are concerned with evaluating those aspects of course design and delivery that should correlate with the formative and summative measures of performance The focus here is on course content (such as its relevance, clarity, and timeliness), course design, appropriateness of methods and media, time allocation and flow, and delivery (such as an instructor's skills, pacing, responsiveness to needs, how learners felt about the instructor or other delivery systems used). Thus we are measuring means rather than ends (that is, the means used to shape the learner's formative and summative performance). These measures are of primary value to the instructor and course designer as input to revisions or modifications before the course is next offered.

In short, formative evaluations measure learners' progress during training. Summative evaluations measure their performance after training and in the workplace. Correlative evaluations measure the performance of the instructional system (how well the course designer and instructor have filled their respective responsibilities).

Table 38-1 reviews the different types of formative, summative, and correlative tools instructors might use to answer different types of questions. As you examine the questions in the table, decide which ones are most useful in meeting your objectives (that is, your reasons for collecting evaluation data). Then decide for each one what method or methods will help you get the answers you want.

Twelve Lessons on How to Evaluate Training

Many potential snares and pitfalls await the unwary trainer when embarking on an evaluation. Since forewarned is forearmed, we have included a dozen lessons that should make your job easier. The first six contain dos and don'ts, and the next six deal with concepts that should provide insights into the evaluation process.

Table 38-1. Questions to ask in evaluating training.

	Questions to Be Answered	Tools and Techniques for Measuring
Formative	1. How well did the learners acquire the knowledge?	Paper-and-pencil text administered in class, as progress test or criterion text, at the end.
	2. What change in attitude took place?	Climate survey, attitudinal assessments that measure values, perceptions, style, teamwork, motivation, beliefs, etc.
	3. What improvement skills does learner show?	Simulations as an assessment, observations in class, measures of competency, etc.
Summative	4. What performance improvement (actual) took place on the job?	Hard data on productivity (output, rejects, etc.) and follow-up on action plan in which each participant spells out new behaviors back at work.
	5. What performance improvement (perceived) took place on the job?	Climate survey, rating by self, manager, etc. on proficiency, and other surveys completed after training.
	6. How much did it cost relative to benefits?	Calculate the dollar value of benefits in 4-5, then compare with total cost of training.
Correlative	7. How relevant was the content to the participant's needs?	Comparison of results of needs analysis with objectives and content of course; end-of-course ratings of relevancy, etc.
	8. How well did the participants like the course?	Evaluation sheets distributed at end of course or sent to the participant back on the job.
	9. How appropriate was the course design?	Critique of course design by instructional systems designer or other expert.
	10. How competent was the instructor?	Instructional skills assessment, instructor evaluation sheet, end-of-course ratings.

1. Evaluation must start before you train. Afterward is too late. It must begin with the needs analysis before you design or conduct training for the following reasons: (a) to get commitment on what to evaluate (course objectives) and how to evaluate after training, (b) to measure gain and document your impact (pre- and postmeasurement improvements), (c) to identify reinforcers and constraints in the workplace that will help or hinder your graduates in applying what they learned, (d) so you can get agreement on expectations of the managers of your

trainees, (e) so you can start to develop a maintenance system that will support and reinforce the desired behavior back on the job.

2. You must evaluate three things before you train. First, evaluate the trainees' entering behavior (E.B.): What knowledge, attitudes, and skills do the trainees bring you that you can build on? Second, evaluate the needs and expectations of the organization. Then establish the terminal behavior (T.B.) that you expect of your trainees after training. Finally, evaluate the workplace in which the trainees are expected to perform to see what factors will support or extinguish the desired behavior, so that you can maximize the reinforcers and minimize the constraints. Trainers are gap fillers who close the gap between E.B. and T.B. Thus, you must know both if you are to evaluate the effectiveness of training.

3. Evaluation must be an integral part of the instructional process. Unlike the public schools, where evaluation is done mainly through tests, training sessions should provide maximum opportunity for hands-on learning and frequent responses by trainees. This gives trainer and trainee alike the frequent feedback they both need to be sure that the learning objectives are being met. By teaching more deductively, using small group exercises, and being learner centered, the trainer does not need a lot of formal testing to evaluate progress. Evaluation can take place informally at each class. Such a course design is more efficient (that is, it makes better use of group time), more pleasant (few people like tests, instructors included), and more effective (it produces higher levels of performance).

4. Formal evaluation should be done by someone besides the trainer. Instructors have a vested interest in getting high evaluations. Moreover, they can develop end-of-course tests and rating sheets to show anything they want. Professionals should develop the tools and techniques of evaluation, and the process of evaluation should be supervised by impartial persons, such as a training advisory committee of line managers, an outside consultant, and the like. Data collected by the trainee and his or her manager are often more acceptable than the trainer's evaluation data.

5. An up-front performance contract makes evaluation easier. Effective training is the responsibility of three persons: trainer, trainee, and trainee's manager. All three must agree on the expected outcomes and on when and how they will be measured. All three must perform if the desired outcomes are to be met. Agreement on roles and responsibilities by the three principles at the start helps to ensure that the training will be more effective, the outcomes will be easier to evaluate, the criteria will be agreed upon in advance, and the responsibility for evaluation will have been established.

6. Delayed evaluation is better. Although it's easier to evaluate trainees while they are still "captive," we can only evaluate their mediating (enabling) behavior in class. However, if we're interested in transfer of training from class to job, then we must go to the workplace and take our evaluation measurements after the intervening variables (reinforcers

and constraints) have had their impact on the trainee's performance. Some trainers will say, "That's not my department. I have no control over what happens after training." However, the strong trend in HRD is toward an organization development (OD) approach that starts with workplace behavior and regards workshop behavior as a subset and supportive (mediating, enabling) element.

7. The higher we train, the harder it is to evaluate the results. Employees at lower levels of the organization chart are relatively easy to evaluate. Job standards and expectations are clearer, more quantitative, more observable. But as we move into professional and managerial positions, evaluating the results of training becomes more difficult. Indeed, in many instances the trainee and his or her manager bear the primary responsibility for giving the trainer feedback on the effectiveness of training. The trainer's role is to help them to define *effectiveness* in operational terms rather than in ratings of relevance, timeliness, and popularity.

8. There are 10 questions to be answered when we evaluate, as shown in table 38-1. Often the trainer lacks the need or the tolerance to answer all of them. Thus, we must decide what objectives we wish our evaluation to accomplish before we decide which of the 10 questions we want to answer. Here are some of the reasons for evaluating: to give remedial instruction, to redesign parts of the course, to improve the delivery, to justify the expenditure, to promote the program, and to maintain new behaviors back on the job. Of the 10 questions to be answered, three are formative, three are summative, and four are correlative.

9. There are five levels on the abstraction ladder, as figure 38-1 shows. Where do we collect our evaluation data? Where should we take our readings? Our data will range from hard to soft, from fact to opinion, from concrete experience to verbal abstractions of it, depending on how far up or down the ladder we choose to evaluate. At the bottom is concrete experience on the job, performance at work. Next comes simulation where we rate the trainee's own performance. Next comes evaluation of the trainee's response to situations via case method or situational analysis, which is often vicarious rather than personal. Next comes appraisal by others, such as peers, boss, subordinates, and customers. Finally, there are verbal abstractions of reality, where trainees describe the correct and incorrect behavior in response to questions or situations.

10. We don't know what we don't know. Perhaps the biggest lesson to be learned on evaluation is the realization that we know what we know, but we don't know what we don't know. Hence, evaluation via any method other than direct observation of hard data back on the job is going to be suspect and shaky. Questionnaires, interviews, survey research are peripheral to the central issue of evaluation: Can we see improved performance on the job in objective, measurable ways? Hence the current interest in competency-based instruction and in assessment in which trainees respond to real-world stimuli rather than classroom stimuli.

Figure 38-1. Five levels of evaluation data.

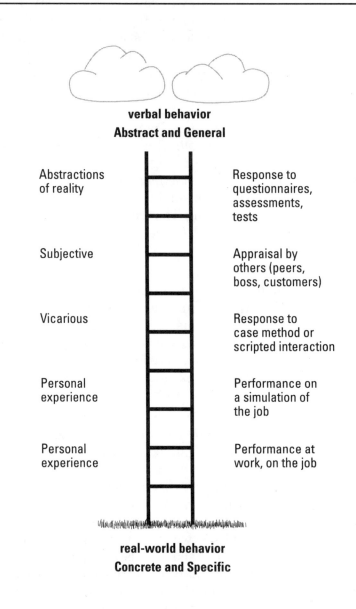

11. Respondents will often say what they think you want to hear. Any form of survey research, whether questionnaires, interviews, or something else, faces this reality. Thus, your trainees and their managers find it easy to take the path of least resistance and give good evaluations to your course. It is more difficult to be objective and analytical in assessing a course and its impact. The questions must be specific, unbiased, and open-ended enough to accommodate for a full range of ratings.

12. Evaluation should yield costs and benefits data for senior management. Although senior management is interested in formative and correlative evaluation data, the bottom-line results that it wants to see can only be answered through summative evaluation. This is the most difficult of the three types of measurements because it must be done in the workplace where the person who has been trained must deal with many constraints that affect transfer of training and the degree of return on the training investment.

CHAPTER 39

MEASURING TRAINING'S ROI

Training doesn't cost...it pays! HRD is an investment, not an expense.

Rare is the trainer who doesn't believe this. Far more common is the trainer who doesn't believe that return on the training investment can (or even should) be calculated.

Should all training programs be required to show a return-on-investment (ROI)? Not at all. However, courses of three days or more that are offered many times to reach a large number of trainees (say 100 or more) represent a significant expense. The professional trainer should justify this expense by calculating the return on this investment.

ROI is level four, results, on Donald Kirkpatrick's (1998) evaluation model, and it's the most difficult result to measure. Level one, reaction, and level two, learning, can be measured with relative ease in class, using paper-and-pencil instruments and simulations. Level three, behavior at work, is more difficult because it means measuring performance on the job where many variables are affecting the performance of our graduates. Level four, results, is usually shown as a return-on-investment: the value in dollars of the benefits of training over and above the cost of the training.

Many factors make this level of measurement the most difficult by far. Here are some of the more common difficulties that are cited as reasons for not doing a level four evaluation:

- The costs of training are known and expressed in dollars, but the benefits are often soft, subjective, and difficult to quantify and convert to dollars.

- We have enough trouble getting managers to send people to training without imposing additional requirements to collect data to document the impact.

- Costs are known up-front, before training, but benefits may accrue slowly over time. At what point after training do you attempt to measure impact?

◆ As trainers, we lack the time and the needed accounting skills to do a cost-benefit analysis. Besides, our requests for data are disruptive of productivity.

◆ We will probably continue to run most of our training programs that are popular even if costs exceed benefits. So why bother? We're not a profit center.

◆ The outcomes could be damaging to the HRD staff and to budget support from top management. We may be better off not knowing.

◆ People at work perform the way they do for many reasons, only one of which relates to training. How can we take credit or blame for their performance?

◆ The very act of collecting data on the dollar value of performance will tend to bias the information we get, making it hard for us to present a true picture.

If you've been looking for some reasons for not evaluating the ROI of your training efforts, read no further. This list should enable you to persuade the most insistent believer that any attempt to prove that training pays for itself is sheer folly! Let sleeping dogs lie. What we don't know can't hurt us. Right?

Wrong! Lest we be accused of favoritism, let's give equal time to a list of reasons why we should take the time and effort to calculate the costs and the benefits of our major training programs. Here are some supporting reasons:

◆ HRD budgets can be justified and even expanded when training can contribute to profit and is not seen as an act of faith or a cost of doing business.

◆ Course objectives and content will become more lean, relevant, and behavioral with the focus on dollar results rather than on the acquisition of information.

◆ There will be a better commitment of trainees and their managers who will become responsible for follow-up and ROI, and not just for filling seats.

◆ Action plans, individual development plans, and managers' briefings will be taken seriously, thus strengthening the trainee-manager partnership.

◆ HRD staff will perform better in containing costs and maximizing benefits. They will become performance managers and not just instructors.

◆ HRD staff has solid data on where training is effective and where it is weak, so that courses can be revised and fine-tuned to produce the best returns.

◆ The curriculum of courses offered can be determined on a financial basis and not just on popularity, rank of the manager requesting it, and the like.

◆ Course enrollments will be serious, with trainees aware of the expectations that follow graduation. We'll get the right faces in the right places at the right times.

◆ By calculating ROI on the courses where it is possible, we are more apt to be trusted on the ones we can't evaluate at level four.

Four Ways to Measure ROI on Training

Following are descriptions of four ways of calculating ROI. The nature of the training and the course objectives will determine which method is most appropriate.

When Hard Data Exist

Performance data are routinely collected on many jobs for which we provide training. Examples include driver safety (dollar value of reduced accidents, lower insurance); machine maintenance (fewer repairs, less down time); sales training (increased volume, fewer returns); bank tellers (fewer overs and shorts, more services and customers handled per hour).

Many technical training programs have data on existing performance before the course was launched. By comparing the costs of inadequate performance prior to training with the reduced costs of better performance after training, we can see the ROI.

Even courses that teach soft skills can have a hard data side to performance. Examples include writing skills (time saved via shorter letters, understood without subsequent clarification); meeting leadership (shorter meetings, better follow-up); equal employment opportunity and diversity (fewer grievances and lawsuits).

Notice that our examples focus on the quantitative aspects of performance—things that can be counted in minutes, dollars saved or gained, and the like. To be sure, these courses also have qualitative aspects of performance. But these are more difficult to quantify (for example, courteous driving, more professional selling, clearer writing, more participative meeting leadership). Hard data probably don't exist to evaluate these qualities, so we have no way of comparing pretraining and posttraining performance.

If we want to take credit for the impact of training on workplace performance, we must establish a bench level of what the performance was before we launched the training program.

Estimates by Trainees and Their Managers

This method is the easiest way to estimate ROI, but also the most subjective. Several months after completing each cycle of a training program, send a memo to each graduate and manager (sponsor). State the actual cost to the organization of the trainee's participation in the course. Ask the two to get together, discuss the actual improved performance that has taken place since the course, agree on a dollar value of this improvement, and project the total value of this improvement over the coming year (or whatever period is appropriate to the application of the concepts and skills that were learned).

The two then send this projected dollar value in, along with a one- or two-paragraph explanation of how the estimate was determined. By comparing the costs of those who responded with their dollar estimates of value added to workplace performance, we can arrive at a crude estimate of the cost-benefit ratio.

In situations where bench levels were not established before launch of the course, this method of estimating ROI has appeal. What it lacks in accuracy it makes up for in getting trainees and their managers to recognize that the responsibility for making training effective is primarily theirs and not the trainer's.

Action Plans, Managers' Briefing

As you saw in chapter 35, each participant in a training program prepares an action plan that spells out how the concepts and skills being learned will be applied back at work. If the course involves the teaching of the entire job to a new employee, then the action plan will resemble a job description. If the course is for present employees (such as supervisors, team leaders, and project managers), then the action plan spells out those actions the participant will take back to the job, which will differ from those of other participants whose needs are different.

After the training program, participants share their action plans with their managers and anyone else who is a stakeholder in their ongoing growth and development. This helps to build the participants' managers into their development, as coaches, mentors, and overseers of the implementation of the action plan. (A pretraining meeting with the participants' managers is important: to cover objectives of the course, how the action plans work, and their role in helping their enrollees on the post-training follow through.)

Several months after the training, participants and their managers come together for a two- to three-hour meeting at which each participant reports on the actions taken as a result of implementing the action plan, along with the cost of doing so and the value of the benefits. Managers work with their participants prior to this meeting to arrive at the dollar value of the costs and the benefits. By tallying the numbers reported by the participants and adding the cost of the course, the return-on-investment is obtained.

Cost-Benefit Analysis via Accounting

This method is the most demanding way to calculate ROI, but also the most accurate.

Costs can be listed under these seven categories:

◆ course development (time) or purchase (price, license fees)

◆ instructional materials: per participant (expendables) and instructor (durables)

◆ equipment and hardware: projectors, computers, video (fair share use)

◆ facilities: rental of conference center or fair share use of classroom overhead

◆ travel, lodging, meals, breaks, shipping of materials, and the like

◆ salary of instructor and support staff (prorated), consultant's fees, and the like

◆ lost productivity (if applicable) or cost of temporary replacements of participants.

These costs are of three types: one time (for example, needs analysis and design), cost per offering (for example, facility rental, instructor's salary), and cost per participant (for example, meals, notebooks, coffee breaks). Costs must therefore be calculated over the life of the training program.

Benefits fall into the following four major categories:

◆ time savings (less time to reach proficiency, less supervision needed, and so forth)

◆ better quantity (faster work rate, less down time, not having to wait for help, and the like)

◆ better quality (fewer rejects, lost sales, reduced accidents, lower legal costs, and so forth)

◆ personnel data (less absenteeism, fewer medical claims, reduced grievances, and the like).

Benefits accrue long after training, and can be projected over the life of the trainees in the job for which they were trained (typically one to five years). Although costs can be calculated by HRD managers, the benefits should be calculated by the trainees and their managers after they have had enough experience in the workplace to collect enough data to project the benefits over the payback period. A comparison of the total costs to the total benefits yields the ROI.

Observations on Conducting a Cost-Benefit Analysis

The list that follows contains eight minilessons or insights that should be helpful to anyone who is attempting to do a cost-benefit analysis for the first time. You might want to circle the number in front of each observation that has particular relevance to your course.

1. Some courses, such as orientation of new employees and retirement planning, should be offered without expectation of a measurable return-on-investment. Because the benefits of conducting such programs are difficult if not impossible to measure and organizations offer them without expectation of any tangible ROI, it would be foolish to attempt a cost-benefit analysis.

2. Training programs for employees whose jobs have well-defined and quantified expectations (namely, standards, goals, and quotas) are the most appropriate ones for measuring return on the training investment since performance measurement systems already exist.

3. In contrast, training for supervisors, managers, technical experts, project coordinators, and others for whom performance measurement systems do not exist are much more difficult to evaluate via a cost-benefit analysis. The responsibility rests with each participant to generate pretraining data and posttraining data on performance, and to assign dollar values to these two sets of data.

4. Most cost-benefit analyses are comparative studies that show how the performance levels obtained by installing a new training program (such as a safety, drug, or stress reduction program) compare with the performance levels obtained by no training or by some alternative form of training (for example, on-the-job training instead of classroom training, individualized rather than group, or centralized versus regional). As in number three, pretraining data on performance prior to installation of the new program may not have been collected. This must be done prior to carrying out a cost-benefit analysis.

5. When training is conducted to accompany the installation of new equipment (or procedures, products, policies, technology, and so forth) and no prior training of a similar nature existed, a cost-benefit analysis is inappropriate for two reasons. First, there are no prior performance measures with which to compare the results of the new training, and second, the impact of installing the new changes make it impossible to separate performance attributable to training from performance attributable to innovation. Training associated with companies' moves from manual to PC operations provides many examples.

6. The costs of training are known up-front and should be calculated by HRD managers and others whose budget is funding the program. The major unknown is based on the shelf life of the course. The shelf life is the number of times (cycles) it will be run before it is no longer needed, which may be because all eligible trainees have received it, changes in technology have rendered it obsolete, or for some other reason. Costs should be calculated over the shelf life of the program.

7. Similarly, the benefits of training should extend well beyond the final offering (cycle) of the program. Different behaviors that were shaped by training have a different life cycle. The payback period on skills that are practiced regularly (for example, time management) might be projected over the employment life of the trainee, whereas skills that are called on less frequently, such as selection interviewing in a downsized economy, may have a much shorter payback period.

8. Although the costs of training are best calculated by HRD managers, the benefits should be identified, quantified, and converted to dollar values by management, whether the trainees' supervisors, department heads, or the like. Management is in the best position to observe changes in performance attributable to training, and their data are more objective and less suspect than if HRD specialists attempted to collect it.

Examples of Applications of Cost-Benefit Analysis

The brief case studies that follow illustrate four ways in which benefits can be shown to exceed the costs of training. They are (1) shortened training time, (2) in-house trainers versus consultants, (3) improved performance of individuals, and (4) improved performance of each supervisor's work group.

1. A rapidly growing fast-food chain had a three-week apprentice training program that prepared employees for promotion as an assistant manager. The corporate HRD manager felt that training time could be reduced to one week with a formal training program at headquarters. The one-week formal program required travel and hotel costs not associated with the three-week local apprentice training program. However, the company's ability to place assistant managers in outlets two weeks earlier resulted in savings that more than offset the cost of developing the program and bringing the trainees to a central location. It also assured uniform quality of instruction, which was lacking in the decentralized apprentice training that had taken place in each outlet.

2. A major corporation had relied on two professors from the state university to come in and conduct their supervisory training program, using their own handouts, visuals, and hands-on exercises. Some 93 supervisors went through the five-day program in classes of 15 to 16 participants each. Three years later the company offered supervisory training again. This time, it purchased a packaged course with videos, workbooks, and instructor guidelines for its own internal instructors. Although the package cost $27,000, the company ended up saving $16,000 (the professors had charged $36,000 for labor and $7,000 for materials). Moreover, postworkshop evaluations showed that transfer of training from workshop to workplace had improved significantly.

3. A government agency ran a three-day workshop on project management, in six offerings for 20 participants each. During the year following each workshop, the trainers surveyed the graduates to see how their posttraining performance on projects compared with their pretraining behavior (as assessed during the needs analysis prior to training). Factors evaluated included: (a) degree of projects completed on time and within budget, (b) level of client satisfaction, and (c) estimate of time and money saved as a result of improved project management. The agency concluded that a $95,000 training investment

had saved an estimated $670,000. This figure did not include one reported savings of $2,000,000 projected over a five-year period and agreed to by the graduate and her manager.

4. An automotive manufacturer installed a management development program as part of the company's total quality management and empowerment efforts and ran 220 managers at an assembly plant through the program. The average length was six days. After the first day of assessment, each manager attended only those workshops that dealt with the competencies and skills that received lower scores. Six months after the training, participants were again assessed. Benefits were evaluated on three factors: (a) the degree to which each manager's individual development plan had been implemented, (b) the change in productivity of the managers work group, and (c) the improvement in scores (percentiles against nationwide norms) by each manager on the two assessments. All three measures showed that the benefits far outweighed the costs.

Conclusion

In this chapter, we've examined reasons for and against doing a level four evaluation of results. We've seen four ways to measure return on the training investment and eight observations or minilessons on conducting a cost-benefit analysis. Finally, we've looked at four brief case studies that illustrate the fact that there are many ways to make training pay for itself and show a return-on-investment.

Reference

Kirkpatrick, D.L. (1998). *Evaluating Training Programs*. San Francisco: Berrett-Koehler.

CHAPTER 40

CONDUCTING A COST-BENEFIT ANALYSIS

In prior chapters you examined the four levels of evaluation on Kirkpatrick's model and concluded that level four is the most difficult. You also looked at four ways to estimate return on the training investment at level four. The last one, cost-benefit analysis via accounting, is the most demanding way to calculate the return-on-investment (ROI) but is also the most accurate.

This chapter contains a case study designed to give you practice in calculating the costs and the benefits associated with a training program. As described in chapter 32, this case study has three parts:

◆ **Stimulus:** This narrative describes the objectives, costs, benefits, and details of Running Effective Meetings, the workshop that B.J. Lewis, a training manager, ran at Southwest Industries.

◆ **Response:** This is an itemization of the costs and benefits that you will calculate and enter in response to the preceding narrative.

◆ **Feedback:** The narrative that follows the response describes the calculations that are appropriate to arrive at a total for costs and benefits.

Case Study: Running Effective Meetings Workshop at Southwest Industries

Southwest Industries was no different from other organizations its size (about 900 employees) when it came to time spent in meetings. The company's managers felt that time was wasted, key players were often absent, and agendas were not followed (or, in some cases, even established). Its training manager decided to do something about it. Using a questionnaire and group interviews with managers in each department, she came up with the design for a half-day workshop to meet the following objectives:

1. Reduced length of meetings: Managers estimated the average meeting to run about 75 minutes and hoped this could be reduced to under one hour.

2. Reduced frequency of meetings: Managers attended an average of 8.6 meetings per week and hoped to reduce the number to five or fewer.

3. Better follow-up and execution: Currently, many decisions reached at meetings didn't get acted on until the next meeting or a reminder went out.

4. Appropriate participants attend: The goal was for no time to be wasted because key people were absent and unnecessary people were present.

5. Better decisions and stronger commitment: By teaching the use of a decision matrix, decisions should be more effective.

The training manager sent these objectives and a cover memo to the company's 95 managers and supervisors, who approved them and added two more:

6. Effective problem solving: By teaching the process and applying it to typical work-related problems.

7. Timely minutes for follow-up: Minutes are often distributed too late to be effective and unclear as to actions to be taken.

They also suggested that a workshop on how to run meetings shouldn't be restricted to managers, since about 250 employees were members of work teams of eight to 10 persons each. These teams typically held one-hour meetings once a week to address problems and improve quality.

During the development of the workshop's methods and materials, the training manager realized that a half-day workshop would not provide sufficient time to have the desired impact. An exercise that would enable participants to prepare results-oriented and measurable objectives for a meeting would be time-consuming, but those skills are important to the success of a meeting. That exercise would have participants evaluate and rewrite a dozen typical meeting objectives and get hands-on practice using two forms—not yet designed—a meeting announcement form and a recap form. Consequently, Running Effective Meetings ended up as a one-day workshop (6.5 hours). Other than one learning exercise that was different for the 95 managers and supervisors and for the 250 team members, the workshop was the same for both groups.

Costs of the Workshop

The company offered the workshop 15 times, with an average enrollment of 21 participants off site to get participants away from the interruptions at the plant. A nearby motel charged $20 per person to cover coffee break, lunch buffet, and afternoon soda and snack. The room itself cost $100 per day.

Other costs of the course were minimal. The biggest expense was the training manager's time in preparing the objectives and getting feedback (one day), preparing course material (five days), and running the program (15 days). The 22 pages of handouts took three days for the administrative assistant to enter in the computer and lay out using desktop publishing. Thereafter, the cost of reproducing, collating, and inserting handouts in folders came to about two dollars per participant. The set of 12 colored overhead transparencies cost about $150 to make.

The training manager felt that it would not be appropriate to consider as a cost of training the participants' salaries during their day at the workshop, and her manager agreed. Similarly, the cost of any productivity lost due to attendance at the workshop was not seen as a cost of training. However, the administrative assistant did spend a total of two hours on each of the 15 workshops in scheduling participants and sending out the invitations.

Benefits of the Workshop

One of the workshop handouts participants received was a log for them to complete about meetings they attended for the three months following the workshop. An analysis of the entries on the 264 logs that were returned indicated the following data (listed in the same sequence as the seven objectives identified earlier):

1. The average length of a management meeting was 55 minutes, a savings of 20 minutes compared to the preworkshop average of 75 minutes. The length of work team meetings remained the same, about an hour.

2. Fewer meetings took place. During the three months following the workshop, managers attended an average of 5.6 meetings per week, down from the pretraining average of 8.6 meetings. (These figures came from the 65 managers who returned their logs. The change in frequency of meetings among members of work teams was not significant, since most teams continued to meet once a week.)

3. All respondents reported that execution and follow-up had improved. No figures were asked for on this question on the log.

4. The responses indicated that three managers who had run their weekly departmental meetings with everyone present (a command performance) were now making participation voluntary on a need-to-know basis. Result: Over the 39 meetings held during the three months, 87 hours were freed up for people who had previously been required to attend.

5.-6. Respondents were asked to estimate the dollar value of better decision making and problem solving. Although participants indicated that they were using the processes taught in the workshop, only eight respondents indicated a dollar value. Their estimates ranged from $50 to $10,000. The training manager decided not to use these data in the cost-benefit analysis.

7. In the workshop, trainees were taught how to use a recap form during meetings to record any decisions, actions, or assignments. This made the writing and distributing of minutes unnecessary, yielding an average savings of 45 minutes per meeting for the participant who served as recorder.

Given this information, the training manager was ready to calculate the dollar value of the time savings (on objectives one, two, four, and seven) that the workshop had made possible. The improved performance reported in response to objectives three, five, and six was a qualitative estimate and hard to quantify, so it was not included in the calculations. Before doing the cost-benefit analysis, the training manager made the following assumptions and verified them by checking with the vice president of human resource development (HRD) and several other managers:

◆ The average annual salary of managers and supervisors at Southwest Industries is $52,000, which amounts to $1,000 per week, or $200 per day, or $25 per hour.

◆ The average annual salary of team members is $36,000, which amounts to $692 per week, or $138 per day, or $17 per hour.

◆ The cost of employee benefits at Southwest Industries (insurance, medical) is figured at 30 percent of salary. In other words, every employee is costing the company 130 percent of his or her gross salary.

◆ The meetings held by managers typically have about five persons in attendance (compared with the team meetings, which nine members typically attend).

◆ The meetings included in the cost-benefit analysis are held at Southwest Industries and have no significant expense other than participants' salaries. (Seminars, conventions, trade shows, and other meetings are excluded from the calculations.)

Now it's your turn. Put yourself in the training manager's shoes. Use figure 40-1 to calculate the cost of the workshop and the benefits. You have all the information you need to estimate costs and benefits. You are working with benefits (savings) for the three months following the workshop, which can be entered on your worksheet as a savings per participant per month (last column). Then answer these questions:

◆ Did costs exceed benefits, or vice versa?

◆ By what amount? What ratio?

◆ Is a year too long, too short, or about right as the payback period?

◆ What was the cost per student hour of this workshop?

◆ Is that high, low, or about average for company-run training? (Guess.)

This cost-benefit analysis is a generic form, so many of the categories of costs and benefits will not apply to Southwest Industries. Make entries only where applicable. When you've added up your costs and your benefits, read the solution to the case on the pages that follow and compare Southwest Industries' calculations with yours.

Costs of the Workshop

The costs of researching, developing, and delivering 15 one-day workshops on Running Effective Meetings are relatively easy to calculate. The training manager spent one day on research and five days on the design and writing of the course material, for a total of six days. Because managers earn $200 per day on average, it is safe to assume that the training manager's salary is about $200 per day. The cost of benefits will add 30 percent. Thus, the entries are $260 and $1,300 under "1. Course development" on the cost-benefit analysis form.

An administrative assistant took three days to type and lay out the materials. Assuming the salary to be about the same as a team member's, the assistant earned $138 per day for three days, or $414. Again, benefits will add 30 percent to this amount, so $538 is the cost of production (typesetting and layout). The other two squares in number one remain blank.

As for "2. Instructional materials," each participant received a presentation folder with handouts. This item cost about two dollars to reproduce and collate. That figure is the cost of participant materials.

There are two costs for the instructor: the $150 for the 12 overhead transparencies, which goes under "One-time costs," and the $20 for lunch and breaks, belongs under "Costs per offering."

Since the only equipment needed was an overhead projector, which the motel provided, there was no cost for "3. Equipment." (If the training manager had purchased a projector or if the course had accounted for a major usage of existing equipment, then it would be appropriate to add a cost for this course's fair share of the equipment.)

The next entry on the cost-benefit analysis form is for "4. Facilities." Since the room cost $100 per day, that amount goes under "Costs per offering."

As for "5. Off-site expenses," Southwest Industries was billed $20 per person to cover refreshments and lunch for each participant, so that amount belongs under "Costs per participant."

Under "6. Salary," it was decided not to include the salary of participants or "7. Lost productivity" as costs of training. However, the salary category that does apply is the instructor's time, which is $200 per day for salary and 30 percent for employee benefits, for a total of $260 under "Costs per offering." Similarly, the administrative assistant spent two hours on each workshop in scheduling participants and sending out invitations. At $17 per hour, this comes to $34, which becomes $44 with the additional 30 percent for benefits. The amount for support staff cost under "Costs per offering" is $44.

The costs just itemized multiplied by the number of offerings (15) and number of participants (315) yields a total of $15,538. This is the sum of all costs in producing and running the one-day workshop 15 times.

Figure 40-1. Cost-benefit analysis for Southwest Industries.

Costs

	One-time costs	Cost per offering	Cost per participant

1. Course development (time) or selection (price, fees)

- ◆ needs analysis and research
- ◆ design and creation of blueprint
- ◆ writing and validating and revising
- ◆ producing (typesetting, illustrating, ready for reproducing)

2. Instructional materials

- ◆ per participant (expendables: notebooks, handouts, tests)
- ◆ per instructor (durables: videotape, film, PC software, overheads)

3. Equipment (hardware)

- ◆ projectors, VHS, computers, flipcharts, training aids

4. Facilities

- ◆ rental or allocated fair share usage of classrooms

5. Off-site expenses (if applicable)

- ◆ travel, hotel overnights, meals, breaks
- ◆ shipping of materials, rental of audiovisual equipment

6. Salary

- ◆ participants (number of hrs. instruction times average hourly rate)
- ◆ instructor, course administrator, program manager
- ◆ fees to consultants or outside instructors
- ◆ support staff (audiovisual, administrative)

7. Lost productivity (if applicable)

- ◆ production rate losses or material losses

- **A.** Total of all one-time up-front costs
- **B.** Total of all costs incurred each time course is offered
- **C.** This sum (B) times number of times course is run (___)
- **D.** Total of all costs incurred for each participant
- **E.** This sum (D) times number of participants (___) over life of course
- **F.** Total costs (sum of A, C, and E)

Figure 40-1. Cost-benefit analysis for Southwest Industries. (continued)

Benefits

	One-time over payback period	One-time per participant	Per participant per month
1. Time savings			
◆ shorter lead time to reach proficiency (hrs. saved times $)	▓		▓
◆ less time required to perform an operation (hrs. saved times $)	▓	▓	
◆ less supervision needed (supervisory hrs. saved times supervisory $)	▓		
◆ better time management (hrs. freed up times $)	▓	▓	
2. Better productivity (quantity)			
◆ faster work rate ($ value of additional units, sales)	▓	▓	
◆ time saved by not having to wait for help (hrs. saved times $)	▓	▓	
◆ less downtime ($ value of reduced nonproductive time)	▓	▓	
3. Improved quality of output			
◆ fewer rejects (scrap, lost sales, returns—$ value)	▓	▓	
◆ value added to output (bigger sales, smoother castings—$)	▓	▓	
◆ reduced accidents ($ value of savings on claims, lost work)		▓	
◆ reduced legal costs (EEO, OSHA, workers' comp settlements—$)		▓	▓
◆ improved competitiveness (change in market share—$)		▓	▓
4. Better personnel performance (attributable to training)			
◆ less absenteeism and tardiness (self or subordinates—$ saved)	▓	▓	
◆ improved health ($ saved on medical and lost time)		▓	
◆ reduced grievances, claims, job actions ($ saved)		▓	
◆ same output with fewer employees ($ on jobs eliminated)		▓	▓
A. Total of all one-time benefits		▓	▓
B. Total of all benefits occurring once per participant	▓		▓
C. Total value of all improvements per participant per month	▓	▓	
D. Length of payback period in months	▓	▓	
E. Number of employees affected during this period (D)	▓		▓
F. Total of B times E	▓		▓
G. Total of C times D times E	▓	▓	
H. Total benefits (sum of A, F, and G)			

Benefits of the Workshop

The benefits of training are the payback that Southwest Industries realized as a result of the workshop. They were calculated as the value of the time saved in addressing objectives one, two, four, and seven.

On objective one, the managers who participated reported an average savings of 20 minutes per meeting. The meetings of work teams did not change significantly. The company's 95 managers reported an average of 5.6 meetings per week, which converts (times 4.33) to 24.25 meetings per month. One-third of an hour is saved at each meeting, for a total of 8.08 hours saved per manager (.33 times 24.25). At $25 per hour, this savings amounts to $202, which we enter under "1. Time savings" as "better time management."

On objective two, a major benefit was realized by reducing the number of meetings from 8.6 to 5.6, a savings of three meetings per week, or 13 meetings per month. Since the time managers spent at meetings had been averaging 75 minutes, or 1.25 hours, the monthly savings is 13 times 1.25, or 16.25 hours at $25 per hour, or $406. We can enter this under "2. Better productivity" as "less downtime" (value of reduced nonproductive time).

On objective four, three respondents to the log and questionnaire reported a savings of 87 hours over the three months, for an average of 29 hours per month. Since the training manager did not know whether managers or nonmanagers accounted for this savings, it was assumed they were nonmanagerial, so the salary figures for team members were applied: 29 hours times $17, for a savings of $493 per month. But this is not a per participant saving, so none of the three column headings on the benefits worksheet apply. The nearest heading is "one time" in the first column. If the length of the payback period were one year (the 12 months following the workshop), the calculation would be to multiply $493 by 12 to get a one-time saving of $5,916, which would go under "4. Better personnel performance" as "same output with fewer employees."

On objective seven, by having participants make their own notes (minutes) during meetings, there's an average savings of 45 minutes per meeting on the part of the recorder. To calculate this saving, we have to determine how many meetings were held during the month following the workshop. This number is different for managers and for work teams. Consider each.

- ◆ **Managers:** Ninety-five managers attend 5.6 meetings per week, for a total of 532 attendees. However, the average number of managers at a meeting is five, for 532 divided by five, for an average of 106 meetings per week times 45 minutes saved at each, for a savings of 79.5 hours per week, or 344 hours per month.

  This converts to 8.6 weeks (344 divided by 40) of a recorder's time saved each month. At $1,000 per week, managers freed from serving as recorders have saved $8,600 per month. This belongs under "1. Time savings" as "less time required to perform an operation." But none of the headings apply. So we divide by our

95 managers so that we can enter it in the last column as a "per participant" saving, for 8,600 divided by 95, which comes to $91.

◆ **Team members:** Teams average nine members, and 250 employees are team members. Thus, 250 divided by nine comes to 27.8 teams. They meet once a week, or 4.33 times per month, for a total number of monthly meetings of 27.8. That figure times 4.33 gives 120 meetings per month.

This total times 45 minutes (for recorder to prepare minutes) comes to a savings of 90 hours, or 2.25 weeks, of recorders at $692 per week, for a total monthly savings of $1,557. This converts to a per participant by dividing $1,557 by 250, or six dollars. The result, six dollar, goes in the last column, sharing a box with the $91 figure for managers in our last entry.

Because the per participant savings are listed for two different populations (managers and team members), the figures must remain separate during multiplication of the number of persons in each population.

The calculations at the bottom of the benefits columns extend the savings per month and per participant over the total number of months (payback period) and the total number of employees affected. In this case, this is 95 and 250, a figure greater than the 315 participants, since the savings at meetings were realized by everyone who attended them and not just by the 315 participants in the workshops.

Summary

The total cost was $15,538. Compared with the total projected benefit in the first year of $820,776, the value of the benefits is 53 times greater than the costs. There is no reason to assume that the ability of managers to run shorter and fewer meetings will end after the first year, but the training manager was content using the figures for one year as the payback period.

As to the cost per student hour, 315 employees attended the 6.5-hour workshop for a total of 2,047.5 student hours. Dividing the total cost by the total number of student hours gives a cost per student hour of $7.59. Notice that the total population to be trained included 95 managers and 250 employees. All of these persons attend meetings. However, they did not all attend the one-day workshop. Thus, the costs of training are based on the total number who attended (15 times 21, or 315), whereas the benefits of training were realized by all those who attend meetings (95 plus 250, or 345). There were undoubtedly other employees who also spent time in meetings, since Southwest Industries has about 900 employees, but they were not surveyed since their participation in meetings was seen as much less frequent.

SUGGESTED READINGS

Argyris, Chris. (1960). *Understanding Organizational Behavior.* Homewood, IL: Dorsey.

Biech, E. (1999). *The Business of Consulting.* San Francisco: Jossey-Bass Pfeiffer.

Biech, Elaine, and John E. Jones. (1996). *The HR Handbook,* volume 1. Amherst, MA: HRD Press; Minneapolis, MN: Lakewood Publications.

Blake, Robert, and Jane Mouton. (1964). *The Management Grid.* Houston: Gulf.

Blanchard, Kenneth. (1982). *The One Minute Manager.* New York: William Morrow.

Bowsher, Jack E. (1989). *Educating America.* New York: John Wiley.

Covey, Stephen. (1989). *The 7 Habits of Highly Effective People.* New York: Simon and Schuster.

Craig, Robert, and Lester Bittel. (1967). *Handbook of Training and Development.* New York: McGraw-Hill.

Daniels, Aubrey C. (1994). *Bringing Out the Best in People.* New York: McGraw-Hill.

Davies, Ivor. (1981). *Instructional Technique.* New York: McGraw-Hill.

DeCecco, John P. (1968). *The Psychology of Learning and Instruction: Educational Psychology.* Englewood Cliffs, NJ: Prentice-Hall.

Dickens, Charles. (1854; reprint 1981). *Hard Times.* New York: Bantam Books.

Drucker, Peter. (1966). *The Effective Executive.* New York: Harper & Row.

Dubois, David D. (1993). *Competency-Based Performance Improvement.* Amherst, MA: HRD Press.

Fitz-enz, Jac. (1995). *How to Measure Human Resources Management.* New York: McGraw-Hill.

Folkman, J. (1998). *Making Feedback Work.* Provo, UT: Novations Group.

Fournies, Ferdinand F. (1999). *Why Employees Don't Do What They're Supposed to Do and What to Do About It.* New York: McGraw-Hill.

Gilbert, Thomas F. (1996). *Human Competence.* Washington: The International Society for Performance Improvement; Amherst, MA: HRD Press.

Hershey, P., and K. Blanchard. (1969). *Management of Organizational Behavior.* Englewood Cliffs, NJ: Prentice-Hall.

Herzberg, Frederick. (1966). *Work and the Nature of Man.* New York: World Publishing.

Keirsey, David, and Marilyn Bates. (1984). *Please Understand Me.* Del Mar, CA: Prometheus Nemesis.

King, David. (1964). *Training Within the Organization.* Chicago: Educational Methods.

Kirkpatrick, Donald L. (1998). *Evaluating Programs, The Four Levels.* San Francisco: Berrett-Koehler.

Knowles, Malcolm. (1973). *The Adult Learner: A Neglected Species.* Houston: Gulf.

Lucia, Anntoinette D., and Richard Lepsinger. (1999). *The Art and Science of Competency Models.* San Francisco: Jossey-Bass/Pfeiffer.

Luft, Joseph, and Harrington Ingram. (1961). *Of Human Interaction.* Palo Alto, CA: National Press Books.

Mager, Robert. (1961). *Preparing Instructional Objectives: A Critical Tool in the Development of Effective Instruction.* San Francisco: Fearon.

Masie, Elliott. (1995). *The Computer Training Handbook.* Minneapolis: Lakewood Books.

Maslow, Abraham. (1968). *Toward a Psychology of Being.* New York: Harper & Row.

McClelland, David. (1961). *The Achieving Society.* New York: Van Nostrand.

McGregor, Douglas. (1960). *The Human Side of Enterprise.* New York: McGraw-Hill.

Munson, Lawrence S. (1992). *How to Conduct Training Seminars.* New York: McGraw-Hill.

Nadler, Leonard, and Garland D. Wiggs. (1991). *Managing Human Resource Development.* San Francisco: Jossey-Bass.

Naisbitt, John, and Patricia Aburdeen. (1985). *Reinventing the Corporation.* New York: Warner Books.

Naisbitt, John. (1994). *Global Paradox.* New York: Avon.

Parry, Scott B. (1997). *Evaluating the Impact of Training.* Alexandria, VA: American Society for Training & Development.

Parry, Scott B. (1997). *Competencies,* volume 1 of *The Managerial Mirror.* Amherst, MA: HRD Press.

Parry, Scott B. (1997). *Qualities,* volume 2 of *The Managerial Mirror.* Amherst, MA: HRD Press.

Peters, Tom, and Nancy Austin. (1985). *A Passion for Excellence.* New York: Random House.

Phillips, Jack J. (1999). *HRD Trends Worldwide.* Houston: Gulf.

Robinson, Dana Gaines, and James C. Robinson. (1995). *Performance Consulting, Moving Beyond Training.* San Francisco: Berrett-Koehler.

Rogers, Carl. (1961). *On Becoming a Person.* Boston: Houghton-Mifflin.

Rothwell, William J., and Henry J. Sredl. (1992). *The ASTD Reference Guide to Professional Human Resource Development Roles & Competencies,* 2 volumes. Amherst, MA: HRD Press.

Schneier, Craig Eric, Craig J. Russell, Richard Beatty, and Lloyd S. Baird. (1994). *The Training and Development Sourcebook.* Amherst, MA: Human Resource Development.

Silberman, Mel, and Carol Auerbach. (1996). *The 1996 McGraw-Hill Training & Performance Sourcebook.* New York: McGraw-Hill.

Syer, John, and Christopher Connolly. (1996). *How Teamwork Works.* London: McGraw-Hill.

Toffler, Alvin. (1970). *Future Shock.* New York: Bantam.

Tompkins, Jim. (1995). *The Genesis Enterprise.* New York: McGraw-Hill.

Weiss, Alan. (1992). *Million Dollar Consulting.* New York: McGraw-Hill.

Woods, J.A., and J.W. Cortada. (1997). *The ASTD Training & Performance Yearbook.* New York: McGraw-Hill.

ABOUT THE AUTHOR

Scott B. Parry is a psychologist, consultant, and trainer and is the chairman of Training House, Inc., creators of instructional programs and assessments. His Managerial Assessment of Proficiency (MAP), an assessment exercise, has been translated into seven languages and is used in 21 countries throughout the world.

He has published numerous articles in training and management journals and is the author of four books and dozens of published training courses. To date, he has run more than 400 train-the-trainer workshops and has addressed human resource development (HRD) conferences in several dozen countries. In 1999, he was inducted into the HRD Hall of Fame.

In private life, Parry plays the organ and harpsichord, has published three collections of music, and has given a carillon concert tour in Europe. He and his wife live in Princeton, New Jersey.